Rewriting the French Revolution

REWRITING THE FRENCH REVOLUTION

The Andrew Browning
Lectures 1989

EDITED BY
COLIN LUCAS

CLARENDON PRESS · OXFORD
1991

Oxford University Press, Walton Street, Oxford OX2 6DP
Oxford New York Toronto
Delhi Bombay Calcutta Madras Karachi
Petaling Jaya Singapore Hong Kong Tokyo
Nairobi Dar es Salaam Cape Town
Melbourne Auckland
and associated companies in
Berlin Ibadan

Oxford is a trade mark of Oxford University Press

Published in the United States
by Oxford University Press, New York

British Library Cataloguing in Publication Data
(data available)

Library of Congress Cataloging in Publication Data
Rewriting the French Revolution/edited by Colin Lucas.
'The Andrew Browning lectures, 1989.'
Includes index.
1. France—History—Revolution, 1789–1799—Political aspects.
2. France—History—Revolution, 1789–1799—Social aspects.
I. Lucas, Colin.
DC148.R49 1991
944.04—dc20 90-27173
ISBN 0-19-821976-8

Typeset by Cambrian Typesetters, Frimley, Surrey
Printed and bound in
Great Britain by Bookcraft Ltd
Midsomer Norton, Bath

Preface

THE essays collected in this volume originated as a series of lectures given in the University of Oxford in 1989 in order to mark the Bicentenary of the French Revolution. Most of the texts appear as longer and revised versions of the lectures. This commemoration of the French Revolution was made possible by the Andrew Browning Fund of Balliol College. Andrew Browning was an undergraduate at Balliol early this century and later became Professor of History at Glasgow University. He endowed a fund for historical studies at Balliol and it is this which supports the Andrew Browning Lectures.

Rewriting the French Revolution is a doubly appropriate title for this volume. On the one hand, it reflects the dominant characteristic of the Bicentenary at large. On the other, it states the general intention of the authors of these essays. Centennial commemorations, especially those with a national dimension, are certainly moments for taking stock; but they are rarely devoted to disreputable events or persons and so usually adopt some tone of harmonious celebration or, at most, amicable differences. Academic reflection at such a time tends to be directed towards marking and exploring the generally defined significance of the subject of commemoration. This has certainly not been the case of the Bicentenary of the French Revolution. Whether as an effect of the inherent imprecisions of a pluralist society or as a result of the late twentieth-century failure of another post-revolutionary system, renewed and divisive relevance has been discovered in the Revolution's claim to be a new beginning, in the revolutionaries' continuous appeal to transcendent, universal principles, and in a history where high and generous aspiration had intolerant brutality as its escort. The political culture of the West has seemed to be brought into question by one of its principal sources.

The controversy among contemporary French politicians over the Bicentenary need not detain us here, nor indeed the more acrimonious attempts to revive a catastrophist interpretation drawn from counter-revolutionary ideology. In a sense, however, they have reflected (and have certainly drawn comfort from) the protracted and as yet unconcluded academic debate over the meaning of the Revolution. The Bicentenary fell at a critical historiographical moment. Some twenty-five years of research, debate, and polemic had, first, challenged and largely undermined the interpretation which had been the orthodoxy in the middle of this century, and then, principally in the 1980s, turned to the more positive task of advancing new general interpretations. By the time of the Bicentenary, there was no new consensus of interpretation. It was not that matters were in disarray, but rather that a number of alternative views were on offer, each with a specific emphasis and none really able to substantiate a claim to be an overarching interpretation of the revolutionary event.

By the end of the 1980s, it could not be said that historians of the Revolution were divided between the revisionists and the orthodox: everyone was a revisionist and the term, so descriptive in the 1970s, was no longer useful. Yet it is certainly true that there were two distinct centres of gravity at the heart of the debate, the one 'political' and the other 'social'. The 1980s were marked by the vigour and the success with which various forms of a 'political' interpretation were developed, whether in terms of the political process and the success or failure of institutions or in terms of the elaboration of a new political culture and the driving force of new principles, language, and representations. The 'social' interpretation had much more trouble in finding an identity in these years. It found it difficult to detach itself from the conflation of social interpretation and Marxist class-conflict thesis operated by the revisionists in the 1960s and 1970s. None the less, although the Bicentenary caught it still seeking a footing for a new general interpretation, there have been distinct signs of renewal, for example in the study of *mentalités*, sociability, and popular culture. Finally, it would be a mistake to see all the work done during these decades as principally concerned to intervene in this debate or as consciously setting itself within the field of one or other of these centres of gravity. The history of the French Revolution was also being rewritten by research and debate in such diverse areas as, for example, peasant history, provincial history, the war and revolutionary expansionism, and élite and popular resistances to the Revolution. Indeed, although in 1989 the informed public perceived academic opinion to be in a state of controversy, it would be more accurate to characterize the situation as a great market-place of different research, hypotheses, and debates. When one thinks back to the premises that held sway thirty years before, one can only conclude that French Revolution studies have become immensely richer and more exciting.

This volume does not claim to present any sort of conclusion or synthesis of the debates through which the history of the French Revolution is being rewritten. However, what it does set out to do is to present a coherent view on a number of issues where the most searching questions have been put in recent years. Each of the authors began his academic work on the Revolution at a time when the old orthodoxy was either still hegemonic or was challenged but not yet displaced. Each author has made a powerful contribution to rethinking the Revolution, more particularly in the area treated by his essay here. Read together, these essays offer an illuminating guide not only to how far the subject had been renewed at the time of the Bicentenary, but also to the directions in which thinking would be going in the early years of the third century of the French Revolution's legacy.

COLIN LUCAS

Contents

List of Contributors

LOUIS BERGERON is Director of the Centre d'Études Historiques at the École des Hautes Études en Sciences Sociales, Paris.

T. C. W. BLANNING is Reader in Modern History at the University of Cambridge, and Fellow of Sidney Sussex College.

ROBERT DARNTON is Professor of History at Princeton University.

ALAN FORREST is Professor of History at the University of York.

FRANCOIS FURET is Director of the Institut Raymond-Aron, Paris.

NORMAN HAMPSON is Professor Emeritus at the University of York.

COLIN JONES is Professor of History at the University of Exeter.

COLIN LUCAS is Professor of History at the University of Chicago.

MICHEL VOVELLE is Professeur d'histoire de la Révolution française at the University of Paris I.

The Forbidden Books of
Pre-revolutionary France

ROBERT DARNTON

I WANT to try to answer a question that was first raised seventy-
nine years ago by Daniel Mornet and that has been dangling
ever since: what did the French read in the eighteenth century?
Whatever it was, according to Mornet, it was not what we
commonly take to be eighteenth-century French literature. We
envisage the literature of every era as a corpus of works grouped
around a core of classics; and we derive our notion of the classics
from our professors, who took it from their professors, who got
it from theirs, and so on, back to some disappearing point in the
early nineteenth century. Literary history is an artifice, pieced
together over many generations, shortened here and lengthened
there, worn thin in some places, patched over in others, and
laced through everywhere with anachronism. It bears little
relation to the actual experience of literature in a given time.

Mornet set out to capture that experience, *la littérature vécue*,
by finding out what people read under the Old Regime. He
began by counting books, a great many of them: 20,000 in all,
which he compiled from auction catalogues of eighteenth-
century private libraries. After accumulating a mountain of
index cards, he decided to determine how many copies of
Rousseau's *Social Contract* had been unearthed. Answer: one.
One copy in a mass of 20,000 works. It looked as though the
greatest political treatise of the century, the bible of the French
Revolution, went unread before 1789. The connecting links
between the Enlightenment and the Revolution seemed to
dissolve. Instead of pondering arguments about popular sovereignty and the General Will, the French appeared to have

amused themselves with the sentimental novels of Madame Riccoboni and the adventure stories of Thémiseul de Saint-Hyacinthe. The Revolution was not 'la faute à Rousseau' and probably not 'la faute à Voltaire', either.[1]

That was 1910. We know now that Mornet made several false steps. He ended his enquiry in 1780, just when the first of many editions of Rousseau's works, the *Social Contract* included, began to appear. He neglected popularized versions of the *Social Contract*, notably the one in Book V of *Émile*, which was incontestably a best-seller. And his source was flawed. Libraries important enough to be sold in public auctions hardly represented a common variety of book ownership, not to mention reading. And the catalogues printed for those auctions had to pass through the censorship. So the ideological element was excluded from the very source where Mornet hoped to find it.[2]

Whatever the adequacy of his answer, Mornet's question remains valid. It has provoked a succession of attempts, in research projects scattered over three-quarters of a century, to identify the literature that Frenchmen actually read under the Old Regime. Each attempt has strengths and weaknesses of its own. Each has added to our knowledge. But cumulatively they tend to cancel one another out, or to contain so many contradictions that no general pattern can be identified. Mornet's question continues to hang over literary history, as tantalizing as ever.[3]

[1] Daniel Mornet, 'Les Enseignements des bibliothèques privées (1750–1780)', *Revue d'histoire littéraire de la France*, 17 (1910), 449–92. In later references to this research, Mornet advanced even stronger conclusions. See Mornet, 'L'Influence de J.-J. Rousseau au XVIIIe siècle', *Annales Jean-Jacques Rousseau*, 8 (1912), 44; id., *Rousseau: L'Homme et l'œuvre* (Paris, 1950), 102–6; and id., *Les Origines intellectuelles de la Révolution française*, 5th edn. (Paris, 1954), 229.

[2] The best criticism of Mornet's work is still Ralph Leigh, 'Jean-Jacques Rousseau', *Historical Journal*, 12 (1969), 549–65. Many scholars have continued to accept Mornet's conclusions, none the less. See Alfred Cobban, 'The Enlightenment and the French Revolution', reprinted in his *Aspects of the French Revolution* (London, 1968), 22; Joan McDonald, *Rousseau and the French Revolution, 1762–1791* (London, 1965); and the more measured interpretation in Norman Hampson, *Will and Circumstance: Montesquieu, Rousseau and the French Revolution* (Norman, Okla., 1983), 28.

[3] For a survey of this literature, see Robert Darnton, 'Reading, Writing, and Publishing', in *The Literary Underground of the Old Regime* (Cambridge, Mass., 1982), 167–82 and my review of Michel Marion, *Recherches sur les bibliothèques privées à Paris au milieu du XVIIIe siècle* in *The Eighteenth Century: A Current Bibliography*, NS 6 (1984), 17–18.

It can easily become a *question mal posée*, because it is far less simple than it seems. In order to trim it down to manageable proportions, I would like to limit my enquiry to the element that Mornet left out of his: illegal literature. That eliminates a vast amount, I know. I simply cannot circumnavigate all of French literature in the eighteenth century, but I think I can map the forbidden sector, and that sector was enormous. In fact, it contained virtually the entire Enlightenment and almost everything that Mornet was later to identify with the intellectual origins of the French Revolution. The censorship, the book police, and the monopolistic practices of the booksellers' guild made it difficult and dangerous to publish anything that had not received official approval, either in the form of a royal *privilège* or under one of the many rubrics by which the officials distinguished graduated nuances of legality: a *permission tacite*, a *permission simple*, a *permission de police*, or a simple *tolérance*. In the baroque world of book administration under the Old Regime, legality shaded off into illegality by almost imperceptible degrees. But at the far end of the spectrum, there existed a category of unalloyed illegality, of books that were clearly forbidden, beyond the pale, outside the law. Those are the books that I propose to study.

This is easier said than done. The irredeemably illegal element in eighteenth-century literature does not stand out to the twentieth-century eye. Some title pages flaunt their forbidden character by gross language—*Le Cul d'Iris* (Iris's Arse)—or by provocative false addresses: 'at the sign of liberty' or 'at a hundred leagues from the Bastille'. But many look anodyne, or at least not perceptibly more illegal than the quasi-legal works that were tolerated by the government. How can one identify the truly 'bad' books, as they were known to the police? The police kept a few lists. The king's council issued individual condemnations. Bishops fulminated from pulpits. And the public hangman lacerated and burned forbidden books with great ceremony at the foot of the grand staircase before the Parlement of Paris. However, none of those activities generated enough documentation for one to be able to study the entire body of illegal literature. In fact, the hangman burned only nineteen 'bad books' during the twenty years before the Revolution, yet thousands of them circulated 'under the cloak' during those years. How can we get our bearings on that vast, uncharted ocean of literature?

The best way is to consult all the available documentation left behind by the professionals of the publishing business. They had to be able to recognize forbidden literature, because it was a hazard of their trade. There could be serious consequences for those who were caught selling it. On 24 September 1768, the Parlement of Paris condemned Jean-Baptiste Josserand, a grocery boy; Jean Lécuyer, a dealer in secondhand goods; and Lécuyer's wife Marie Suisse, for peddling *Le Christianisme dévoilé*, *L'Homme aux quarante écus*, *La Chandelle d'Arras*, and similar works. They were exposed in chains for three days on the Quai des Augustins, Place des Barnabites, and Place de Grève, wearing a sign saying 'Purveyor of impious and immoral libels'. The two men were then branded on their right shoulders with the letters GAL for *galérien* and sent to row in the galleys, Lécuyer for five years, Josserand for nine years, followed by perpetual banishment from the kingdom. Madame Lécuyer spent five years in prison.[4] More distinguished booksellers such as the masters of the Paris guild did not receive such harsh punishment, although in principle, according to a royal edict of 16 April 1757, they could be hanged for dealing in such literature. Instead, they generally spent five or six months in the Bastille. But the Bastille was no three-star hotel, despite the attempts of some revisionist historians to brighten up its reputation. A half-year in one of its cells could ruin a bookseller's business as well as his health. So the men in the book trade had to know how to tell the difference between a quasi-legal work and an egregiously illegal one. To them, the distinction could be a matter of commercial survival, if not a question of life or death.

They expressed the distinction in many ways. First, in their use of language. As already mentioned, the police referred to forbidden books as 'mauvais livres'. Journeymen printers had a special term for them in the argot of their craft: 'marrons' (chestnuts), whence 'marronner' (to print an illegal work).[5] Booksellers used a more elevated expression: 'livres philo-

[4] Bibliothèque Nationale (hereafter BN), ms. fr. 22099, fos. 213–21.

[5] A.-F. Momoro, *Traité élémentaire de l'imprimerie, ou le manuel de l'imprimeur* (Paris, 1793), 234–5 and Nicolas Contat, *Anecdotes typographiques*, ed. Giles Barber (Oxford, 1980, from the original manuscript of 1762), 71.

sophiques'. Thus a typical remark from a letter by Gabriel Regnault, a bookseller in Lyon: 'My line is all philosophical, so I want almost nothing but that kind.' He then indicated what 'that kind' meant by ordering eighteen works and marking all the 'philosophical' ones with an X. They ranged from *De l'esprit* by Helvétius to *L'An 2440* by Mercier and *La Fille de joie*, a translation of *Fanny Hill*.[6]

Publishing houses developed alliances for marketing their work. When one publisher completed a new edition, he often traded a quarter or a half of the copies for an equivalent number, calculated in printed sheets, which he chose from the stock of an allied house. In this way he could market the edition quickly and vary the assortment in his own stock. 'Philosophical books' commanded a special exchange rate—usually one sheet for two of a legal book or a pirated version of a legal book. Thus the terms proposed by Gabriel Grasset, a Geneva printer who specialized in forbidden books, in negotiating an alliance with the Société Typographique de Neuchâtel: 'As all the other booksellers give me two sheets for every one of the philosophical kind, I propose the same exchange to you.'[7] 'Philosophy' was not an empty abstraction for eighteenth-century publishers. It was embedded in the routine of their daily business.

They often issued two kinds of catalogues: one for legal books, which carried their name and address, and another entitled 'livres philosophiques', which contained nothing but highly illegal works and excluded all kinds of incriminating information. Sales representatives carried the second kind 'under the cloak' when they made their rounds, and the home office mailed it to booksellers whose discretion could be relied upon. The booksellers, in turn, signalled 'philosophical books' in their orders. They marked the titles of egregiously illegal works with an X, or drew lines to separate them from the legal section of the order, or scribbled them on scraps of *papier volant*, which were to be burned after the arrival of the covering letter.

[6] Regnault to the Société Typographique de Neuchâtel, 19 Sept. 1774 in Papers of the Société Typographique de Neuchâtel (hereafter STN), Bibliothèque publique et universitaire, Neuchâtel, Switzerland. For a full discussion of such usages in the book trade, see my article, 'Philosophy under the Cloak', in Robert Darnton and Daniel Roche (eds.), *Revolution in Print: The Press in France, 1775–1800* (New York, 1989), 27–49.
[7] Grasset to STN, 19 June 1772.

When the 'philosophical books' came back in shipments from the publisher, they were stashed in the bottom of the crate, or hidden in the packing, or buried inside legal works by a technique known in the trade as 'marrying'. The supplier would slip sheets of illegal works in legal ones—books were shipped in unbound sheets—and could be confident that the inspectors in the guild halls would not look closely enough to detect them. Marriages inevitably brought together ill-sorted couples: thus an order to a Swiss firm from a bookseller in Loudun asked that *La fille de joie* be married to *Le Nouveau Testament*.[8]

Everywhere in the practice of their trade, in selling, ordering, shipping, and talking about books, eighteenth-century bookmen singled out the truly illegal works for special treatment. By studying their letters, therefore, one should be able to identify the 'philosophical' element in the trade. And by studying enough of them—order by order, title by title, copy by copy—one should be able to reconstruct the entire corpus of illegal literature that actually circulated in prerevolutionary France.

That is what I have been doing for most of the last twenty years. I have systematically worked through the archives of the Société Typographique de Neuchâtel (STN), the only papers of an eighteenth-century publisher–wholesaler to survive, in order to follow the play of supply and demand on book markets everywhere in France from 1769 to 1789. The archives contain 50,000 letters and a full supply of account books. They cover all the cities and most of the towns in France. They are rich enough, I believe, to provide an answer to Mornet's question, or at least the part of it concerning illegal literature.

However, the history of literature is littered with so many failed answers, including those of Mornet himself, that it seems worth while to pause for a moment in order to consider some methodological problems. The greatest problem concerns the representativeness of the STN papers. It may be exhilarating to take a great trek through some virgin archives, but why expend so much effort if the archives do not lead anywhere in particular? Can one piece together the whole world of forbidden French books from a single collection of documents that happened to survive in the attic of an old house in a small Swiss

---

[8] The order appears in an entry for 24 April 1776 in the 'Livre de commission' of the STN.

city?[9] I must admit to having lost some sleep over those objections. In order to answer them, I would turn once more to the practices of the eighteenth-century book trade, especially two of them: the practices of exchanging books among publishers and of ordering books among booksellers.

Because publishers swapped large proportions of new editions among themselves, they built up large stocks of *livres d'assorti-ment*; and publishing shaded off into wholesaling. In fact, the functions of publisher, printer, wholesaler, and retailer blended into one another and were often difficult to distinguish before the nineteenth century.[10] Yet while combining several functions, some houses specialized in the production of certain kinds of books. 'Philosophical books' tended to be put out by obscure entrepreneurs from small shops in the tiny principalities across France's borders. Everything about these businesses was marginal—the location, the product, and the producers: men who set up shop between bankruptcies and risked prison by publishing anything the market would bear. Gabriel Grasset and Jacques Benjamin Téron in Geneva, Gariel Décombaz in Lausanne, Samuel Fauche in Neuchâtel, Louis-François Mettra in Neuwied, Clément Plomteux in Liège, Jean-Louis de Boubers in Brussels—their names are forgotten today, but they produced the bulk of France's forbidden literature. Instead of selling it all themselves, they traded it, at the advantageous rates for 'philosophical' goods, against the less dangerous works printed in the larger and better established houses. In this manner, they accumulated a stock that they could sell without difficulty in their home towns, while the big firms, like the STN, acquired

---

[9] On the origin and character of the STN archives, see John Jeanprêtre, 'Histoire de la Société typographique de Neuchâtel, 1769–1798', *Musée neuchâtelois* (1949), 70–9, 115–20, and 148–53; and Jacques Rychner, 'Les Archives de la Société typographique de Neuchâtel', *Musée neuchâtelois* (1969), 1–24.

[10] The publisher did not emerge as a professional occupying a clearly defined place in the system for producing and diffusing books until the nineteenth century. True, the word had come into existence; thus 'éditeur' according to the 1762 edition of the *Dictionnaire de l'Académie française*: 'Celui qui prend soin de revoir et de faire imprimer l'ouvrage d'autruil.' A few entrepreneurs such as Charles-Joseph Panckoucke began to specialize in publishing under the Old Regime, but the functions of the publisher, as distinct from the printer and bookseller, were not well established before the era of Balzac, who described them vividly in *Les Illusions perdues*. We still need a study of the rise of the publisher, but there is some information scattered through Roger Chartier and Henri-Jean Martin (eds.), *Histoire de l'édition française* (Paris, 1984), ii.

the illegal books that they needed to satisfy customers throughout their own networks of retailers.[11]

The exchange system meant that the same general stock was
available to all the major wholesale houses. Therefore, in
ordering with one or two wholesalers outside France, a French
retailer could get virtually everything he wanted. This practice
suited the big houses, which promoted it by improvising
informal alliances among themselves, even though they were
competitors. In a letter to one of its customers, the STN
explained: 'Despite the fact that we compete with several of our
neighbours, we nevertheless co-operate with them. Having by
now a very extended business, we succeed in selling their books
along with our own.'[12] The STN's catalogue in 1785 contained
700 titles. An inventory of its stock in 1787 ran to 1,500 titles.
Already in 1773 it boasted, 'There is no book of any importance
that appears in France that we are not capable of supplying.'[13]

Seen from the perspective of the bookseller placing orders,
this system had one feature that made it fundamentally different
from the book-ordering practices of today: it did not permit
returns. Retailers therefore tended to be cautious. They ordered
only as many copies as they felt sure of selling. In fact, they
often arranged sales in advance and adjusted the size of their
order accordingly. A typical order from a provincial city like
Orléans or Nancy would contain only four or five copies per title
(though occasionally the bookseller would request a dozen
copies in order to get the free thirteenth) but it would include a
great many titles. The point of this practice was to save on
transport costs. Costs were cheapest in bulk shipments that
went by wagon (*voiture*), but the wagoners would not take
anything that weighed less than 50 pounds. The lighter
shipments had to travel by coach (*carosse*) at a rate that could be
ruinously expensive. So the *voiture–carosse* distinction served as
a guideline in the ordering strategy of booksellers. It meant that
they ordered large assortments of books from a small number of
suppliers instead of scattering their orders among many houses

[11] The account of these trade practices is derived from the dossiers of the
printers and booksellers who did business most regularly with the STN, notably
Gabriel Grasset, Jacques Benjamin Téron, and Gabriel Décombaz.
[12] STN to Mossy of Marseille, 10 July 1773.
[13] STN to Astori of Lugano, 15 Apr. 1773.

according to whatever advantages they could find in the wholesale prices.

Of course, when booksellers caught the scent of an unusual bargain or a possible coup, they would order from anyone who could supply the goods. But they tended to develop stable relations with a few wholesale houses. So a compilation of their orders with one major supplier over several years can reveal the general pattern of their business. And since they often accompanied their orders with comments on their trade, their correspondence provides plenty of qualitative evidence to supplement the statistics. By the same token, the trade of one big supplier like the STN can serve as a window, which provides an accurate view of the illegal commerce as a whole.

Admittedly, there is bound to be some distortion. The STN sold its own publications in larger numbers than the books it procured from other publishers, and it specialized slightly in a few genres such as travel and Protestant devotional works. However, one can allow for those factors. By studying the STN's business with a dozen of its most regular customers distributed everywhere in France, one can calculate the demand for illegal literature with considerable precision. It is even possible to construct a retrospective best-seller list and thus, at last, to answer Mornet's question—all because the STN archives really are representative of the illegal book trade in general.

However, I *want* them to be representative. After twenty years and 50,000 letters, the hunger for significant conclusions can be overwhelming—and that is dangerous, because as soon as a historian desires a certain result, he is likely to find it. So, in order to control for bias built into my work in Neuchâtel, I have undertaken three research projects in other archives. It would be misleading to refer to them as 'control' studies, because no attempt to measure literary demand two hundred years ago can be conducted with scientific rigour. All the sources are imperfect, and none of the methods for studying them is foolproof. Worst of all, there are no publisher's papers comparable to those of the STN. But it is possible to find some points of comparison by culling statistics from three other kinds of documents: registers of books confiscated in the Paris customs, inventories of bookshops made during police raids, and catalogues of *livres philosophiques* from other Swiss publishers.

A detailed description of all this supplementary research would be out of place here. Suffice it to say that the STN papers yield a list of 457 titles of illegal books, which can be compared with lists compiled from the other three sources. The French authorities kept a record of all the books that they confiscated in the Paris customs from 1771 to 1789, and in each case they noted the reason for the confiscation—that is, whether the book was pirated, or relatively inoffensive but *non permis*, or unambiguously illegal. The total number of titles among the illegal books comes to 280, of which 166 (59 per cent) appear on the STN list.[14]

Police inspectors often raided bookshops after receiving tips about suspicious activities. When they caught a bookseller with a substantial stock of illegal works, they confiscated the books and listed them in inventories. The archives of the Bastille contain nine such inventories from raids in Paris, Strasbourg, Caen, Lyon, and Versailles between 1773 and 1783. They also contain a list of all the confiscated books in the *pilon* (pulper) of the Bastille. These lists yield 300 titles, of which 179 (60 per cent) are on the STN list.[15]

Finally, the manuscripts in Neuchâtel and the Bibliothèque Nationale in Paris contain six catalogues of *livres philosophiques* issued by publishers in Geneva, Lausanne, and Berne between 1772 and 1780. The catalogues indicate the character of the stock of illegal books kept by a half dozen houses like the STN. Altogether they include 261 titles, of which 174 (67 per cent) are on the STN list.[16]

All this compiling and comparing confirms the conclusion that the STN list does indeed represent the illegal trade in general, although of course it does not cover every book that

[14] BN, ms. fr. 21933–4. I will give a full account of this and the other two projects in a later publication.

[15] Bibliothèque de l'Arsenal, ms. 10305. The papers from the *pilon* of the Bastille are badly scrambled and require unusual caution in their study. I have limited myself to unambiguous accounts of *perquisitions* during raids on bookshops and to one inventory of the *pilon* itself, made in 1774.

[16] The catalogue from Berne, which was almost certainly issued by the Société Typographique de Berne, is in the BN, ms. fr. 22101, fos. 242–9. The others can be found in the archives of the STN, included in the following letters: Gabriel Grasset to STN, 25 Apr. 1774; Gabriel Décombaz to STN, Jan. 1776; Jean-Samuel Cailler to STN, 30 Apr. 1777; Jean-Abram Nouffer to STN, 4 Feb. 1778; and J.-L. Chappuis and J.-E. Didier to STN, 1 Nov. 1780.

circulated outside the law. The representativeness can be seen most clearly at the top of all four lists, where the overlap is greatest. That is, the books ordered in the largest quantity and with the greatest frequency from the STN were also the books most confiscated in the Paris customs, most impounded in the police raids, and most often listed in the clandestine catalogues of other publishers. By amalgamating all four sources, one can produce a fairly complete bibliography of the illegal literature in prerevolutionary France, 720 titles in all. And by closer analysis of the orders to the STN, one can measure the relative importance of individual works, authors, and genres.

This analysis is based primarily on the compilation of every illegal book in every order from twelve regular customers of the STN, the 'major dealers' indicated on Map 1. The statistics make it possible to draw a profile of the business of a dozen booksellers scattered around the kingdom. I have supplemented those case-studies with surveys of the illegal market in three especially active areas—Paris, Lyon, and Lorraine—where I could amalgamate statistics from many different businesses. Then, to extend the enquiry further, I compiled the orders from seventeen 'minor dealers' in other locations (see Map 2), and from *colporteurs* (hawkers). They did not place enough orders with the STN for me to draw firm conclusions about their trade as individuals. But taken as a whole, their orders fall into a significant pattern. In fact, it is virtually the same as the overall pattern that emerges from the orders of the 'major dealers'. So all the statistics can be combined in a survey which, by eighteenth-century standards, is remarkably exhaustive. It covers 28,212 books and 3,266 orders. It is as valid, I believe, as most best-seller lists today.

Table 1 shows the top thirty-five best-sellers from the illegal trade in France from 1769 to 1789. It should not be read literally, because the place of individual books cannot be determined with absolute accuracy. Also, it over-represents the importance of books published by the STN, which are indicated by an asterisk, and it underrates a few works published at the very end of the period, when the STN had cut back on its business in France. But the table provides enough information for one to allow for irregularities. The first column on the right shows the total number of copies ordered for a title. The second column

Major (provincial) dealers

Bergeret, Bordeaux
Blouet, Rennes
Buchet, Nîmes
Charmet, Besançon
Letourmy, Orléans
Malherbe, Loudun
Mauvelain, Troyes
Manory, Caen
Mossy, Marseille
Pavie, La Rochelle
Rigaud, Pons, Montpellier
Robert et Gauthier, Bourg-en-Bresse

Lorraine:
Audéart, Lunéville
Augé, Lunéville
Babin, Nancy
Bergue, Thionville
Bernard, Lunéville
Bertrand, Thionville

Bonthoux, Nancy
Carez, Toul
Chénoux, Lunéville
Choppin, Bar-le-Duc
Dalancourt, Nancy
Gay, Lunéville
Gerlache, Metz
Henry, Nancy
L' Entretien, Lunéville
Matthieu, Nancy
Orbelin, Thionville
Sandré, Luneville

Lyon:
Baritel
Barret
Cellier
Flandin
Jacquenod

Paris:
Barré
Barrois
Cugnet
Desauges
Lequay Morin
Prévost
Védrène

MAP 1 Major provincial dealers in illegal books, including three areas with composite statistics: Lorraine (centred on Nancy), Paris, and Lyon

Minor (provincial) dealers:

Boisserand, Roanne
Billault, Tours
Bonnard, Auxerre
Caldesaigues, Marseille
Cazin, Reims
Chevrier, Poitiers
Fontaine, Colmar
Habert, Bar-sur-Aube
Jarfaut, Melun
Lair, Blois
Laisney, Beauvais
Malassis, Nantes
Petit, Reims

Resplandy, Toulouse
Sens, Toulouse
Sombert, Châlons-sur-Marne
Waroquier, Soissons

Itinerant hawkers:

Blaisot
Giles
Planquais
'Troisième'

MAP 2 Minor provincial dealers in illegal books

TABLE 1 *Best-sellers: total orders (major and minor dealers)*

Title [Author]	Books	Orders	Editions	Sources
1. *L'An 2400* . . . [Mercier]	1,394	(124)	25	ABCD
2. *Anecdotes sur Mme la comtesse Du Barry* [Pidansat de Mairobert? or Théveneau de Morande?]	1,071	(52)	5?	ACD
3. *Système de la nature* . . . [d'Holbach]	768	(96)	13	ABCD
4. *Tableau de Paris* . . . [Mercier]	689	(40)	2?	AD
5. *Histoire philosophique* . . . [Raynal]	620	(89)	8?	ABCD
6. *Journal historique* . . . *par M. de Maupeou* . . . [Pidansat de Mairobert and Moufle d'Angerville]	561	(46)	3?	ACD
7. *L'Arrétin* [Du Laurens]	512	(29)	14	ABCD
8. *Lettre philosophique* . . . [Anon.]	496	(38)	9	ABCD
9. *Mémoires de l'abbé Terray* . . . [Coquereau]	477	(24)	2?	AC
10. *La Pucelle d'Orléans* . . . [Voltaire]	436	(39)	36	ABCD
11. *Questions sur l'Encyclopédie* . . . [Voltaire]	426	(63)	5	ABCD
12. *Mémoires de Louis XV* . . . [Anon.]	419	(14)	1?	AD
13. *L'Observateur anglais* . . . [Pidansat de Mairobert]	404	(41)	3?	ABCD
14. *La Fille de joie* . . . [trans. by Lambert? or Fougeret de Montbrun?]	372	(30)	16	ABCD
15. *Thérèse philosophe* . . . [d'Arles de Montigny? or d'Argens?]	365	(28)	16	ABCD
16. *Recueil de comédies et* . . . *chansons gaillardes* . . . [Anon.]	347	(27)	1?	ABCD
17. *Essai philosophique sur le monarchisme* . . . [Linguet]	335	(19)	2?	A

18. Histoire critique de Jésus Christ . . . [d'Holbach]	327	(36)	3	ABCD
19. Les Plus Secrets Mystères . . . de la maçonnerie . . [trans. by Bérage?, ed. by Koeppen]	321	(36)	6?	A
20. *Requête au conseil du roi . . . [Linguet]	318	(17)	1?	AD
21. La Putain errante . . . [Aretino or Nicolo Franco]	261	(27)	10	ABCD
22. Le Christianisme dévoilé . . . [d'Holbach]	259	(31)	12	ABCD
23. Œuvres [Rousseau]	240	(58)	21	ABCD
24. Le Paysan perverti . . . [Restif de la Bretonne]	239	(19)	10	AD
25. L'École des filles . . . [Milot]	223	(16)	3	ABCD
26. Le Bon-Sens . . . [d'Holbach]	220	(16)	11	ABCD
27. Lettre de M. Linguet à M. le comte de Vergennes . . . [Linguet]	216	(4)	1?	A
28. De l'homme . . . [Helvétius]	215	(21)	6?	ABCD
29. Système social . . . [d'Holbach]	212	(32)	4	ABCD
30. Le Monarque accompli . . . [Lanjuinais]	210	(18)	3?	ACD
31. Dictionnaire philosophique portatif . . . [Voltaire]	204	(27)	11	ABCD
32. La Vie privée de Louis XV . . . [Moufle d'Angerville? or Laffrey?]	198	(17)	4?	AD
33. La Lyre gaillarde . . . [Anon.]	197	(14)	2?	ABCD
34. Les Lauriers ecclésiastiques . . . [Rochette de la Morlière]	191	(22)	13	ABC
35. Histoire de dom B, portier des Chartreux . . . [Gervaise de Latouche? or Nourry?]	190	(20)	20	ABCD

* An STN edition.

Sources: A = STN; B = Catalogue; C = Police confiscations; D = Customs confiscations.

indicates the number of orders placed for that title—that is, it permits one to study the incidence of repeated orders. The third column summarizes the available information about the number of editions of the work, although bibliographical studies are so uneven that it can provide only rough approximations. And the fourth column shows which books appeared most frequently in the four sources that I studied.

Are there any surprises on this list? One might expect to find Raynal's *Histoire philosophique* near the top of it along with Voltaire's *Pucelle*. But *L'An 2440*? *Anecdotes sur Mme Du Barry*? *L'Arrétin*? The literary market-place in the eighteenth century overflowed with best-sellers that have been completely forgotten today.

Table 2 lists the writers whose works sold best. Almost all illegal books appeared anonymously, but most of their authors can be identified. Some authors, like Raynal, conquered the market with a single work, while others, like Voltaire, wrote several best-sellers. Indeed, Voltaire's output was amazing: 68 of the books on the STN list, in nearly all the genres of illegal literature. Second to Voltaire but far below him in importance were d'Holbach and his collaborators, who composed, translated, and adapted a small library of anti-Catholic and atheist tracts. The Holbachean current of irreligion reached far more readers than is generally believed, although none of them at the time could trace its source to d'Holbach's salon. Then, following those two familiar names, comes a string of others that are now extinct, except among a few specialists in eighteenth-century literature: Pidansat de Mairobert, Théveneau de Morande, Du Laurens, Coquereau, d'Argens, Fougeret de Montbrun, de Pauw, Goudar, Moufle d'Angerville, Rochette de la Morlière . . . These were the men who wrote the best-sellers of pre-revolutionary France, yet they have disappeared from literary history.

Their disappearance may seem less surprising if one views literary history itself in the manner that I mentioned earlier—as an artificial construct, passed on and reworked from generation to generation. 'Minor' authors and 'major' best-sellers inevitably got lost in the shuffle. We do not expect the best-sellers of our own day to be read two hundred years from now. Yet do we not think that literary history should take account of the literature

TABLE 2 *Authors by number of books ordered*

1. Voltaire, François-Marie Arouet de	3,545
2. Holbach, Paul-Henri-Dietrich Thiry, baron d' (and collaborators)	2,903
3. Pidansat de Mairobert, Matthieu-François (and collaborators)	2,425
4. Mercier, Louis-Sébastien	2,199
5. Théveneau de Morande, Charles	1,360
6. Linguet, Simon-Nicolas-Henri	1,038
7. Du Laurens, Henri-Joseph	866
8. Raynal, Guillaume-Thomas-François[a]	620
9. Rousseau, Jean-Jacques	505
10. Helvétius, Claude-Adrien	486
11. Coquereau, Jean-Baptiste-Louis[b]	477
12. Argens, Jean Baptiste de Boyer, marquis d'[c]	457
13. Fougeret de Montbrun, Charles-Louis[d]	409
14. Restif de la Bretonne, Nicolas-Edmé	371
15. Bérage/Koeppen, Karl-Friederich[e]	321
16. Mirabeau, Honoré-Gabriel Riqueti, comte de	312
17. Aretino, Pietro Bacci[f]	261
18. Pauw, Cornelius de	235
19. Milot (or Mililot)[g]	223
20. Goudar, Ange	214
21. Lanjuinais, Joseph[h]	210
22. Moufle d'Angerville, Barthélemy-François-Joseph[i]	198
23. Rochette de la Morlière, Charles-Jacques-Louise-Auguste	197

[a] One title: *Histoire philosophique . . . deux Indes.*
[b] One title: *Mémoires de l'abbé Terrai.*
[c] Includes *Thérèse philosophe* (365 books, 28 orders) which is also attributed to d'Arles de Montigny. D'Argens, however, has six other titles attributed to him, so he is not disproportionately high on the list.
[d] Includes *La Fille de joie*, his translation of *Memoirs of a Woman of Pleasure* (*Fanny Hill*) by John Cleland. This translation has also been attributed to a certain Lambert.
[e] One title: *Les Plus Secrets Mystères des hauts grades de la maçonnerie dévoilés, ou le vrai Rose-Croix; traduit de l'anglais, suivit du Noachite traduit de l'allemand.* By usage, the translator is cited as 'Bérage' (e.g. Barbier and Caillet). Fesch gives Koeppen as the editor, without citing any original English or German works.
[f] One title: *La Putain errante.*
[g] One title: *L'École des filles.*
[h] One title: *Le Monarque accompli.*
[i] One title: *La Vie privée de Louis XV*, attributed to both Moufle d'Angerville and Arnoux Laffrey (198 books, 17 orders).

that actually reached most people? Should not literary historians study the ordinary varieties of *la littérature vécue*, the sort of thing that we refer to loosely by expressions such as 'taste' and 'demand' among the 'general public'?[17] Table 3 provides some preliminary answers to those questions by showing which genres of illegal literature were most popular. To be sure, its categories, like those in any classification system, are arbitrary. They may be inadequate as a means of sorting out data, and the sorting involves a great deal of subjective judgement: is a work primarily irreligious, or seditious, or pornographic, or does it manage to be all three at the same time? None the less, the rubrics in the table work reasonably well; the classifying proved to be a manageable task; and the result, however approximate, provides a general picture of the proportions within the corpus of forbidden literature as a whole.[18]

The main surprise in this picture is the relative unimportance of pornography: only 13 per cent of the total, or 19 per cent if one adds bawdy works that were primarily anticlerical. A poor score for the century of Restif de la Bretonne and the marquis de Sade, even though it does not do justice to the selling power of a few classics such as *La Fille de joie* and *La Putain errante*. Political works, by contrast, stand out as the most important general category. They did not include many theoretical treatises like Rousseau's *Social Contract*, however. In fact, the *Social Contract* did not figure among the top 400 books ordered from the STN. It

[17] In putting these questions in this manner, I do not mean to imply that literary historians should abandon the study of great books, even though 'greatness' is a culture-bound category. Nor am I arguing for a revival of positivism. I think it important to discover patterns of literary demand by means of empirical research, but I also consider it crucial to go on to questions about how books were read, taste was formed, and literature was related to other elements in culture and society. Finally, I should explain that my statistics cover supply as well as demand. Thanks to its extensive stock and the system of exchanges, the STN was able to fill a very large proportion of the orders it received. And despite occasional mishaps, it usually got the books to its customers.

[18] A full account of this research, with details on how individual best-sellers were classified, will be given in a book-length study of the subject. But even in this shorter version, the reader can allow for possible bias by shifting subheadings. For example, 'irreligious ribaldry' could be shifted from the general heading 'religion' to 'sex' because it contains works that were both bawdy and anticlerical. I think the irreligion predominates in books like *La Chandelle d'Arras*, but others may disagree. When all the data are published, they will be able to determine patterns of their own.

TABLE 3 *General pattern of demand*

Category and sub-category	Titles		Copies ordered	
	No.	%	No.	%
Religion				
A. Treatises	45	9.8	2,810	10.0
B. Satire, polemics	81	17.7	3,212	11.4
C. Irreligious ribaldry, pornography	18	3.9	2,260	8.0
Subtotals	144	31.5[a]	8,282	29.4
Philosophy				
A. Treatises	31	6.8	723	2.6
B. Collected works, compilations	28	6.1	1,583	5.6
C. Satire, polemics	9	2.0	242	0.9
D. General social, cultural criticism	33	7.2	4,515	16.0
Subtotals	101	22.1	7,063	25.1[a]
Politics, current events				
A. Treatises	20	4.4	986	3.5
B. Topical works	50	10.9	2,213	7.8
C. Libels, court satire	45	9.8	4,085	14.5
D. *Chroniques scandaleuses*	17	3.7	1,051	3.7
Subtotals	132	28.9[a]	8,335	29.5

TABLE 3 *General pattern of demand* (cont.)

Category and sub-category	Titles		Copies ordered	
	No.	%	No.	%
Sex	64	14.0	3,654	12.9
Other				
A. Occultism	2	0.4	111	0.4
B. Freemasonry	6	1.3	639	2.3
Subtotals	8	1.7	750	2.7
Unclassified	8	1.8	128	0.5
TOTALS	457	100.0	28,212	100.0

[a] Rounding creates the discrepancy in the subtotals of percentages.

did not appear in any of the clandestine catalogues and did not get seized in any of the police raids, although it was confiscated four times in the Paris customs. So Mornet was probably right in stressing the poor diffusion of Rousseau's treatise. But he overstated his case, because the *Social Contract* was included in many editions of Rousseau's works, and those editions appear near the top of the best-seller list, even though they contained as many as 38 volumes and often cost 24 livres or more. (The common and relatively cheap duodecimo edition published in 31 volumes by the Société Typographique de Genève sold for 25 livres in 1785.) In any case, it is clear that political theory sold far less well than topical works, personal libels, and *chroniques scandaleuses*. These sub-genres overlapped so much that they cannot always be distinguished. But, when taken together, they can be seen to have constituted a kind of muckraking journalism, which was all the more sensational in that modern political journalism did not yet exist in France. These books operated on the still unannounced principle that names make news; so they concentrated their fire on the most eminent personages of the kingdom. They began with the king himself, working their way down through ministers and royal mistresses to the common run of courtiers and *filles d'Opéra*; and they blasted away so effectively that they made the whole regime look rotten.

Whether it actually looked that way to the readers of the books cannot be determined. The archives say very little about the social composition of the readership and almost nothing about the experience of reading. They raise a host of new questions, which lie beyond the range of statistical analysis and which make Mornet's old question seem simple in comparison. But this is not the place to take on a new set of problems. Instead, after so much quantification, it may seem time to stop counting and start reading the forgotten best-sellers. Although we cannot read them exactly as they were read in the eighteenth century, we can study the way the texts work and try to capture something of their flavour. Without pretending to be immune from anachronism or to provide anything more than an introduction to this literature, I would like to discuss three forbidden books that were most popular then and are least familiar now.

Thérèse philosophe, by the marquis d'Argens or d'Arles de

Montigny, comes about as close as a book can get to 'pure' pornography.[19] The narrative consists of orgies strung together with bits of conversation while the partners gather their forces for the next round of pleasure. It has little redeeming social comment. Like most of the older varieties of bawdy literature, it mixes sex with anticlericalism; but it remains explicitly respectful of all the secular authorities.

The novel is actually a *Bildungsroman*, recounted in the first person by Thérèse herself. She tells the story of her education, an education in pleasure, which leads from her first exploration of her private parts as an infant to the full flowering of her sexuality as the mistress of the comte de ***. As in many *romans galants*, the narrative takes the reader inside nunneries and brothels; and its tone remains consistently voyeuristic, in keeping with the illustrations, which show couples copulating and spying on one another in bowers and boudoirs.

It is all very genteel, and rather passionless, too; for pleasure, as Thérèse presents it, is not so much an emotion as an idea—a tingling in the epidermis, which passes through the animal spirits to the brain, where it is stored as food for thought. Ultimately, then, sex becomes cerebral. By instructing Thérèse in its mysteries, her lover provides her with an education in metaphysics, like the tutor in *Émile*. He strips away the spiritual side of Cartesianism, revealing a world of matter in motion, devoid of any ethical reality beyond the pleasure principle. Principled pleasure, however, turns out to be a hedonistic calculus in which the first principle is: thou shalt not get pregnant.

The comte de *** therefore provides Thérèse with a hundred lessons on how to reach orgasm without conceiving. They masturbate and philosophize deliciously until the culminating moment of the narrative. Then, in a paroxysm of pleasure, Thérèse begs the count to bury himself in her. He agrees, but at the climactic moment, by a supreme effort of the will, he withdraws, spilling his seed safely outside her. It is a lesson in coitus interruptus, a lesson fraught with implications for demographic history.

[19] *Thérèse philosophe, ou mémoires pour servir à l'histoire du P. Dirrag et de Mlle Eradice*, 2 vols. The first edition, which lacks a place and date of publication, appeared in 1748. Most authorities attribute it to Jean-Baptiste de Boyer, marquis d'Argens.

Childbirth was a dangerous business in the eighteenth century. Thérèse decides it is not worth the risk, her own mother and her best friend having nearly died in labour. She resolves to take charge of her fate, rejects the role of wife and mother, and lives out her life as the voluptuary companion of her philosophic count. Instead of becoming a sex object, like Fanny Hill, she provides an object lesson in the self-determination of woman. But above all, she embodies a lesson in philosophy—that is, in the importance of regulating the pleasure principle and of subordinating it to reason, all in the name of achieving the greatest possible happiness. That was a revolutionary idea, one that would appear twenty-eight years after the original publication of *Thérèse philosophe* in the American Declaration of Independence.

As a philosopher, Thérèse understands that there is no god, or no monotheistic being beyond nature itself, but that two deities can be said to preside over man and womankind, Voluptuousness and Philosophy. They appear in the frontispiece to the book, with a caption that summarizes its message: 'Voluptuousness and Philosophy create the happiness of the sensible man. He embraces Voluptuousness by taste. He loves Philosophy by reason.'

L'An 2440 reads like a Rip Van Winkle tale.[20] The narrator falls asleep and wakes up in the year 2440, when he has reached the age of 700 and France has turned into a utopia. He can barely recognize Paris, it has become so clean and orderly. Carriages proceed slowly along the right-hand side of the immaculate streets, stopping deferentially before pedestrians. The Bastille has been replaced by a 'Temple of Mercy'. The Hôtel de Ville has been moved next to the Louvre, leaving room for civic festivals at the Place de Grève. The Pont Neuf, now called Pont Henri IV, is lined with statues of patriotic statesmen, which make it function as a 'book of morals'.[21] In fact the entire city can be read as a book proclaiming a civil religion. The Catholic Church has been reduced to a deistic cult preached in glass-covered temples and transmitted through an initiation rite, the 'communion of the two infinites', in which adolescents develop an ecstatic

[20] Louis-Sébastien Mercier, *L'An deux mille quatre cent quarante: Rêve s'il en fût jamais* (Amsterdam, 1771). The following quotations come from the expanded text published in 1775 under the false address of London.
[21] Ibid. 37.

sense of the Supreme Being by means of telescopes and microscopes.

But the most important cult is devoted to writers. Their statues preside over the public squares, celebrating their triumph over superstition and tyranny. Corneille stands with the head of Richelieu under his foot, and Voltaire and Rousseau bestride pedestals that proclaim them to be the greatest prophets of the third millenium. Writers rule the world, not directly, but by guiding public opinion, which has become the supreme force in society, thanks to an enlightened system of education and a free press. While the greatest patriots devote themselves exclusively to enlightenment, every citizen contributes to the collectivity as a writer; for everyone distills the essence of his experience into an autobiography, which serves as a monument to him after his death, and the French as a whole govern themselves as a collective 'author' ('tout un peuple auteur'.)[22] Writing and reading combine in the same way as active and passive citizenship, according to Rousseau. Print culture and the General Will have been fused in the ideal society, a political version of the Republic of Letters.

It is a curious fantasy, at least for the modern reader. But the readers of the Old Regime loved it. *L'An 2440* was the supreme best-seller in the entire corpus of forbidden literature. It went through twenty-five editions between 1771 and 1789. Mercier expanded the text from edition to edition without bothering much about the plot. In fact, the book hardly has a plot at all. It is presented as a walk through Paris in the future just as Mercier's other best-seller, *Le Tableau de Paris*, was a walk through the Paris of the present. The two works complemented one another, providing a positive and a negative picture of the same subject. But *L'An 2440* seems to have struck the imagination of his contemporaries with particular force. It was not the first utopian novel, far from it; but it was the first to be set in the future. Readers could enjoy a new kind of mental experiment, imagining their own world transformed in time. Mercier helped them along with abundant descriptions of daily life. He gave a detailed account of how people dressed, for example. They wore Roman-like smocks, gathered at the waist by a sash, in place of the unnaturally constrictive clothes of the Old Regime.

---

[22] Mercier, *L'An deux mille quatre cent quarante*, 52.

Of course no one wore a sword, 'an old prejudice of gothic chivalry',[23] or any of the gear that made clothing such a strong social code in the eighteenth century. Distinctions existed only in the form of embroidered hats, which were awarded to citizens who had performed some great act of humanitarianism or who excelled in their craft.

Nothing could be further in spirit from the science fiction of today. When we read about the future, we expect to find technological marvels. Mercier's future had none—no ray guns, no intergalactic television, no zipping about in space machines, no star wars. Utopian gadgetry was unthinkable in the fantasies of the Old Regime. The dimensions of Mercier's utopia were moral, and the elements missing from it, as he made clear in footnotes to the text, were the abuses that he found most objectionable in contemporary France. The France of 2440 had no priests, no Parlements, no *lettres de cachet*, no censorship, and no oppressive taxes. Mercier did not go so far as to conjure up a France purged of all social distinctions. In fact, his imagination seemed bounded by the outer limits of society under the Old Regime. He described a world of rich and poor, of noble and common, fixed in the economic and demographic conditions of the eighteenth century. True, he eliminated the extremes of wealth and poverty. He turned his princes into innkeepers and required them to give free meals to the old and the infirm. But he did not envision any basic change in the social structure or the standard of living.

Mercier did not show much interest in political institutions, either. He indicated that France was ruled by the General Will but did not explain how it operated. The state seemed to run on civic virtue, fraternal love, and general openness. Mercier allowed for a few officials, a Senate, and a king. But none of them had much power, the king least of all: he merely presided over civic festivals and laboured with peasants in the fields for a certain period every year. Apparently, like Marx, Mercier felt no need to produce a blueprint for the government of the future, or perhaps utopian tinkering of that sort had little appeal for the French before 1789. Whatever the reason, Mercier's argument remained essentially negative. It kept returning to the evils of the Old Regime and presented them, not as the consequence of

[23] Ibid. 17.

faulty institutional design, but rather as a matter of public morality—that is, of corruption at the top of society where power was monopolized by decadent courtiers, overweening ministers, and despotic monarchs.

The book ends with an account of a visit to Versailles, written in the overblown style of Young's *Night Thoughts*. The palace has fallen into ruins. The gardens have run wild, forming a melancholy anti-Eden at the other end of time. In the midst of the desolation, the narrator comes upon Louis XIV, who has been reincarnated as an old man and condemned to inhabit the site of his former glory, contemplating the folly of his pride and weeping over the misery he inflicted on his people. In the midst of a tearful lamentation, a serpent crawls out from under a rock and bites the narrator, causing him to wake up back in the eighteenth century.

The futuristic fantasies of *L'An 2440* provided a powerful indictment of the Old Regime, but they did not give Frenchmen a way to think the unthinkable—that is, to imagine something comparable to the Revolution, which was only a few years away. Instead of predicting the future, Mercier translated the utopian vision of Rousseau into terms that could be grasped by everyone and turned against abuses in the present. It is a pity that Mornet did not study *L'An 2440* as well as the *Social Contract*, for Mercier's dream disseminated radical Rousseauism more effectively than Rousseau's own treatise.

Anecdotes sur Mme la comtesse Du Barry by Pidansat de Mairobert ranks second to *L'An 2440* on the best-seller list. In a way it can be considered even more of a success,[24] for it contains many episodes that can also be found, sometimes word for word, in the other libels and *chroniques scandaleuses* on the list: *Journal historique . . . par M. de Maupeou*, *Mémoires de l'abbé Terray*, *L'Observateur anglais*, *Vie privée de Louis XV*, *Correspondance secrète et familière de M. de Maupeou*, *Les Fastes de Louis XV*, *Mémoires secrets pour servir à l'histoire de la république des lettres*, *Le Gazetier cuirassé*, *Mémoires authentiques de Mme la comtesse Du Barry*, *Précis historique de Mme la comtesse Du Barry*, and *La*

---

[24] *Anecdotes sur Mme la comtesse Du Barry* (London, 1775). Standard bibliographies and catalogues refer to four other editions between 1775 and 1778; but considering the lack of bibliographical information about this kind of literature, it seems likely that the number was much higher.

Chronique scandaleuse, to name the most popular in the order of their popularity. It is difficult to know who copied whom, because the authors of these works drew on the same gossipy sources, and they lifted material from one another without the slightest concern for plagiarism, or intertextuality, as it is known among literary theorists today.

The result was an enormous body of literature which purveyed the same set of themes. But *Anecdotes sur Mme la comtesse Du Barry* stood out above the others, because it told the common tales with exceptional skill. The narrator presents himself as a historian, the chronicler of a life bound up with the deepest secrets of the times. He promises to cull through all the sources—private letters, interviews, underground gazettes—in order to extract nothing but the hardest facts. Although he is obviously writing a libel (the French term, *libelle*, had a specific resonance for eighteenth-century readers), he pretends to despise the genre. He claims to restrict himself to the most sober version of Du Barry's biography. Indeed, he insists on refuting the worst calumnies—and proceeds to do so in such an unconvincing manner, while serving up so much damning evidence, that he makes his own account seem modest in comparison. This technique reinforces the authority of the narrator while providing the greatest possible *frisson* for the reader: everything in the rhetoric works to promote the illusion of an inside view of the innermost corridors of power.

The narrative combines a biography of Madame Du Barry with a political history of the reign of Louis XV. It is a sexual success story organized around a single theme: from brothel to throne. The plot leaves plenty of room for salacious detail about key questions such as: Who first had the heroine's maidenhead? The narrator refuses to pronounce. He finds too many possib-ilities, too much ambiguous evidence, to make a responsible judgement. But one thing is certain, he assured us: she was sold as a virgin half a dozen times in the whore-house of Madame Gourdan. It was here that Du Barry received her education. She ran through the full gamut of the classical positions and the main variations with a whole array of bishops, courtiers, and magistrates—mainly for the fun of it, because she took to the profession by inclination and usually asked for nothing in compensation beyond a few baubles or clothes. Her career as a whore turned out to be profitable in the long run, however, because she picked up tricks in Madame Gourdan's that later proved to be crucial in arousing the jaded libido of Louis XV and thus in conquering Versailles.

While chronicling the stops as Du Barry sleeps her way to the top, the narrator brings out two subsidiary themes. First, her commonness. He dwells on the disparity between her humble origins and her elevation to the summit of society. Writing for a readership that was especially sensitive to parentage, he ends the book with a genealogical appendix about the Du Barry family (they are fake aristocrats who agree, in exchange for a sum, to provide the heroine with a title by means of an arranged marriage so that she can appear at court), and he begins it with an account of her birth. She was the offspring of a cook and a *rat de cave* (tax inspector), he explains, indignantly rejecting the story that her father was a monk. He also insists that his heroine's career as a whore was limited almost entirely to a short stint at Madame Gourdan's, which was the classiest establishment in Paris. Honesty forces him to admit, however, that Du Barry spent some time as a streetwalker. Thus a motif in the popular songs and verse that he quotes throughout the text: anyone could have had her for a few pennies only a few years before she became the mistress of the king—and a great many did, including 'all of our lackeys'.[25]

But as Du Barry rises through society, she becomes a plaything of the rich and the well-born; and when they get between the sheets—our omniscient author takes us everywhere—they prove to be incompetent or perverted. Dukes cannot have erections; prelates require flagellation; countesses are lesbians. When she wants to satisfy herself, Du Barry has to descend to the servants' quarters. This second theme reverses the direction of the first. Instead of exposing violations of the social hierarchy, it asserts the native superiority of the common people. It is implicitly democratic. In fact, Du Barry makes it explicit at an early point in her career, when she expounds her philosophy in a letter to one of her lovers, a pretty boy who is trying to seduce his way upward along a path parallel to hers.

---

[25] *Anecdotes sur Mme la comtesse Du Barry* (London, 1776), 167: 'Tous nos laquais l'avaient eue, | Lorsque traînant dans la rue, | Vingt sols offerts à sa vue | La déterminaient d'abord.'

The letter proclaims that all men are equal when it comes to love, although servants tend to be better value than masters, and that all women are divided into two classes, the beautiful and the ugly.[26] Instead of making Du Barry into the embodiment of evil, the text comes close in places to glorifying her. True, she nearly ruins France. But she has no personal ambition and no particular taste for riches or social advancement. She just loves sex. Although she lets herself be used by wicked courtiers, she remains curiously innocent, protected from the corruption around her by her healthy appetite and indominable naïveté. In the end, she can be considered, at least in one possible reading, as a genuine heroine, a forerunner of Marianne.

But the story concentrates on her role in the political crisis that nearly crippled France during the last years of the reign of Louis XV. Du Barry reaches the royal bed through the offices of Le Bel, the king's valet and procurer, who scours the country for 'game', 'real pieces fit for a king'—the narrator's favourite terms derive from hunting and eating—and produces two a week on average. They are cleaned up ('décrassées'), dressed up, and pensioned off after one-night stands at 200,000 livres apiece—or 10 million a year, according to the author's estimate; enough to bankrupt the kingdom.[27] Unlike the others, thanks to her temperament and training, Du Barry manages to retain the king's favour. She becomes *maîtresse en titre* and is presented at court.

At that point, her personal story intersects the history of France, and the book turns into a behind-the-scenes account of politics in Versailles. It takes the reader through all the major events during the latter part of Louis XV's reign: the fall of Choiseul, the partition of Poland, and the destruction of the Parlements by Maupeou. In each case, the decisive factor is not a matter of principle, not even reason of state, but rather the vilest variety of personal intrigue. Bored with incest and driven by jealousy, the duchesse de Grammont tries to supplant Du Barry in the king's bed and brings down a ministry. The duc d'Aiguillon climbs into power by wooing Du Barry with presents—they include a carriage whose price, according to the narrator, was the equivalent of what it would have cost to feed the poor in an entire province for several months—and then

---

[26] Ibid. 31.   [27] Ibid. 54–6.

seduces her, effectively cuckolding the king. Meanwhile Terray, the controller-general of finance, tries to cut out d'Aiguillon by sprinkling gifts of châteaux and estates through the Du Barry clan; and Maupeou, the chancellor, tries to undermine both d'Aiguillon and Terray by cultivating the so-called 'devout party', which has formed around the dauphin, the future Louis XVI. The dauphin himself will have nothing to do with Du Barry, because she has mocked his impotence and criticized his wife's complexion. And so it goes; politics reduced to trivia in round after round of plotting and bickering.

Through it all, the real power behind the throne turns out to be not Du Barry herself—to the end she remains interested only in sex and clothes—but her brother-in-law and former lover, and comte Jean Du Barry, who is not really a count at all but a pimp. He operates out of gambling dens in Paris and governs France by means of couriers whom he dispatches regularly to Versailles with secret orders for the royal mistress. Once she has received her instructions, Du Barry fills the king with drink, drags him to bed, and gets him to sign anything she asks. It was by this procedure, the narrator explains, that Du Barry led Louis XV to destroy the country's parlementary system in the judicial coup of 1771.

The narrator spices up his account of such episodes with excerpts from poems, songs, placards, gossip, and *bons mots*. In fact, he cites so many that the story-line sometimes disappears, and the last part of the book reads like a digest from the *Mémoires secrets*, which was also written in large part by Mairobert. Each item has its shock value, however. We get the story of how the papal nuncio and the cardinal de la Roche-Aymon held the favourite's slippers for her as she slid, naked and giggling, out of the royal bed. And her famous remark as the king began to spill his coffee: 'Eh! La France, prends donc garde, ton café fout le camp' ('Look out, France! Your coffee's running away').[28] And also the poisonous paternoster:

Our Father who art in Versailles. Abhorred be thy name. Thy kingdom is shaken. Thy will is not done, neither on earth nor in heaven. Give us back our daily bread, which thou hast taken from us. And forgive the trespasses of thy Parlements, which have upheld thy interests, as you

[28] *Anecdotes sur Mme la comtesse Du Barry*, 215.

have forgiven your ministers, who have betrayed them. Do not succumb to the temptations of the Du Barry. But deliver us from the satan of a chancellor. Amen![29]

This material often dwells on the symbolic aspect of the monarchy and systematically desecrates it, as if the libellers meant to destroy the aura of sacredness that surrounded the king. The poems and anecdotes picture Du Barry as fouling the *fleurs de lys*, the crown, and the throne. One popular song even associates the feebleness of the sceptre with the debility of the royal penis. Thus, when at last Du Barry has succeeded in arousing the dirty old monarch, he says

> Viens sur mon trône,
> Je veux te couronner,
> Viens sur mon trône:
> Comme sceptre prends mon vit.
> Il vit, il vit!

> (Come on my throne,
> I want to crown you,
> Come on my throne:
> As sceptre take my cock.
> It's alive, it's alive!)[30]

All the narrative devices seem to be aimed at the same effect, the desacralization of the monarchy. The moral of the story stands out on every page: France has become mired in decadence and despotism. In fact, according to the narrator, the kingdom would have collapsed, had it not been saved by the death of Louis XV. And how did he die? The narrator revealed the awful secret. As Madame du Barry became increasingly incapable of exciting the aged monarch, she turned procuress and held on to his favour by slipping fresh young girls into his bed. One girl had an undetected case of smallpox. She gave it to the king; he died; and everyone in France breathed a sigh of relief.

But that was not the end of the story. The reign of Louis XVI did not promise to be much better, because the new king inherited the old system of corrupt court politics. To be sure, he was not a sexual monster. On the contrary, he was impotent.

---

[29] Ibid. 153.
[30] Ibid. 76. For similar examples, see ibid. 160, 211, 258, 260, and 297.

But that made him monstrous in his own way, while Marie-Antoinette was succumbing to nymphomania. The stage was set for the Diamond Necklace Affair and a still more vicious flood of libels, which would continue unabated until the overthrow of the monarchy.

If one studies the *Anecdotes sur Mme la comtesse Du Barry* in company with its sister libels, they seem to constitute a full-blown political mythology. They all have the same motifs, and they all spread the same theme: moral rot had made the monarchy degenerate into a despotism. Their cumulative effect, in so far as one can guess at it, was to corrode the sense of legitimacy that bound the people to the king. It took a great deal more to bring the monarchy down, but the collapse that occurred in 1792 seems unthinkable without the delegitimation perpetrated by the illegal literature of the previous two decades.

Thus Mornet's question leads to the larger question of the ideological origins of the French Revolution, just as it did when he pursued it seventy-nine years ago. But the issues now seem infinitely more complex. One cannot string an argument along a series of inferences that link the buying of a book to the reading of a book to the assimilation of the reading in personal convictions and the expression of those convictions in political engagement. Linear causality does not operate in literary history any more than it does in history *tout court*.

Nevertheless, in order to advance some conclusions that have a semblance of conclusiveness, I would say that the 'philosophical books' undermined the legitimacy of the Old Regime in two ways. First, in theory: the Voltairean and Holbachean works directly attacked the Church and the Crown and all the values that supported them. Secondly, on a visceral level: the scandalous political libels reduced the baroque world of Old Regime politics to a mythology built around the theme of decadence and despotism. But the illegal best-sellers contain so many themes that a single essay cannot do justice to them. There is a whole world of forgotten literature waiting to be explored. Once one ventures into it, all literary history begins to look different, and all kinds of possibilities open up—even a fresh view of the French Revolution.

2

The French Revolution
or
Pure Democracy

FRANCOIS FURET

THE repercussions of the French Revolution are universal because it proclaimed itself to be universal. Independent of the particular conditions of its birth and even of the country in which it broke out, it gave itself the mission not of adjusting institutions to the circumstances of national history or to the state of opinion, but rather of remaking the social contract from top to bottom, as though it were an artefact to be completely reworked, remodelled according to the principles of reasoning will. It was thus an event that was inextricably political and philosophical, and contemporary observers immediately saw it as a blend of these two aspects, hailing 1789 as the victory of Enlightenment philosophy in the realm which it had made its speciality—the reorganization of the polis. The unique character of the French Revolution in modern history derives from this combining of genres, by virtue of which 1789 was to be accompanied by a laicized religious annunciation where the promise of democracy was substituted for that of God.

Not that they are mutually incompatible. The promise of democracy can indeed be accommodated by the promise of God, which can provide it with a more time-honoured and sacred shelter, as in the American case. Yet in the French case, it set itself up alongside the religious message: not against it, but separate from it, basically very different and at the same time comparable in form, limited to the earthly domain but completely filling it with the idea that there is an essence of man to be realized in society. Democratic universality reduces religious belief to something private if it takes up all the public space of the community of individuals. This is exactly what it did in late eighteenth-century France, giving rise furthermore to the most enigmatic characteristic of the French Revolution—its temporal discontinuity. Like the birth of a religion, 1789 divided time into a before and an after.

This was indeed an enigmatic characteristic; and yet, it has been so domesticated by modern political culture that it has become a commonplace. The French in particular have made it into such a widespread belief that they have ceased to see it as anything strange. For two hundred years, they have been the people for whom 1789 represents the originating division into Right and Left, into those who liked the Old Regime and hence detested the Revolution and vice versa. However, in accordance with the wishes and ambitions of the men of 1789, this political schizophrenia has spread beyond the history of France. Since their time, it has become the revolutionary political universe, which is conceived in terms of secular Messianism as a foundation following upon a long period of oppression. This is so much the case that a good starting-point for a contemporary reflection on the French Revolution is the rediscovery of this peculiar idea that a temporal discontinuity can become the necessary substance of history.

Very early on, the Frenchmen of 1789 mapped out this idea in both its negative and its positive aspects, through what their actions abolished and through what they inaugurated that was radically new. They destroyed the so-called Old Regime and founded a new order of free and equal individuals under the sovereignty of the law, that other name for the General Will. It is easier to establish the date of the Old Regime's death than the date of its birth or the length of its existence, because the term only appeared with its dissolution. In early spring 1789, the expression was not yet in use when the *cahiers de doléances* were written by the parishes in order to instruct their delegates. It came into being little by little during the summer in the course of the circumstances, events, and decisions taken by the Assembly, which had become a Constituent Assembly. Even if the words 'ancien régime' were not actually uttered during the most famous night in French parliamentary history (the night of 4–5

August 1789), one can discover here the sentiment, the almost sacred emotion that gave birth to the term. The debate of that evening was born of the pressures of circumstances: France had risen up, burning châteaux in a number of places. However, the debate was marked not so much by a preoccupation with cutting losses as by the transports of enthusiasm that united the hearts and minds of the Assembly. The deputies shared the conviction that they were producing a twilight and a dawn, casting themselves as the almost divine stage-hands of a show in which the past disappeared and a new world began. In giving way to circumstances, they thus accomplished something of a completely different order.

That something was the 'destruction of the feudal regime'. By this, the deputies did not mean only the rights derived from the regime of seigneurial property and the fiefs. They also meant the tithe levied in kind by the Church on all harvests, as well as other things infinitely more recent such as venality of office—a practice to which the monarchy had had recourse since the early seventeenth century in order to fill its coffers by selling hereditary functions in the law courts, the financial administration, or the municipal authorities. Thus, what disappeared with 4 August concerned not only the residual institutions characteristic of feudal property, but also the entire corporative structure of the realm. The Assembly's vote undid the contradictory situation in which the absolute monarchy had found itself for one or two centuries: it had been both the bestower of privilege and also attacked in the name of privilege. The destruction of the *corps* liquidated all the particular rights which constituted the liberties of the king's subjects and which were linked to their Estate in society—that is, to the existence of juridically defined privileges. There would henceforth be only an identical common law for each member of the nation; all the private associations—intermediaries between the citizen and the public sphere of the law—were henceforth banned, perceived as no more than impediments.

Thus, what was destroyed in 1789 under the designation of 'feudal' was in fact more characteristic of the absolutist period, when the central State erected itself by converting privileges into cash and power. In this respect, the men of the Revolution completed the drive towards uniformity undertaken by that

state, suppressing that which it had had to concede to the
particularist spirit of feudalism. In every other respect, they took
care to transform the abolished rights (or the great majority of
them, at least) into good bourgeois currency, a precaution not in
the least at odds with the general spirit of liquidation which
inspired them, contrary to the belief of so many twentieth-
century historians. These historians have been so obsessed with
the socialist idea that they see 4 August merely as the passage
from noble inequality to bourgeois inequality. They are incapable
of conceiving that something much more essential occurred
with the end of aristocratic society: the disappearance of the
hierarchy of dependence among men, the birth of the modern
individual, and the birth of the idea of the universality of law.
The socialist world stands in the same relation to this historical
breakpoint as does the bourgeois world: it is simply a development of the promises of equality. Thus, the patriotic enthusiasm
of the deputies on 4 August was not incompatible with the
circumstantial character of the order of the day and the decrees
they voted. The peasant revolution crystallized a set of decisions
which had their source in the eighteenth century's books: they
were taken a little earlier than predicted and were perhaps more
wide-ranging, but that was all.

Nevertheless, the term 'ancien régime' did not appear in the
debates of 4–11 August. It was not to be forged until later on, the
course of the discussion on the constitution during the succeed-
ing weeks. That is because this discussion brought up a second
issue which had not yet been visible when 'feudal' society was
being dissolved: 'monarchical government'. What contemporaries meant by this term was a collection of principles and
political mechanisms which made the king the key element of
public authority, whether in the absolutist version corrected by
the idea of 'enlightened despotism' or in a more 'constitutional'
form, that is to say in the old sense of the word, starting from an
immemorial contract between the monarchy and the nation,
guaranteed by fundamental laws and the consultation of the
'estates' in the formation of laws. On 17 June, the Third Estate
proclaimed itself to be a 'National Assembly'. All the consequences of that term were not immediately explored, but six
months earlier, one of the men who proposed it—Sieyès—had
already explained its implications in his celebrated *Qu'est-ce que*

le Tiers État? It implied nothing less than a transfer of sovereignty or rather, a recovery (by seizure) by the nation of its imprescriptible rights, delegated to a constituent assembly. Thus, between mid-June and early September, the sharing of public authority between Louis XVI and the deputies was ambiguous. On the night of 4 August, the liberal noble Lally-Tollendal, one of the great lawyers of the *monarchien* Right, sought to associate the king with the Assembly's votes: *in fine* (at 2 a.m.), Louis XVI was proclaimed the 'restorer of French liberty'. Yet that ambiguity was short-lived. It was resolved to the advantage of the anti-king deputies when the discussion about the new constitution took place, beginning in late August.

The traditional 'constitution of the realm' (the binding element of 'monarchical government') was no longer at issue, because in that case it would be necessary to allow the prince at least a co-sovereignty in the English style. This was what the *monarchiens*, the first moderates of the French Revolution, advocated. They were not hostile to the Revolution, for up until then they had participated in, encouraged, and supported it; but they were already intent on curbing its effects and even on bringing its effervescence to an end, citing the English example of 1688. It was their misfortune to hark back to a precedent that had not actually existed in French history: there was no French tradition of a 'King in Parliament'. What the Bourbon monarchy had brought forth was a sovereignty which was at once indivisible and in escheat: it was easier to settle it upon the people than to reinvent a sovereignty shared by a King, a House of Lords and a House of Commons—a trio whose subtle equilibrium had never existed in the nation's past.

In order to get to that position, they would have had to go back into France's past to the moment when the monarchy had given up the practice of consulting the estates; they would have had to go back to the time (if it had ever existed) when the aristocracy constituted an organized political power and not a caste of courtiers. The idea of an upper chamber, which the *monarchiens* deemed inseparable from monarchical government, whitewashed centuries of absolutism. Even when partisans of this idea tried to domesticate it (by making it elective, for example), it continued to be saddled with the ghost of the Second Order of the realm, defined by its privileges and meeting in its own assembly, an Order which had to be dissolved into the Third Estate in order to constitute the nation represented. Moreover, the aristocratic structure of society had been destroyed on 4 August. It had left behind only equal individuals, who were all but new, and it had placed them in the situation which contractualist philosophy had so often imagined: to remake the conditions of the social contract in order to enter into it. The dissolution of 'feudal' society, which thereby abolished the 'Gothic' diversity of the rights and franchises of communities, also delegitimized the notion of particular social interests. It inspired the idea of a unitary political body where each contracting member recovered his equal share of sovereignty through a unitary representation, identical for all.

It follows that the idea of bringing together national history and the Revolution by means of 'monarchical government' is an impossible one for two reasons. First, the *monarchiens* referred back to a tradition which did not exist or which had ceased to exist if it had ever begun an existence in the French past. Second, the attempt to 'restore' that tradition after two centuries of absolutism became even more unrealistic in the light of the complete condemnation of the feudal principle which both surrounded the absolute monarchy and also preceded it. Such a search for an Old Regime capable of founding new institutions was therefore a hopeless venture. In the manner of a testamentary legacy, the *monarchiens* would have liked to settle upon the new institutions the co-sovereignty of the king (that is, his veto over the legislative power) and bicameralism. However, all they accomplished was, on the contrary, to highlight the failure of a monarchical history of liberty which, notwithstanding, they claimed as their principal justification.

To this extent, the radical segment of the revolutionary camp was unwittingly more traditional than the moderate segment: it appropriated the sovereignty produced by the labours of absolutism, whereas the *monarchiens* sought to reinvent sovereignty in a form which it had never had. This gave the Constituent Assembly sovereign power to reconstruct the body politic; the king remained only its delegate, soon to become the first functionary of the realm. Thus, the 'Old Regime' took on its full meaning as a rejected past. Thenceforth, the term condemned both the 'feudal' and the monarchical, both the social and the political past of France. However, the peremptory affirmation of chronological discontinuity, which gave the word 'revolution' its new meaning, cannot be separated from the readoption by the 'patriots' of 1789 of a notion of political sovereignty that owes its character to absolutism: the people took the place of the king and pure democracy replaced absolute monarchy. Just as was the case under the old sovereign power, when nothing was left to anyone but the monarch, under the new sovereign power, consent came exclusively from the people, or that which supposedly represented it. Thus, the idea of 'Old Regime' which appeared at this point contained a symbolic and an actual overthrow of the throne which, though half-cloaked in the recycling of the king as the first servant of the people, was nevertheless experienced and affirmed as such by the great majority of the members of the Constituent Assembly.

However, if the idea of discontinuity is so compelling, it is because it contains the idea of a recomposition of politics on the basis of principles instead of the legacy of time. The most spectacular manifestation of this reinstitution of the social contract is the vote on the Declaration of the Rights of Man of 26 August 1789. The idea was to base the new collectivity upon a statement of the rights that each individual brings with him upon entering into society and which that society must, in return, protect and guarantee; in short, to replay in real life the primordial scene of contract philosophies, whereby the man of nature becomes a citizen and must, as a social being, conserve that which was imprescriptibly his as a natural being. This famous passage, the object of so much speculation, had been accomplished by the Americans several years before the French and they had enshrined it in Declarations of Rights. However, in their case, was that crucial, quintessentially philosophical moment what really founded the contract? The American documents contain no brutal rupture with a prior social state. They contain no affirmation of the rights unrecognized by the small emigrant communities that had progressively populated the future republic. On the contrary, they 'declare' rights felt to be fundamental by the colonists since their arrival on that virgin soil in a society newly formed and based upon voluntary membership. America was a new world, still close to nature, barely tainted by inequality, for which the Declarations carried no subversive dynamic. 'Je vous prie de songer', said Lally-Tollendal addressing his colleagues on 11 July after Lafayette finished reading out his project, 'combien la différence est énorme d'un peuple naissant qui s'annonce à l'univers, d'un peuple colonial qui rompt les liens d'un gouvernement éloigné, à un peuple antique, immense, l'un des premiers du monde, qui depuis quatorze cents ans s'est donné une forme de gouverne-ment'.

That incomparability can, however, lead to opposite conclu-sions. Lally-Tollendal's friends took advantage of it in order to reiterate their warnings: the proclamation of the liberty of the individual in a society where men have been dependent for so long, the proclamation of equality when they are destined to remain so unequally endowed by the fortunes of existence, can only give rise to unreasonable expectations which are destructive of social unity. Thus, one needed to compensate by having a declaration of civic duties in order to fix the limits of social obligation. The particular nature of the French situation could, however, foster the ambition to create a Declaration of Rights even more exemplary than those of the young American republic. In the oldest kingdom of Europe, in that powerful and populous monarchy, a Declaration of the Rights of Man and of the Citizen would need that much more force in order to break with the past and to usher in the new era. There, more than anywhere else, that proclamation could draw its universal emancipatory spirit from the separation between the Old Regime and the Revolution. 'Suivons l'exemple des États-Unis', declared Mathieu de Montmorency, one of the deputies of the liberal nobility, on 1 August; 'ils ont donné un grand exemple au nouvel hémisphere; donnons-le à l'univers.' On that same day, the same man wrote in the *Courrier de Provence* (which was Mirabeau's newspaper) that the French should perfect the example of America by giving their hemisphere the advantage over the other of 'une invocation plus élevée de la Raison', which would allow it to speak a purer language.

It was not so much that the French deputies were of a particularly abstract turn of mind. Many of them perceived and weighed the risks of a general proclamation of individual rights in such a populous society, a society so unequal and one in which the work of centuries had wrought a disposition much to the contrary. Yet, on the other hand, they all needed to redeem the rickety origins of their own sovereignty by affirming all the more loudly their mission, carried away as they were by the logic of what they had voted on 4 August. The Americans had not had to destroy an aristocratic society based upon the hierarchy of birth. For the French, however, the traditional social nexus had been completely undone and the only way left for them to reconstruct the body politic was to build it out of equal individuals based on the universality of the law. Finally, it was upon this infinite multiplicity of contracting parties that they had had to found a will of the people as sovereign and as indivisible as that of the king. The text of 26 August was the product of this set of constraints, and it was the bearer of an unlimited ambition: to secure the entirety of natural rights with the law and to retain for the citizen all that belonged to man. The moderates viewed the strong affirmation of public power as a guarantee against the risks of social dissolution threatened by the idea of rights. The patriots, such as Sieyès, saw in it the assurance that political association would have no other end, no other foundation, than the autonomy of man. In the phrase 'La loi est l'expression de la volonté générale' there lies the optimistic belief of French political voluntarism: the liberty of natural individuals is buttressed by a power born of their collective consent and participation. There is no place for an eventual rift between the law and its foundation; and thus no antidote is provided to dispel the appearance of such a rift except for the right to resist oppression, which would bring the whole contract into question and for the legitimate conditions of whose exercise no definition is furnished.

Therefore, with amazing rapidity during several months of the summer 1789, the principles and modalities of a new society took form. Starting from the autonomy of the individual, they were reinvented upon the ruins of what had been the individual's ancestral dependence. To that extent, there is a common logic at work in the texts of 4 August and the Declaration of Rights and in the discussion about public powers in early September 1789. The Old Regime and the Revolution had been assigned their essential characteristics: pure monarchy versus pure democracy.

The adversaries of the Revolution of 1789 were no less certain that it constituted an absolute break with the past. In some ways, it was even more so for them because the period I have just described began and ended with two waves of emigration. The most privileged, with the comte d'Artois to the fore, or the most fearful sounded the alarm the day after 14 July and the king's capitulation before Paris. After 6 October, the first partisans of the Revolution began in their turn to distance themselves from it. Mounier left Paris and the Assembly, withdrawing to his native Dauphiné prior to abandoning France altogether the following year. In this way, the separation of national history from the Old Regime culminated in these deliberate departures from a realm where those who left had found themselves estranged from their compatriots and from their customs. However, that demarcation was to be even more evident the following year, the year in which Burke was to write and publish his *Reflections on the Revolution in France*. It took the English parliamentarian no longer than the summer 1789 to reject entirely the undertaking of 1789. Between May and October, the theatre of revolutionary France had produced a spectacle such as to convince him that he should condemn it. In his appraisal of that short stretch of time, Burke was the first person to analyse the French Revolution as an undivided whole, *comme un bloc*.

He did not know—obviously—what was to come, especially not the dictatorship and the Terror, and this would endow his book *a posteriori* with predictive value and bring it immense popularity in Europe. He discussed only the events of the summer 1789 and the principles set forth to guide and justify those events. He fitted the whole of the Revolution into those few months by taking seriously, just as the men of the Revolution had done, the new ideas that issued from it and which he considered to be its essence. It was this conflictual complicity with the men of 1789 that gave his critique a large part of its profundity.

Nevertheless, in his eyes, the ideas of 1789 were not the ideas of the century. Burke's refutation of 1789 derives its special character not only from its early date but also from his wonder at an event whose philosophical character was quite obvious to the English observer, although he failed to see—in contrast to the majority of his contemporaries—its natural filiation from the

Enlightenment. Thus, it was the Revolution's sternest critic who saw it as it would itself have wished to be seen—as a rupture in the chain of time. That very pretension to historical discontinuity, which constituted its pride, provoked the stunned indignation of its adversary.

It is an understatement to say that Burke condemned that pretension: he could hardly bring himself to conceive of it. For him, a people without a past was both an absurdity and a hopeless endeavour; it was a human collectivity devoid of its essence, of the centuries of accumulation during which successive generations acquire their rules of civility, their morals and their customs, their mode of being together, their political constitution. Like any good Whig parliamentarian, Burke never doubted the failings of the Bourbon absolute monarchy. Yet, for him, it was not sufficiently bad, not sufficiently 'despotic', as one might have put it then, to have prevented the development of civilization, for the propensity and good manners of the late eighteenth-century French testified to the contrary. Furthermore, the political treatises of the prerevolutionary years often referred to an ancient 'constitution' of the realm and the Estates-General of 1789 were convoked in function of that constitution.

So how was it that, immediately after those years, the French wished to deny absolutely that heritage, their heritage? Burke bore witness to that denial, proffering expressions of indignation more than explanations. He had put his finger on the moment and the characteristics of that rupture: the momentous votes of August 1789 and in particular the Declaration of the Rights of Man. This last decreed the new organizing principle of society which the Revolution had brought to the world, the imprescriptible rights that belong to each and which are the only possible foundation for a society made up of free and equal individuals. Burke understood that this idea held within it the constitutive abstraction of modern democracy, the universalism of citizenship. He held up against it real society, prejudices, passions, and interests, thus defining one of the major themes of conservative thought and even, more generally, of the critique of democracy whether it be from the Right or from the Left—the difference between flesh-and-blood individuals as opposed to the claim to found a society upon their abstract common identity.

In the same way, the natural rights of individuals keep men from thinking of, let alone constituting, power. What is there to unify a society if it defines itself by what belongs only to individuals? Burke inherited the central question of the eighteenth century, which he treated in the light of 1789. Thus, he was the first observer of the events in France to understand the degree to which the problem of political representation stood at the heart of the French Revolution, inasmuch as the Revolution was a manifestation of the radical individualism of natural rights. The Revolution, as could be seen just about everywhere in 1789, but most especially in Sieyès, passed directly from the individual to the universal, dismissing all the intra-social powers as so many filters or barriers to the General Will. Inescapably, it brought into question the representation of interests in the formation of sovereignty.

The year 1789 separated the political from the social, the State from civil society: Marx was to say this after Burke. For the Whig parliamentarian, however, once the image of individuals at the same time private and equal had been taken as the point of departure, there was no longer any space left for the body politic except in the abstract exaltation of the state-community, an abstract exaltation that was both illusory and dangerous. It was illusory because political society has nothing to do with real society; it was dangerous because the emancipation of individuals from social dependencies superior or anterior to them does not bring about a diminution of authority over them, but rather a shifting and enlarging of authority in the form of the State as incarnation of the sovereignty of the people. What lent Burke's analysis its enormous influence in Europe was this anticipation of democratic despotism, whose realization would be manifest in the Terror one or two years later.

Thus it was that a hostile way of thinking about the Revolution, which rejected it as a collection of false and dangerous principles, was established early on. Set forth in 1790, it condemned in advance as irremediably evil the events born of that disastrous rupture in the continuity of French history. It thus imbued those events with a second nature, derived from the initial error. The Terror presents no particular problem to thought posterior to Burke, no more than can be found in the work of the first German critics of the first French

Declarations of Rights, such as Moser or Jacobi. In direct but opposing echo to the men of 1789, the most profound adversaries of the Revolution positioned themselves to condemn the undertaking from the most general and abstract perspective. If the attempt to reinstitute the social order upon reason, *tabula rasa*, is absurd, what ensued can be deduced from it as its logical consequence. Later on, Bonald was to use such terms to condemn Madame de Staël: 'Je ne connais pas, je l'avoue, ce qu'on appelle les excès de la révolution. Tous les crimes qu'elle a produits n'en ont été que les conséquences naturelles et prévues par les bons esprits, pour horribles qu'elles aient été.'

Counter-revolutionary thought had little trouble constituting itself early on, once and for all, in opposition to revolutionary abstraction: its proponents needed only to take seriously the ambition proclaimed by the men of 1789. By manifesting the philosophy of modern democracy in a universal setting, that famous year provoked the inverse reaction of systematic critique of that philosophy. Since that time, in a conflict which has nourished all of European culture, the ancients and the moderns continue to confront each other.

3

The Heavenly City of the French Revolutionaries

NORMAN HAMPSON

BY way of preface, I should like to emphasize as vigorously as I can that what follows is not intended to suggest that the French Revolution was all about the construction of a heavenly city or a New Jerusalem. Authentic—and radical—revolutionaries like Danton would have ridiculed any such idea. Even the most ideologically inclined were also practical politicians who were concerned about their victory—and personal survival—in a singularly bloody arena. As politicians, they had to deal with concrete problems and to accommodate such pressures as they did not have the resources to resist, which often arose from economic causes. From start to finish the Revolution existed in three dimensions: political, economic, and ideological. In one sense each of these constituted an autonomous force but each reacted upon the other two and was influenced by them, so that the particular form of each was partially shaped by the simultaneous existence of the three. What I have done here is to isolate one of these factors, without implying that it was the most important or that it had more effect in moulding the other two than they had on shaping it. I am dealing with one thread in the revolutionary skein or, to put things in another way, with a single way of looking at a very complicated and multi-dimensional historical epoch. I hope that my account is 'true', in the sense that it is part of the explanation of the behaviour of some of the revolutionaries during part of the time. I am quite certain that it is not the whole truth, but I should regard as inadequate any attempt at a synthesis that failed to incorporate this aspect of the Revolution, which is not to pretend, of course, that I regard my own interpretation of revolutionary ideology as the only one possible.

The heavenly city of the revolutionaries was no vague dream of some ideal future state. It had a local habitation and a name, and the name was Sparta. Robespierre, admittedly, thought it politic to deny this: 'Nous ne prétendons pas jeter la République française dans la moule de celle de Sparte', but he went on to praise that *vertu* that had wrought so many prodigies in Greece and Rome. Saint-Just had fewer inhibitions about telling his hearers what was good for them: 'nous vous offrîmes le bonheur de Sparte et celui d'Athènes dans ses beaux jours'.

For their conception of the qualities that made Sparta so exemplary they owed a good deal to Montesquieu, although he usually coupled it with Athens and republican Rome. For Montesquieu, the activating principle of the classical city-state had been *vertu*, which he defined as 'L'amour de la patrie et de l'égalité'. As he had demonstrated in the parable of the Troglodytes, in the *Lettres persanes*, a community of the *vertueux* would need no coercive government since all its citizens could be relied on to discharge their civic duties of their own accord. This was perhaps a heavenly city, but it was no City of God. By locating his model societies in pre-Christian Europe, Montesquieu escaped any awkward questions about a dual allegiance to God and Caesar. He went further than that, insisting that *vertu* was not a Christian or a moral quality, but a purely political one. This attempt to define the principle of the classical republic as no more than a particular political cast of mind proved impossible to sustain. In practice, he found it impossible to keep *vertu* separate from virtue—especially since he had to use the same word for them both—and the city-state therefore came to take on attributes of moral excellence that were denied to other forms of political organization.

As *De l'esprit des lois* progressed, Montesquieu began to change his mind. Liberty came to be his criterion of good government and he realized that liberty, in the sense of the individual's freedom to develop his own potentialities in his own way, could not flourish amongst the self-imposed restraints of the classical republic. 'La vertu même a besoin de limites.' We are all do-gooders at heart and we need protection from other people's concern for our moral welfare. Montesquieu therefore turned away from the collective joys of the polis to the kind of state in which the necessarily divergent views of the inhabitants checked and balanced each other as the result of a contrived political equilibrium.

The cause of the classical republics and especially of Sparta, deserted by Montesquieu, was taken up by Rousseau. Like Montesquieu, Rousseau was primarily concerned with liberty, but he conceived of it in an entirely different way. Burke said of him, 'Rousseau is a moralist or he is nothing', and for him freedom meant essentially freedom from political sin. Putting society in the place of God, he saw the individual as becoming a moral being only when he agreed to participate in a society whose collective well-being became the sole determinant of his civic and moral duty. In its service was perfect freedom. The General Will of such a society, in other words, what was actually beneficial to it, assumed some of the attributes of God. It was infallible: 'la volonté générale, par cela seul qu'elle est, est toujours ce qu'elle doit être.' It was also omnipotent, in the sense that deviants could—and should—be 'forced to be free'. To invoke one's conscience against the General Will was as meaningless as to invoke it against God. Rousseau's problem was to find a working relationship between the General Will, or the 'objective' interest of a society, and what its members actually thought they wanted. Considering that they might be ignorant as well as virtuous, and that their virtue itself would need sustaining against what the Christians called 'the world, the flesh, and the devil', Rousseau was driven to invoke an omniscient Legislator, to provide a new society with the institutions necessary to confirm it in the ways of right-eousness and subsequently to explain to the sovereign people what political choices actually involved, or what it was for their own good that they should believe them to in-volve.

This way of conceiving of society as the vehicle for the moral regeneration of its members involved several logical conse-quences. Once the General Will had been established in connection with any particular issue, those who had initially misjudged it were expected, not merely to obey, but to admit that they had been wrong and to adopt the policies that they had formerly opposed. Persistence in opposition could only imply a wilful preference for personal advantage over the common good. The more perfect a society, the more unanimous it would be. A community of political saints would be one where the views of the individual members would always be in harmony with each other and with the General Will. Those who found the prospect of life in such a society asphyxiating had no need to join. Those who accepted the terms and then went on to contest them had broken the initial contract and declared themselves to be rebels against the General Will. Rousseau was never consistent about what he regarded as matters of detail and one should perhaps not make too much of the fact that in one place he argued that such revolt justified putting people to death. He certainly upheld the Stoic view that the scale of a crime or misdemeanour was less significant than the fact that it constituted a violation of the social contract on which everything depended. He was quite extraordinarily vague about how, in practice, one could distinguish the General Will from the will of all. The one represented the real interest of a community and was morally binding on the entire population, whereas the other was merely the sum of its individual interests. The General Will was therefore not to be equated with a majority vote but Rousseau, in an incautious moment, said that it was always located within the majority.

When one tries to understand the extent to which ideas of this kind influenced the theory and practice of the French revolutionaries, two questions arise: how far were the politicians consciously trying to implement Rousseau's ideas and how did they adapt his abstract theories when dealing with concrete political problems. There is an obvious danger of misplaced erudition seizing upon a few casual references to Montesquieu or Rousseau, tacked on to speeches in the hope of making them sound more important, and interpreting them as commitment to an ideology. Anyone who reads the reports of debates, particularly those of the Constituent Assembly, will soon realize that this was far from being the case. References to Rousseau in particular were continual and frequently specific: deputies turned for support not merely to his name but to his ideas. Some of these could be borrowed as they stood, but others had to be adapted. As he himself insisted, when he wrote the *Social*

Contract, Rousseau had in mind a community of the size of the classical city-state or his own native Geneva. He claimed to have destroyed the original manuscript in which he described the federal structure that would be necessary if his ideas were to be applied to the government of a state of any size. This was fundamental to his theory, since he insisted that the General Will could not be expressed through representatives but could only emerge from an actual meeting of the entire body of citizens. This was why he maintained that the British were free only on polling day. Most of the revolutionaries chose to disregard this, arguing that the people, by the electoral process, transferred the exercise of its sovereignty to its deputies. In strictly theoretical terms this disqualified them from being considered as Rousseauists, but only if one conceded that Rousseau's ideas had no relevance to the modern world. They certainly believed themselves to be his followers and if they had never read him they would not have behaved as they did. If one wants to understand their sense of mission, their passion for moral regeneration, and their adoption of policies that sometimes bore only a very distant relationship to the social and economic realities of eighteenth-century France, one has to start with Rousseau.

Rousseau's *political* influence only became significant after 1789. It was scarcely visible in the prerevolutionary 'Roman' posturing that came naturally to a classically-educated society. In a rough-and-ready way, one can say that all opponents of the monarchy adopted Roman poses, whereas Rousseau was more concerned with the kind of transformation of society that he believed to have occurred in Sparta. *Parlementaires* had fancied themselves to be patricians and talked about the *patrie* instead of the *royaume*. The diarist Barbier described them admiringly as *véritables Romains*. Voltaire glorified Brutus and Montesquieu had himself painted in a toga. This sort of thing was common to both England and France and it did not get anyone very far. Rousseau did indeed enjoy a unique reputation in France, but as a sentimental moralist rather than a Spartan. This was something that tended not to cross the Channel and it puzzled Burke: 'I have often wondered how he seems to be so much more admired and followed on the Continent than he is here. Perhaps a secret charm in the language may have its share in this extraordinary difference.'[1] The British have never been very good at foreign languages. It was indeed Rousseau's hypnotic prose, harnessed to a boastful exhibition of his human frailty and an appeal to the emotions of a generation desiccated by the logic of the Enlightenment and the conventions of polite society, that gave 'Jean-Jacques' his unique influence in France. To the generation that grew to maturity in the 1780s he was a kind of guru, a sort of Wesley who inspired them, if not exactly to repentance and to God, at least to Nature and morality. His effect was that of a revivalist preacher, inviting men to discover their souls and to awaken to a new moral existence. Brissot and Madame Roland recorded their reaction to *Émile* and to the *Nouvelle Héloïse* in the language of religious conversion. Rousseau's moral empire in a France awash with *sensibilité* was eatablished well before the Revolution, but his political writings did not seem to have much relevance to the ritualistic ballet that passed for politics in the Old Regime. When a political crisis developed in 1787 it was Montesquieu who supplied the *parlementaires* with most of their ammunition. It was the miracle of 1789 when, as the British ambassador put it, 'the greatest revolution that we know of' had made France a free country, the inconceivable had already happened and all things seemed possible, that made Rousseau's political message sound like prophecy. Had he not written in the *Social Contract*, 'Les bornes du possible, dans les choses morales, sont moins étroites que nous ne pensons; ce sont nos faiblesses, nos vices, nos préjugés, qui les rétrécissent.' After 1789 that seemed equally true of *les choses politiques*. Whatever might be the case where foreigners were concerned, the French people at least had responded to Rousseau's challenge. From 1789 onwards, as Roger Barny has shown, he became a kind of totem whom one criticized at one's peril.[2]

François Furet has stressed the extent to which a Rousseauist ideology came to dominate and explain the course of the Revolution, describing it as 'un système de croyances qui constitue la légitimité nouvelle'. 'Sa pensée politique constitue

[1] E. Burke, 'Letter to a member of the National Assembly' [1791], in *Reflections on the Revolution in France* (Everyman Edition; London, 1935), 267.
[2] R. Barny, *Rousseau dans la Révolution: Le Personnage de Jean-Jacques et les débuts du culte révolutionnaire* (Oxford, 1986).

bien par avance le cadre conceptuel de ce qui sera la jacobin-
isme.' Furet then seems to assume that the revolutionaries were
unaware of the source of their ideas when they substituted
ideology for the normal play of political institutions, going so far
as to claim that 'la plupart des hommes de 89 n'ont pas lu
Rousseau'.[3] A glance at the reports of the debates in the
Constituent Assembly is enough to demonstrate that this was
far from being the case. This is not a matter of claiming every
casual reference to a General Will or the sovereignty of the
people as a Rousseauist scalp. People arguing about his ideas
did not find it necessary to spell them out but could refer to
them in a kind of shorthand. Robespierre in particular treated
his name as too holy for casual mention and usually preferred to
speak of the sage of Geneva or the preceptor of the human race.
When Mounier found it odd that those who proclaimed the
sovereignty of the assembly should do so in the name of a man
who said that the General Will could not be represented, he did
not need to say who that was. The debates about the royal veto
and a unicameral assembly were seen by everyone as a battle
between Montesquieu and Rousseau. The duc de La Roche-
foucauld summed up his conversion to the radical viewpoint by
simply saying, 'Montesquieu sera combattu par Rousseau.'
Robespierre, apparently about the time of his election in 1789,
wrote a solemn invocation to Rousseau in which he swore to be
true to his example. Five years later, in the most ideological of all
his speeches, he quoted the only passage in the *Social Contract* in
which Rousseau said that the regeneration of an old and corrupt
society was possible.[4] This is not to deny, of course, that
Rousseauists sometimes decided that the Master's principles
were better honoured in the breach than in the observance.
Most of them accepted, with reservations, the legitimacy of
representation, which Rousseau denied. When an over-
enthusiastic Jacobin, in the spring of 1794, wanted to deport the
deputy Lequinio, on the ground that he was an atheist,
Robespierre shut him up with the observation that there were
some truths that were better left in the pages of Rousseau. The
point is simply that whether they followed him, or occasionally

---

[3] F. Furet, *Penser la Révolution* (Paris, 1978), 44, 51.

[4] M. Bouloiseau and A. Soboul (eds.), *Œuvres de Maximilien Robespierre* (Paris,
1967), x. 355. The reference is to *Du contrat social*, II. 8.

decided not to, they were quite well aware of what they were doing. He provided them with their vision of the New Jerusalem and their justification for all the sacrifices they imposed on the French people in order to effect its regeneration.

Rousseau's influence was so powerful that even those who started out from different premisses were caught up in the current. Saint-Just believed man to be a social animal whose natural state was one of co-operation and harmony. Any talk of 'rights' or 'contracts' was only appropriate to an unnatural or political state that rested, in the last resort, on force. In his early writings he was quite critical of Rousseau, whom he could not pardon for his acceptance of the death penalty, and accused him of strangling liberty with its own hands. Once elected to the Convention, in 1792, Saint-Just's ideas soon came into line with those of the citizen of Geneva. By the spring of 1793, the man who had once objected to Rousseau's 'vigorous methods' was virtually quoting him on the need for a Legislator: 'C'est à lui de rendre les hommes ce qu'il veut qu'ils le soient' (Rousseau had written: 'les rendre tels qu'on a besoin qu'ils soient'). In theory, when he dreamed of his social state, Saint-Just was as far from Rousseau as ever; he comforted himself from time to time with the thought that his Draconian remedies were applied only to the wicked, while the innocent were *indépendants sur la terre*. There did not seem to be many of the latter and when he talked about re-creating Sparta he must have realized that most of his audience would have to be bullied into becoming Spartans. What had originated as a rejection of Rousseau's ends came to rely on his means, and even where ends were concerned, Sparta was not how Saint-Just had originally conceived of the social state. The French revolutionaries were not simply millenarians; they were Rousseauist millenarians.

The implications of trying to apply Rousseau's principles to France's problems were soon apparent. Virtually all the members of the Constituent Assembly, with the possible exception of a handful of royalist cavaliers, believed in popular sovereignty. Most of them acted as though they also thought of *vox populi* as *vox dei*. For the Right, whose members liked to quote Rousseau on the impossibility of representing the General Will, the sovereign people consisted of the silent majority whose instructions to its *mandataires*, as expressed in the *cahiers* of 1789, had been limited to the redress of grievances and had been very respectful of the authority of the king. The Left, which normally enjoyed a majority in the assembly, insisted that the people had transferred the exercise of its sovereignty to the assembly itself which had been 'elevated to a constituent power by the unanimous wish of all Frenchmen', as one deputy put it, though he would have been hard pressed to say when and how. The extreme Left, whilst usually content for business to be transacted on this basis, insisted that nothing could deprive the sovereign people (which in practice meant the Parisian crowd) of its right to resume the exercise of its sovereignty whenever it chose, as had allegedly happened in July 1789.

Men from different parts of the political spectrum might disagree about the location of sovereignty. They were all convinced that it coincided with the will of their own political group and as Rousseauists they believed that all opposition to their and the people's will was illegitimate and immoral since it consisted in subordinating what the men concerned knew to be in the general good, to whatever looked like serving their selfish and sectional interests. In the words of Alexandre de Lameth, 'La volonté de l'Assemblée Nationale est l'expression de la volonté générale. Le résultat des opinions de la majorité des représentants de la nation est, quoi qu'en dise un petit nombre d'hommes, l'expression de la volonté générale.' If this was the case, the minority consisted of people who had been mistaken about what was in the national interest. If they were honest they would admit this and change their minds, or if that was asking rather too much of human frailty and *amour-propre*, at least they would keep their mouths shut. What was intolerable was for them to go on parading their disagreement, which one deputy described as a *conspiration contre le pouvoir législatif*. To claim the right to conscientious objection in cases of disagreement was mere hypocrisy for, as Mirabeau put it, 'S'il est contraire à la morale d'agir contre sa conscience, il ne l'est pas moins de faire une conscience d'après des principes faux et arbitraires. L'obligation de faire sa conscience est antérieure à l'obligation de suivre sa conscience.' This was a conception of political conscience with which the Right had concurred—in 1789, when it hoped to form the majority, and Lally-Tollendal had said: 'Il n'est pas permis de protester, de réserver, c'est un attentat à la puissance de la majorité.' From the summer of 1789 onwards the Right was rarely in a majority, so it had few opportunities to proclaim its allegiance to democratic centralism as defined by Rousseau.

This comfortable doctrine had even more convenient corollaries, which Duport expounded for the benefit of those who were not very good at political theory. The *cahiers* had merely been an expression of the opinions of isolated groups of people. The General Will only emerged with the coming together of the National Assembly, which alone embodied the will of the entire people. Its function was therefore to 'faire vouloir le peuple. Sa volonté est ici.' There might actually be times when it was necessary for the deputies to rectify public opinion. As Charles Lameth put it, 'Il faudrait éclairer l'opinion; il faudrait la régir pour lui rendre les bienfaits que nous tenons d'elle.' Barère agreed that it was for the 'pouvoir constitué, devenu législatif, à remédier aux abus du pouvoir constituant'. It was, in other words, for the elected to disregard the views of the electors whenever it was necessary for their own good. This may have been the opposite of what Rousseau had in mind, but it was what his Legislator was supposed to do and the deputies were rather fond of describing themselves as legislators.

When the assembly turned its attention to the place of religion in regenerated France it became obvious that its conception of a heavenly city was more than a matter of dressing up certain political options in grandiloquent language. It applied to every aspect of human existence. Mirabeau claimed that the assembly enjoyed all the powers that had belonged to the people who first united to form the French nation. Treilhard, on the same tack, said to his colleagues, 'Nous pourrons faire tout ce que nous ferions s'il s'agissait d'admettre la religion dans le royaume.' Camus who, not long before, had represented the French clergy in the Paris Parlement, agreed that 'Nous avons assurément le pouvoir de changer la religion', even if he disclaimed any intention of doing so. Robespierre asserted that *les officiers religieux* were established for the good of society; hostile noises prevented him from going on to say that they should therefore be encouraged to marry. The deputies in general, and this included some of the clergy, saw priests as *officiers de morale*. They did not intend to interfere with Roman Catholic dogma, but they saw this as an indication of their moderation rather than a limitation of their power. Popular sovereignty left no room for the imperatives of canon law and the *morale* that was preached would be determined by the assembly and not by the Church. Heavenly cities have no room for dissenting preachers.

The actual practices of the Constituent Assembly, except when it blundered into the disastrous conflict with the Church, were much less extreme than the language of some of the deputies would have led one to expect. A few oratorical swallows did not necessary imply the arrival of a Rousseauist summer. The course of the Revolution was not entirely determined by its ideology, but the debates of 1789–91 had shown that, if circumstances were propitious, the theoretical foundations had already been laid on which to begin building a heavenly city that would not have much in common with traditional views about town-planning.

What transformed the political situation was the war, the virtual overthrow of the monarchy on 10 August 1792 and the proclamation of a republic in the following month. To eighteenth-century ears the word 'republic' had the sort of connotations that 'soviet' would have today. It implied a qualitatively different kind of regime. Montesquieu had taught the revolutionary generation that a republic was not merely a state without a king, but a community whose principle was *vertu* and whose survival depended on its citizens subordinating their private interests to the general good. This posed problems. As Robespierre informed his readers in the first issue of the newspaper that he launched in the autumn of 1792, France had put the cart before the horse. 'Pour former nos institutions politiques, il nous faudrait les mœurs qu'elles doivent nous donner un jour.' Rousseau had had to face the same problem: 'Pour qu'un peuple naissant pût goûter les saines maximes de la politique et suivre les règles fondamentales de la raison d'état, il faudrait que l'effet pût devenir la cause.' Robespierre's problem was even worse since the French were anything but a *peuple naissant*, since they had been corrupted by centuries of 'despotism'. 'Vous avez chassé les rois, mais avez-vous chassé les vices que leur funeste domination a enfanté parmi vous?' It was rather sinister that he should have switched from 'nous' to 'vous' when he began to talk about vice. He went on to give a long quotation from the *Social Contract* about the qualities required of a Legislator. Robespierre had no immediate solution to the problems of trying to build a republic with 'des mains encore flêtries des fers du despotisme'. For the moment he consoled himself with the thought that 'le peuple est bon'; France was now a democracy, in the sense that all adult males were allowed to vote—for republican candidates, and that might see her through, although Robespierre obviously had his doubts.

Saint-Just, whose public career began when he was elected to the Convention, shared Robespierre's conviction that creating a republic involved rebuilding the whole edifice of the state in a new way. This was the leitmotiv of all his contributions to the debates of the first six months. His maiden speech, which established his reputation overnight, was about what to do with the king. In his *Esprit de la Révolution*, published in 1791, he had adopted a rather patronizing but not unduly critical attitude towards Louis XVI. Things were very different in a republic. The character and policies of Louis had become irrelevant. 'On ne peut régner innocemment.' The king was not a party to the social contract and from the point of view of the French people he was an alien 'qui doit être jugé comme un ennemi étranger'. There was a certain logic to this, but it did not extend to Saint-Just's conclusion that Louis should therefore be put to death without trial. For this at least Rousseau was not to blame: he had specifically condemned the killing of prisoners of war. Regeneration, if Saint-Just ever got his way, looked like bearing hard on the unregenerate. If, as Robespierre said, only republicans were citizens in a republic, quite a lot of Frenchmen were going to find themselves in the same situation as the king.

In a remarkable speech on 29 November, Saint-Just went on to call for the creation of a republican economy. Under the monarchy, employment and the circulation of wealth had been assured by the extravagant expenditure of the aristocracy. That would have to be replaced by a new kind of economy, based on the exchange of necessities. 'Si vous voulez une république, faites en sorte que le peuple ait le courage d'être vertueux.' 'On a fait une république avec des vices; faites-en des vertus.' In January it was the turn of the War Office. Whatever Montesquieu was believed to have said about the separation of powers, it was not safe for a belligerent republic to entrust its armed forces to ministers who would be tempted to use them in pursuit of their personal power. The Convention should therefore make itself directly responsible for the war ministry. In the spring he argued that electoral constituencies were territorial areas in a monarchy, but communities of people in a republic.

Before one could set about building the heavenly city one had to choose the architects. This led to a war—literally to the death—between Montagnards and Girondins. Both groups shared a common ideology. Virtually all of the revolutionaries saw themselves as Rousseauists of one kind or another, but Montagnards and Girondins were Rousseauists of the same kind. Both were democrats, republicans, and anticlericals; both believed the 'laws' of liberal economics to be laws of nature that could not be defied with impunity or for long. Robespierre and his followers had initially opposed the war but they had become as chauvinistic as the Girondins and both factions united to extend the war to England, Spain, and The Netherlands. By 1793 the Girondins appealed to the provinces and to law and order, the Montagnards to Paris and the sansculottes, but that was the product of political tactics, rather than of ideology or of economic policy. What really divided the two was the claim of each to be the custodian of the General Will. This led the Girondins to accuse their rivals of aspiring to dictatorship and the Montagnards to retort with accusations of federalism. Each was convinced that there could be no question of compromise with the other, which would have been tantamount to condoning political sin.

The elimination of the Girondins on 2 June 1793 should at last have cleared the site for building operations. The majority of the deputies were committed, or at least resigned, to the construction of an ideal republic, in accordance with plans that owed more to Lycurgus than to Adam Smith. The naïve might have thought that the time was ripe for the first general signs of the coming social state of Saint-Just's dreams. In fact, the real struggle was only just beginning. As Saint-Just explained in October, 'Les lois sont révolutionnaires; ceux qui les exécutent ne le sont pas.' 'La République ne sera fondée que quand la volonté du souverain comprimera la minorité monarchique et régnera sur elle par droit de conquête.' This was the language of the *état politique*, in the days when Saint-Just had seen all force as oppressive. Times had changed with a vengeance. 'Vous avez à punir non seulement les traîtres, mais les indifférents mêmes; vous avez à punir quiconque est passif dans la République et ne fait rien pour elle; car depuis que le peuple français a manifesté sa volonté, tout ce qui lui est opposé est hors le souverain; tout ce qui est hors le souverain est ennemi.' It was King Charles's head again, or rather, Louis XVI's.

There was, of course, the possibility that the vigorous methods of the Committee of Public Safety would produce a situation where there were more French people outside the heavenly city than within it. This need not cause anyone undue concern. Rousseau had explained that although the General Will was infallible, the people were not always reliable judges of what it was, and it was not to be confused with the will of all. This could take one rather a long way. Barère enlarged on the principle that he had already put forward in the Constituent Assembly, that the elected were superior to their electors and the whole process of election was a monarchical sort of thing. This was being rather too blunt and the unctuous Couthon supplied the necessary qualification: 'Le droit d'élection appartient essentiellement au peuple souverain. On ne peut y porter atteinte sans crime, à moins que des circonstances extraordinaires ne le demandent pour le bonheur même du peuple.' It all depended on who was to be the judge of that. Saint-Just was of the same opinion: 'Il s'est fait une révolution dans le gouvernement; elle n'a point pénétré l'état civil.' The sovereign people, in other words, was not up to the level of its leaders. As Robespierre had feared all along, that was to be expected. Generations of men who had learned deference and hypocrisy in the vicious society of the Old Regime were not going to respond spontaneously to the bracing demands of the new Sparta. Ever since the autumn of 1793 Saint-Just had been reiterating that what were needed were 'republican institutions', which, like Rousseau's Legislator, would transform human nature itself. That was what a republic was really about and until that victory had been won all the rest was precarious and insecure.

In the meantime France had to be governed and the war won, in circumstances of exceptional difficulty. The measures taken

by the revolutionary government were to some extent dictated
by external pressures, but its reaction to these pressures was
quite unlike the behaviour of any other eighteenth-century
government, and this was partly due to the ideology of the
revolutionaries. It would scarcely be going too far to say that the
whole course of the Revolution was dominated by the war. The
republican response to the military challenge was national
mobilization of a kind that was not to be seen again until the
twentieth century. As in classical times, the republicans made
no distinction between public and private, military and civilian.
All unmarried adult males between 18 and 60 were declared
mobilized, although only those aged 25 and below were
incorporated into the army. The remainder could be sent
wherever their services were needed: coopers from the Channel
ports to make barrels in Brest, dockyard workers from Bayonne
to the arsenal at Toulon. This was a practical demonstration of a
republic exercising its right to dispose of all its citizens in its own
defence.

The revolutionaries were sufficiently influenced by the values
of their own century to treat property rights as sacred—but not
when this might detract from the war effort. Items of military
use were requisitioned, cannon foundries put under the control
of state managers, shipowners forbidden to send out their
vessels without a certificate saying they were not required by
the navy. The means employed were modern but the attitude
behind the policies went back to Sparta.

War on this scale could not be financed by taxation. The
government pressures were turning out assignats as fast as they
could be printed. To avoid uncontrollable inflation the price of
necessities was regulated by the state. That meant abolishing
the grain trade and supplying the towns and armies by
requisition. The Commission des Subsistances became the first
Ministry of Food in European history. Much of this was of
necessity a hit-or-miss business: when the navy minister
reduced the wages of dockyard workers for the second time in
six months, he was under the impression that he was increasing
them. In such circumstances, carpenters and caulkers were
perhaps unlikely to share the government's view that it alone
was in a position to distinguish the General Will. Some of the
economic controls were imposed on a reluctant government by

pressure from the streets, rather than adopted from ideological conviction, but when the pressure had been overcome, the regulations were modified but not abolished. There were probably two views, within the government, about how one should regard all this. For the more conservative, like Carnot, it was all a question of temporary expedients that would be abandoned as soon as the war was won. For Robespierre and especially Saint-Just it was a demonstration that, within a republic, even the 'laws' of economic liberalism had to march in step.

The war became one of national extermination, in the classical rather than the eighteenth-century tradition. When the Committee of Public Safety introduced a Bill to exclude British trade, an enthusiast persuaded the Convention to order the arrest of all British civilians. This was eventually extended to include all enemy aliens, despite Saint-Just's denial of any intention to 'nationalize' the war. Robespierre declared himself shocked by a man who said that France's quarrel was with the British government and not the people. More remarkable, indeed reaching a depth of barbarity that our own century has yet to equal, was the decision of 26 May 1794 that no British or Hanoverian prisoners were to be taken. The more enthusiastic historians of the Revolution, when they do not pass this over in silence, find easy comfort in reassuring their readers that the order was never applied in practice. This would not excuse it and there is at least one case where it was applied. After all, like Louis XVI, the British were not part of the city and so they had no rights.

Where politics was concerned, the course of events owed as much to circumstances as to ideology. The scale of the war effort, in a divided country, parts of which were in open revolt, made the creation of a war cabinet with dictatorial powers virtually inevitable. The constitution of 1793 was a blueprint for a democratic society some way along the road to Saint-Just's social state. It was not necessarily disingenuous to argue that it could not be applied in the desperate conditions of 1793. Nevertheless, when Saint-Just persuaded the Convention that government must remain 'revolutionary' until the end of the war, he was also committing it to revolutionary methods, which meant ferocity in the repression of whatever was considered to

be vice or crime. 'Il faut que le glaive des lois se promène partout
avec rapidité . . . Il faut . . . placer partout le glaive à côté de
l'abus.' As some Montagnards were complaining within a
month, that meant intimidating the Convention as well as the
faceless friends of monarchy and corruption. The decree of
4 December empowered the government to replace elected
officials with its own nominees and to control the representatives
on mission in the provinces.

The centralization of government was something that might
well have happened as a response to the pressure of circumstances, and the bloody civil war within the Montagnards owed
more to politics than to ideology. The government had its
reasons for wanting to destroy possible rivals, both in Paris and
within the assembly itself. Some of the deputies *were* corrupt,
and royalist plots were not wholly imaginary. The Cordelier
Club did talk vaguely about starting a new insurrection, and the
government may have feared that if Fabre d'Églantine were
tried for corruption, his friend Danton might overthrow the
government in order to rescue him. François Furet has argued
persuasively that revolutionary ideology presupposed the existence of a ubiquitous but undefinable Enemy: there had to be
some explanation for the fact that the adoption of the 'right'
policies never produced the expected results. This is true
enough but not the whole truth. There are conspiracies as well
as conspiracy theories, and there was more to revolutionary
politics than the rationalization of an ideological need.

What does seem to call for a particular explanation is the fact
that the Terror was greatly intensified just when victory in civil
and foreign war diminished the justification for it. The law of 22
Prairial (10 June) transformed not merely the procedure but the
rationale of the revolutionary tribunal. It established within the
judicial process the distinction made by the ideologists between
public and private relationships. However desirable humanity
might be in civil law, where the state was concerned Terror was
emphatically the order of the day. Crimes against the state were
defined in the most general terms, which allowed human
weakness, avarice, or bloody-mindedness to be treated as
treason or sabotage of the war effort. Presumed enemies of the
Revolution, who had excluded themselves from the community,
were not to be treated as though they were citizens. They were

denied counsel and the right to call witnesses. As soon as the jury had convinced itself of their guilt—on moral rather than judicial grounds—it could bring a trial to an end. This was to give a new meaning to 'conviction'. For the guilty, and henceforth that was almost synonymous with the accused, the only penalty was death. This was not a panic measure to terrify opposition during a temporary crisis. It constituted, and was defended as constituting, a new conception of justice. In the heavenly city, innocence and guilt was to be determined by moral conviction rather than by legal niceties. Innocent men were assumed not to tremble, for fear of conviction was proof of guilt. In a world increasingly divided into the innocent and the enemies of the people, the salvation of the former depended on the extermination of the latter, who had chosen to forfeit their claim to be treated as members of the city. This was indeed being true to Sparta.

In the end, therefore, it is difficult to see revolutionary politics, in the summer of 1794, as motivated any longer by what are usually regarded as political norms. It was, however, a logical extension of the idea that Saint-Just had put forward and Robespierre adopted at the time of the king's trial, that whoever separated himself from the republican community—and the government was the judge of that—forfeited his right to exist. If the world were to be made safe for the sheep, every wolf had to be destroyed, and to talk of pardoning or converting wolves was to reveal that one was a wolf oneself.

Attempts have been made to present the economic policies of the revolutionary government as a quest for an impossible compromise between the class interests of the bourgeoisie and those of the sansculottes. Any economic policy is going to benefit some sections of the community more than others and, to the extent that the ideologists had a sentimental hankering after a society of independent small producers, their sympathies were directed towards the poor rather than the rich. In practice, this meant pacifying the relatively small number of urban poor by extracting food from the peasant majority at less than its market price. This had been the practice of the Old Regime, when times were difficult, and there was nothing very new about it, except that it was now being done on a national scale. But, as always, there was an ideological dimension to the thinking of some at least of the members of the government. It was for the state to regulate the economic side of communal life in a manner appropriate to the community that it was trying to create. The urban artisan was entitled to a secure, if frugal, existence and the extension of peasant proprietorship was to be encouraged by the division of commons and the sale of émigré land in small lots. Saint-Just, in his speech of 26 February 1793, made it clear that the rationale behind this was moral rather than economic.

La première loi de toutes les lois est la conservation de la République . . . L'opulence est dans les mains d'un assez grand nombre d'ennemis de la Révolution; les besoins mettent le peuple qui travaille dans la dépendance de ses ennemis . . . La Révolution nous conduit à reconnaître ce principe que celui qui s'est montré l'ennemi de son pays n'y peut être propriétiare . . . Les propriétés des patriotes sont sacrées mais les biens des conspirateurs sont là pour tous les malheureux.

The decree that concluded his speech provided for the expropriation of enemies of the republic and their banishment at the end of the war. This was not class war; it corresponded to Robespierre's 'il faut moraliser le commerce'. Everything had to be *moralisé* if the New Jerusalem was to work.

When Rousseau published *Émile* he excused himself for not writing about public education since there was no *patrie* that might give the subject any meaning. In January 1793 Robespierre began an article on education in his newspaper by paraphrasing the first sentence of *Émile*: 'L'homme est bon, sortant des mains de la nature . . .'. If evil institutions had perverted him, better ones might reform him. Like Rousseau, however, Robespierre thought that the time was not ripe: Girondin domination of the Convention had to be destroyed before 'vous serez dignes de commencer le grand ouvrage de l'instruction publique'. By the summer of 1793 this condition had been met and on 13 July Robespierre read to the assembly a plan for a system of national education that had been written by the murdered deputy Michel Lepeletier. This provided for compulsory education for all boys from 5 to 12 and for girls from 5 to 11, in State boarding schools. It specifically rejected a Platonic or Spartan system, in which the State provided the same education for everyone, on the disingenuous ground that the republic needed *des hommes de tous les états.* The intention, in other words, was to use the educational system as a means of political indoctrination rather than of social levelling. At the age of 12 some would become ploughboys and other devote themselves to *des belles lettres, des sciences ou des arts agréables.* By that time, seven years of communal life, Spartan conditions and military exercises should have endowed each of them with 'les aptitudes physiques et morales qu'il importe à tous de retrouver dans le cours de la vie, quelle que soit la position particulière de chacun . . . nous préparons, pour ainsi dire, une matière première, que nous tendons à rendre essentiellement bonne.'

When Saint-Just discussed education in his 'institutions républicaines', he was more laconic in every sense of the word. 'Les enfants appartiennent à leur mère jusqu'à cinq ans, si elle les a nourris, à la république ensuite, jusqu'à la mort.' All boys were to receive the same education until 16, after which they would work for five years in agriculture, in industry, or as seamen, before doing four years of military service. Girls were to be educated at home. Robespierre and Saint-Just shared a common intention to create a race of Spartans, but where Robespierre saw this as an initial period of character formation before they took their places in society as it was, what Saint-Just had in mind was a primitive society where everyone would be artisans, peasants, or soldiers. He had obviously not much use for *belles lettres, des sciences et des arts agréables.* Whatever the Spartans had found unnecessary was of no use to anyone else.

Where religion was concerned, Robespierre derived his inspiration from the penultimate chapter of the *Social Contract*, with its *profession de foi purement civile.* His speech of 7 May 1794 amounted to the dedication of France to Rousseau's conception of the divinity and the beginning of a new age.

L'art de gouverner a été jusqu'à nos jours l'art de tromper et de corrompre les hommes; il ne doit être que celui de les éclairer et de les rendre meilleurs . . . Le fondement unique de toute société civile, c'est la morale . . . La Révolution n'est que le passage du règne du crime à celui de la justice . . . L'idée de l'Être Suprême et de l'immortalité de l'âme est un rappel éternel à la justice; elle est donc sociale et républicaine.

What was not republican had forfeited its right to exist in the republic and whatever *was* republican enjoyed divine endorsement and protection. The heavenly city was entirely self-sufficient, in religion as well as in everything else, and everything served to emphasize both its unanimity and its separation from the rest of the world.

Robespierre who, in his Arras days, had defended lightning conductors against the prejudices of the unscientific, now rejected the *philosophes—fiers dans leurs écrits et rampants dans les ante-chambres*—as materialists and egoists whose only criterion of virtue was success. Their descendants had been no better: 'Les hommes de lettres en général se sont déshonorés dans cette révolution.' Rousseau alone 'parla avec enthousiasme de la divinité; son éloquence mâle et probe peignit en traits de flamme les charmes de la vertu'. And so Robespierre dedicated France to a republican deism that was modelled on the national religion of the *Social Contract*. Four great annual fêtes were to commemorate the great days of the Revolution as religious events, with minor festivals every tenth day. For Robespierre at least, the ideal city was indeed a heavenly one. He had asserted his belief in providence at a time when it was more fashionable to be a sceptic; he had staked his political career on opposition to what he declared to be atheism, and there can be no question of the sincerity of his faith. Everything that the Revolution stood for was guaranteed and sustained by a republican god.

Towards the end of his life Saint-Just began to draft the republican institutions that were both to create and to consolidate his own heavenly city. He did not have the time to reduce these fragmentary jottings to any kind of systematic order, but enough has survived to indicate the fatal paradox that transformed what was intended as a utopia into a nightmare. True to the vision of the ideal society that he had sketched in *De la nature*, he continued to insist that men were naturally good, spontaneously social beings who had no need of a *société politique* with its contracts and coercive laws. Private life should be subjected as little as possible *aux lois de l'autorité*. That was the goal, but its attainment called for something more than the punishment of the corrupt and oppressive. The people in whose name and for whose benefit all this was to be done had been perverted by centuries of misgovernment. It was therefore necessary *d'enchaîner le crime par des institutions*. The people had made the Revolution but only a Legislator could make the Republic. His objective was therefore to 'rendre à la nature et à l'innocence la passion de tous les cœurs'. In other words, as things stood, nature was unnatural; it was something that had to be taught to a people by its government. Only when this had been done would it be safe to leave the private citizen to his own devices. *L'innocence* might be *indépendante sur la terre*, but it was for the government to make men innocent.

The regeneration of the French people was not merely a matter of moral exhortation; it called for a transformation of the economy. If men were to recover their independence they had to be made self-sufficient, which meant growing their own food. 'Il faut donner quelques terres à tout le monde . . . Il ne faut ni riches ni pauvres . . . L'opulence est une infamie.' Even inequality of talent was suspect, and he shared Robespierre's mistrust of intellectuals. 'Il faut ramener toutes les définitions à la conscience; l'esprit est un sophiste qui conduit les vertus à l'échafaud.' His conception of a republican economy was as ruthless as it was impracticable. He disapproved of slavery but the colonies had to be developed; and so he proposed buying Africans, shipping them across the Atlantic, and then establishing them as free settlers. He believed himself to be liberating the citizens whom he proposed to enslave, but behind everything—laws, customs, institutions, and economy—loomed the shadow of Sparta.

What the visionaries failed to realize was that the basis of the General Will, as they conceived it, was narrowing all the time. In 1789 it had been the people as a whole, minus the counter-revolutionaries. After 10 August 1792 it was the republicans and then the Convention, which quickly came to mean the Convention minus the Girondins. When the Montagnards themselves split into hostile factions, it became, at least in its own eyes, the Committee of Public Safety. In the summer of 1794 the committee itself disintegrated; Saint-Just was at loggerheads with Carnot, and Robespierre suspected all his colleagues except Saint-Just and Couthon. On 26 July 1794 he denounced them to the Convention, and the frightened deputies took advantage of their opportunity to put an end to the revolutionary dictatorship and the ideology that had sustained it.

When the Paris Commune called for an insurrection to rescue the Robespierrists, it became clear that their whole doctrine, indeed the entire conception of popular sovereignty, rested in the last resort on the assumption that might was right. Unless the General Will was to have a purely metaphysical existence, there was only one way to determine whether the Commune's revolt was an assertion of the will of the people, as the insurrections of 14 July 1789 and 10 August 1792 were assumed to have been, or a criminal uprising by the people's enemies. It all depended on who won. The defeat of the Commune was not enough in itself to determine the future of France. Both sides within the Committee of Public Safety were tarred with the totalitarian brush: Barère had been as bloodthirsty as anyone, and Billaud-Varenne and Collot d'Herbois were no moderates. In the event, both were defeated when the deputies seized their opportunity to take power back into their own hands. The Thermidorian regime that followed saw a revulsion against every sense of the word Spartan and the mirage of the New Jerusalem faded into the light of common day. It would be hard to imagine anything more common than the light of Thermidor but at least it was daylight.

4

Bourgeois Revolution Revivified: 1789 and Social Change

COLIN JONES

THE decision on 16 July 1789 to demolish the Bastille presented a wonderful opportunity to Pierre-François Palloy.[1] The 34-year-old building contractor, who—so he said—had helped to storm the Bastille on 14 July, took on the job of demolition. The grim medieval fortress was soon a building site, offering much-needed employment to about 1,000 hungry Parisian labourers and providing a diverting and edifying spectacle for the leisured élite. The famous Latude, who had made his name by publishing an account of his imprisonment in the state fortress, was on hand to act as tourist guide to the site. Latude's publishers rushed out extra editions of his work, and Bastille commemorative volumes were soon among the best-sellers. A further wave of popular interest accompanied the discovery by Palloy's workmen in early 1790 of subterranean cells filled with

Alfred Cobban, launching his famous broadside against the so-called 'Marxist interpretation' of the French Revolution in 1964, regretted that 'one cannot criticise an historical interpretation without appearing to criticise the historians who have held it'. As I am sure was the case with Cobban, it is not my intention to launch *ad hominem* (or *ad feminam*) attacks—all the more in that number of the historians whose arguments I here criticize offered helpful and constructive comments following earlier versions of this paper read in Oxford, London, and Washington, DC. Particular thanks are due to Jonathan Barry, Bill Doyle, Colin Lucas, and Michael Sonenscher.

[1] For a brilliantly written account of some of Palloy's activities, see S. Schama, *Citizens: A Chronology of the French Revolution* (London, 1989), 408–16. Cf. Romi [pseud. Robert Miquel], *Le Livre de raison du patriote Palloy* (Paris, 1962); and H. Lemoine, 'Les Comptes de démolition de la Bastille', *Bulletin de la Société de l'histoire de Paris et de l'Île de France*, 1929.

chains and skeletons. This was not the Man in the Iron Mask, but it was something.

Palloy, however, was attracting some unwanted attention. When he presented accounts to the National Assembly in October 1790, certain right-wing deputies suggested that he had made a huge profit from the whole enterprise. Bertrand Barère, the future colleague of Robespierre in the great Committee of Public Safety, sprang to Palloy's defence. 'Ce n'est pas un marché qu'on a fait . . . C'est une destruction politique; c'est un acte vraiment révolutionnaire . . . Ainsi la démolition de la Bastille tourne au profit de la Nation et à l'honneur de la liberté.'[2] Fine words and flattery: but Palloy's books seem not to have balanced. Although he managed to avoid investigation, he seems to have made a considerable profit from merely selling off the stones of the Bastille; many went, for example, into the construction of the Pont de la Concorde. He went further than this, moreover, setting up a manufactory in his home in which huge numbers of the stones were carved into little replicas of the Bastille. Chains and irons found on the site were created into similar memorabilia: medals, dice-boxes, paperweights, snuff-boxes, inkpots, and the like. Palloy enrolled a host of fellow *Vainqueurs de la Bastille* to act as his travelling salesmen—he called them his *apôtres de la liberté*—taking stocks around the departments to meet what was clearly a great demand. Three parcels of Bastille memorabilia were presented gratis to each of France's eighty-three departments—though the latter did pay the transport costs, which allowed a profit to be made, and doubtless further stimulated local demand.

As he protests at his stone Bastille models being undercut by cheap plaster imitations, we should perhaps tiptoe quietly away from this interesting entrepreneurial figure who clearly awaits his Samuel Smiles—or better still, his Richard Cobb. From the vantage-point of the Bicentenary in 1989, with its chocolate guillotines and Bastille boxer shorts, his story nevertheless neatly demonstrates that the commercialization of the French Revolution is as old as the Revolution itself. The character sketch does, moreover, illustrate some of the themes I wish to develop here: namely, the Revolution and economic opportun-

---

[2] *Archives parlementaires de 1787 à 1860*, 1st ser., 19 (1884), 433 (session 4 Oct. 1790).

ities; bourgeois entrepreneuralism; consumerism and fashion; civic sensibilities; the interlocking of business and rhetoric.

To bring a bourgeois to the centre of the stage may, however, appear gloriously *dépassé*. After all, 1989 marked not just the bicentenary of the Revolution, but also the twenty-fifth anniversary of the publication, in 1964, of Alfred Cobban's *Social Interpretation of the French Revolution*, the classic text of the Revolutionist school which has come to dominate French Revolutionary historiography.[3] Over the last quarter of a century, the Revisionist current has virtually swept from the board what is now identified as the Orthodox Marxist view. The idea, almost axiomatic to the historians whom Cobban attacked— Mathiez, Lefebvre, Soboul—that the Revolution marked a key episode in the passage from feudalism to capitalism is now either widely discounted or else viewed as a *question mal posée*. And the idea—regarded as a truism before the 1960s—that the Revolution was a bourgeois revolution is now held up to ridicule. Indeed, George V. Taylor, one of the Grand Old Men of Revisionism, recently warned off historians from using the term 'bourgeois' which is, he contends, 'freighted with too many ambiguities to serve in research as a general analytical tool or operational category'.[4]

In the place of the old Marxist orthodoxy—the Revisionists always talk of the Marxist interpretation in the singular, as if Marxists never disagreed, or else robotically took their cue from the Politburo—a New Revisionist Orthodoxy has gradually sprung up, which by now has permeated into general interpretations and views, in much of French publishing as well as in English and American scholarship. The New Orthodoxy will have little truck with social interpretations in general, and the bourgeois revolution in particular. Far from being the heroic, world-historical, almost transcendental force which Karl Marx had seen him as, the bourgeois now cuts a shabby figure. Revisionist historians view him as pathetically insecure,

---

[3] A. Cobban, *The Social Interpretation of the French Revolution* (London, 1964). Cobban's line of argument can to traced back to his Inaugural Lecture in 1954, 'The Myth of the French Revolution', reprinted along with other of his polemical and scholarly pieces in *Aspects of the French Revolution* (London, 1968).

[4] G. V. Taylor, 'Bourgeoisie', in B. Rothaus and S. F. Scott, *Historical Dictionary of the French Revolution*, 2 vols. (Westport, Conn., 1985), i. 122.

anaemic, transitional—zombie-esque, in the view of Simon Schama.[5] The Old Regime bourgeoisie, so the New Orthodoxy goes, burnt its candle at both ends. At the top, merchants and manufacturers who built up sufficient wealth were swift to disinvest from productive activities and sink their capital in land, seigneuries, and venal office. Their propensity to ape their social betters was exemplified by their wish to achieve noble status, and indeed many former traders and manufacturers referred to themselves as *bourgeois vivant noblement*. The preference for status over profit which this behaviour is alleged to exemplify can be dated back centuries, as Colin Lucas and William Doyle have reminded us, and may thus be dubbed, as George Taylor would have it, atavistic.[6] At its bottom end, the Revisionists tell us, the bourgeoisie was equally undynamic. Peasants who might have enriched themselves by production for the market preferred risk-avoidance and subsistence strategies, and coralled themselves away from their bourgeois betters in the ghetto of a 'popular culture' they shared with guild-dominated, and equally 'traditionalist' urban workers.[7]

---

[5] Schama, *Citizens*, p. xiv for the zombies. This is little improvement on Colin Lucas's reference to 'indeterminate social mutants': C. Lucas, 'Nobles, Bourgeois and the Origins of the French Revolution', *Past and Present* (henceforth *P&P*), 60 (1973), 90.

[6] G. V. Taylor, 'Noncapitalist Wealth and the Origins of the French Revolution', *American Historical Review* (henceforth *AmHR*), 72 (1967), 482; Lucas, 'Nobles, Bourgeois and Origins', 89–92 and *passim*; W. Doyle, 'The Price of Offices in pre-Revolutionary France', *Historical Journal*, 27 (1984), 844. These are major articles within a relatively small range of classic texts which together form the much remasticated pabulum of Revisionist argument. Other key works in the litany include G. V. Taylor, 'Types of Capitalism in Eighteenth-Century France', *English Historical Review*, 79 (1964); id. 'Revolutionary and Non-Revolutionary Content in the *Cahiers* of 1789; An Interim Report', *French Historical Studies* (henceforth *FHS*), 7 (1972–3); E. Eisenstein, 'Who Intervened in 1788?', *AmHR*, 71 (1965); C. B. A. Behrens, *The Ancien Régime* (London, 1967); id., 'Nobles, Privileges and Taxes in France at the End of the Ancien Régime', *Economic History Review* (henceforth *EcHR*), 15 (1962–3); W. Doyle, *Origins of the French Revolution* (Oxford, 1980); F. Furet and D. Richet, *The French Revolution* (London, 1970); F. Furet, *Interpreting the French Revolution* (London, 1981). T. C. W. Blanning, *The French Revolution: Aristocrats versus Bourgeois?* (London, 1987) is a brilliant summation of the debate and itself stands as a major contribution to Revisionism.

[7] A good example of a 'traditionalist' reading of Old Regime society from an authoritative Revisionist source in W. Doyle, *The Oxford History of the French Revolution* (Oxford, 1989), esp. ch. 1. Cf. id., *The Ancien Régime* (London, 1986), 20 ff. For popular culture, see the classic R. Mandrou, *De la culture populaire aux*

This was a bourgeoisie more deeply riven by internal schisms than by class antagonisms—and indeed the Revisionists reserve some of their sharpest barbs for those starry-eyed 'Marxist' idealists who retain some attachment to the concept of class struggle. Indeed, the New Orthodoxy has it that there was less unity shown by the bourgeoisie as a class than, for example, by the inter-class élite of upper bourgeois and nobles. One must admire the Revisionists' sleight of hand, for the Old Regime nobility, normally portrayed (they tell us) as monolithically parasitic and feudal in its outlook, are nowadays viewed as hyper-dynamic and entrepreneurial. The nobility dominated the key sectors of the economy, Guy Chaussinand-Nogaret assures us, exercised overwhelming cultural hegemony, and generously held out a co-operative hand to those awestricken bourgeois wishing to enter France's social élite.[8] Once viewed as the agents of a 'feudal reaction' which shut out talented commoners, the nobility is now seen as the leading partner in an enlightened élite, entry into which through venal office was still surprisingly easy.[9] The term 'open élite' is now being used less in regard to eighteenth-century England, following the broadsides of

XVIIᵉ et XVIIIᵉ siècles (Paris, 1964); and, as a recent example, T. Brennan, *Public Drinking and Popular Culture in Eighteenth-Century Paris* (Princeton, NJ, 1988). For spirited onslaughts on the conceptual framework of much research on 'traditional society' and 'popular culture', see M. Sonenscher, *Work and Wages: Natural Law, Politics and the Eighteenth-Century French Trades* (Cambridge, 1989), 44–6; and R. Chartier, 'Culture as Appropriation: Popular Cultural Uses in Early Modern France', in S. L. Kaplan (ed.), *Understanding Popular Culture* (Paris, 1984).

[8] G. Chaussinand-Nogaret, *The French Nobility in the Eighteenth Century: From Feudalism to Enlightenment* (Cambridge, 1985). Much of Chaussinand-Nogaret's evidence on entrepreneurship is culled from the (refreshingly unrevisionist) scholarship of Guy Richard, notably the latter's *La Noblesse d'affaires au XVIIIᵉ siècle* (Paris, 1975). See too Chaussinand-Nogaret, *Une Histoire des élites, 1700–1848* (Paris, 1975); R. Forster, 'The Provincial Noble: A Reappraisal', *AmHR*, 78 (1968); and D. Sutherland's trenchant views on the social élite in his *France 1789–1815: Revolution and Counter-Revolution* (London, 1985), 19–21. A good counter-argument to Chaussinand-Nogaret is mounted by P. Goujard, ' "Féodalité" et lumières au XVIIIᵉ siècle: L'Exemple de la noblesse', *Annales historiques de la Révolution française* (henceforth *AhRf*), 227 (1977).
[9] See W. Doyle, 'Was There an Aristocratic Reaction in pre-Revolutionary France?' *P&P*, 57 (1972); D. Bien, 'La Reaction aristocratique avant 1789: L'Exemple de l'armée', *Annales: Économies, sociétés, civilisations* (henceforth *AnnESC*), 29 (1974).

Lawrence and Jeanne Stone, than to Old Regime France.[10] The Revolution's persecution of this enlightened noble-dominated group can only, in its injustice, its economic irrationality, and its lack of humanity, be compared to anti-Semitism (the comparison is Chaussinand-Nogaret's).[11] Yet the nobility would have the last laugh, for once the Revolution was over, they formed the backbone of the class of landowning and professional notables which dominated nineteenth-century France.[12]

The idea that France's late eighteenth- and nineteenth-century history essentially concerns the formation of an élite of notables (the latter, incidentally, every bit as much a portmanteau term as that of 'bourgeois', against whose vagueness Cobban inveighed), with the Revolution as an unwelcome intrusion or even an irrelevant footnote, has become a keystone of the New Revisionist Orthodoxy.[13] It fits in very snugly with the systematic disparagement of the economic significance of the Revolution. Far from marking the passage from feudalism to capitalism, the Revolution could not even transform the economic structures and shortcomings of the economy: agrarian productivity only registered progress, Michel Morineau tells us, after 1840, and industrial capitalism had generally to await the railway age.[14] Late eighteenth-century France was in any case only just emerging from *l'histoire immobile*, Emmanuel Le Roy Ladurie's description of a kind of neo-Malthusian prison-camp in which

[10] L. and J. Stone, *An Open Elite? England, 1540–1880* (Oxford, 1984). Cf. A. Milward and S. B. Saul, *The Economic Development of Continental Europe, 1780–1870* (London, 1973), esp. 30–1. On the French side, note the important calculations on social mobility in Bien, 'Réaction aristocratique', 505–14.

[11] Chaussinand-Nogaret, *French Nobility*, 1.

[12] An authoritative overview of this widely held perspective in Doyle, *Ancien Régime*, 25–6.

[13] W. G. Runciman, 'Unnecessary Revolution: The Case of France', *Archives européennes de sociologie*, 23 (1983).

[14] M. Morineau, 'Was There an Agricultural Revolution in Eighteenth-Century France?', in R. Cameron (ed.), *Essays in French Economic History* (London, 1970); and id., *Les Faux-semblants d'un démarrage économique: Agriculture et démographie en France au dix-huitième siècle* (Paris, 1970)—both key texts for the Revisionists case which is also buttressed on this point by socio-economic historians who view structural economic change in France as a post-railway phenomenon. See, for example, R. Price, *The Economic Modernization of France, 1730–1914* (London, 1981); and E. Weber, *Peasants into Frenchmen: The Modernisation of Rural France, 1870–1914* (London, 1979). The gloomy diagnosis is confirmed in the non-scholarly but well-argued R. Sedillot, *Le Coût de la Révolution française* (Paris, 1987).

French society had been interned since the fourteenth century.[15] The Revolution thus becomes little more than a minor fold in the flowing fabric of that *longue durée* so beloved of the *Annales* school.

This tendency within the Revisionist camp to minimize the social changes associated with the Revolution has led to most recent historiographical running being made by historians of politics and culture. Lynn Hunt has chided social historians for concentrating their interest on mere 'origins and outcomes',[16] and for failing to recognize that the revolutionary character of the 1790s resides in the fabrication of a new political culture. The outstanding work of Keith Baker, and the 1987 Chicago conference proceedings, *The Political Culture of the Old Régime*, which have been published under his direction, buttresses that view.[17] In the Brave New Revisionist World, discourse reigns supreme and social factors bulk exceeding small. It often seems, for example, as if the new political culture had no long-term social roots, but emerged in a process of inspired and semi-spontaneous politico-cultural *bricolage* in 1788–9. François Furet, for example, the veritable pope of contemporary Revisionism, sees 1789 as ushering in a political logic and a proto-totalitarian discourse which lead in unilinear fashion to the Terror.[18] The idea that the Revolution's shift to the left in the early 1790s might have something to do with the counter-revolution is roundly dismissed: the revolutionaries are diagnosed as suffering from a plot psychosis predating any real threat to their work. The Revolution was on the track to Terror from the summer of 1789, socio-political circumstances notwithstanding.[19]

---

[15] E. Le Roy Ladurie, 'L'Histoire immobile', *AnnESC*, 29 (1974). This influential article, highly symptomatic of much contemporary writing on rural history, is available in English translation as 'History that Stands Still', in id., *The Mind and Method of the Historian* (London, 1981).

[16] L. Hunt, *Politics, Culture and Class in the French Revolution* (London, 1986), 9.

[17] K. M. Baker (ed.), *The French Revolution and the Creation of Modern Political Culture*, i. *The Political Culture of the Old Regime* (Oxford, 1987). Reviews of this important work by J. Censer, 'The Coming of a New Interpretation of the French Revolution?', *Journal of Social History*, 21 (1987); and P. R. Campbell, 'Old Régime Politics and the New Interpretation of the French Revolution', *Renaissance and Modern Studies*, 32 (1989). The second volume of the series, ed. Colin Lucas, was: *The Political Culture of the French Revolution* (Oxford, 1988).

[18] Furet, *Interpreting the French Revolution*, esp. 47 ff., 61 ff.

[19] Ibid. 53 ff. Cf. F. Furet and R. Halévi, 'L'Année 1789', *AnnESC*, 44 (1989), esp. 21. This view by Furet contrasts with his own views as expressed in Furet

François Furet has been a devastating critic of the unreflective sociologism of the old Marxist approach as exemplified in some of the writings of Albert Soboul.[20] The pendulum has now swung to the other extreme, however, and many Revisionists seem to wish to reduce the history of the Revolution to political history with society left out. A typical recent example of the way in which discourse analysis and high politics override the social angle is the treatment which a number of recent authors have given to the famous Night of 4 August 1789, when the National Assembly issued a decree formally abolishing feudalism. Overlooking or discounting evidence about the blatant fixing of this session, ignoring the ridiculously high rates of compensation for losses of feudal rights the deputies awarded, turning a blind eye to stories of violent peasant revolution which, magnified by rumour, were pouring into Paris and Versailles at the time, William Doyle, Norman Hampson, Michael Fitzsimmons, and Simon Schama all view the explanation of the behaviour of the deputies as lying in the altruism of the old 'enlightened' élite.[21] One of the key moments in the social transformation of France, the zenith of peasant influence on the course of events, thus merely becomes a vacuous chapter in group psychology, with the Assembly acting as if hermetically sealed from outside social influences. What Simon Schama characterizes as a 'patriotic rhapsody' becomes for Michael Fitzsimmons a kind of beatific vision, a Close Encounter of the 4 August Kind, in which the deputies self-denyingly pledged themselves to 'the sublimity of the Nation'.[22] The Revolution as a whole thus becomes 'the reaction of groups and individuals to the imposition by the National Assembly of its new vision of France', an approach congruent with George Taylor's famous characterization of the

and Richet, *The French Revolution*—where the Terror is seen as taking place as a result of the Revolution 'skidding' unpredictably to the Left. Cf. the forceful statement of much of the Furet case (Mark II) in Schama, *Citizens*, esp. 446–7, 623, 792, etc.

[20] Notably Furet's essay 'The Revolutionary Catechism' in *Interpreting the French Revolution*, ch. 2.1.

[21] M. Fitzsimmons, 'Privilege and Polity in France, 1786–91', *AmHR*, 92 (1987); and id., *The Parisian Order of Barristers and the French Revolution* (Cambridge, Mass., 1987), 41–2, 193–4; N. Hampson, *Prelude to Terror: The Constituent Assembly and the Failure of Consensus, 1789–1791* (Oxford, 1989), 56; Doyle, 'Price of Offices', 859–60; Schama, *Citizens*, 439.

[22] Schama, *Citizens*, 439; Fitzsimmons, *Parisian Order of Barristers*, 41–2.

Revolution as a 'political revolution with social consequences rather than a social revolution with political consequences'.[23]

This denigration of the popular and collectivist aspects of the Revolution and the downplaying of social origins to the political crisis of 1789 keys in with some other recent accounts, moreover, which view French society as largely the opponent or the victim of the new political culture. From Donald Sutherland's account, for example, one gains the impression that nine-tenths of French society in the 1790s was objectively counter-revolutionary.[24] (This, incidentally, is a view which calls into question François Furet's diagnosis of plot psychosis.) If there was a popular revolution at all, Douglas Johnson tells us, it was the Counter-Revolution.[25] From evacuating the Revolution of all positive social content to viewing the repression of counter-revolution as 'genocide' by a 'totalitarian' power is only a short step—and one which certain historians have not been afraid to take.[26]

Perhaps we are wrong to judge the views of the New Revisionist Orthodoxy by the uses to which they are being put by the political Right; after all, the Old Marxist Orthodoxy was shamelessly exploited by the Left. What is, however, worrying for a social historian is the extent to which social change is disparaged in or omitted from the New Revisionist Orthodoxy. It is not my intention to pose as King Canute, vainly bidding the Revisionist wave to recede. On the contrary, I would contend that a great deal of Revisionist research being done in fact subverts the main, rather brittle assumptions around which the New Revisionist Orthodoxy has hardened.[27] In this essay, I

---

[23] Fitzsimmons, *Parisian Order of Barristers*, 197; Taylor, 'Noncapitalist Wealth', p. 491.

[24] Sutherland, *France, 1789–1815*: see esp. 333–5, 438–42.

[25] D. Johnson, 'Fire in the Mind', *Times Educational Supplement*, 14 Oct. 1988, 24.

[26] See in particular the recent work of R. Sécher, *Le Génocide franco-français: La Vendée-Vengé* (Paris, 1986) and *La Chapelle-Basse-Mer: Révolution et contre-révolution* (Paris, 1986), dealing in highly contentious fashion with the repression of revolt in western France in the 1790s. For a sober assessment of some of the statistics involved, cf. F. Lebrun, 'Reynald Sécher et les morts de la guerre de Vendée', *Annales de Bretagne* (henceforth *AB*), 93 (1986).

[27] There are clear signs that historians are becoming increasingly dissatisfied with many Revisionist arguments. See, as a sampler, B. Edmonds, 'Successes and Excesses of Revisionist Writing about the French Revolution', *European History Quarterly*, 17 (1987); P. M. Jones, *The Peasantry in the French Revolution*

would like to mine that seam in a way which suggests that we need to rethink our attitudes towards some of the key problems associated with the relationship of the Revolution to social change. While many may prefer cosily to relax in the platitudes of the New Revisionist Orthodoxy, we may in fact be moving towards a situation in which new research allows us to relate afresh to some of the problems of causation which concerned Marxist French Revolutionary historiography. This may come as a shock to many Revisionists, who tend to relate to that historiographical tradition by presenting a knockabout pastiche of the views of the alleged Old Marxist Orthodoxy, a kind of pantomime in which a succession of Revisionist Prince Charmings rescue Marianne from the clutches of a wicked, mean-spirited old Stalinist Baron—a part reserved in most scripts for the late Albert Soboul. Using the research of both Revisionist and Marxist scholars, I am going to be foolhardy enough to suggest that the Revolution did have long-term social origins. I will go on to suggest that these related directly to the development of capitalism and indeed that the much-disparaged term 'bourgeois revolution' retains much of its force and utility.

One of the cardinal tenets of the New Revisionist Orthodoxy is that eighteenth-century France was—with the possible exception of the enlightened élite—'traditionalist', preferring a flight from capitalism rather than its warm embrace. Much of the force of this view has in the past resided in unfavourable comparisons made with the allegedly more mature capitalist economy of Great Britain, undergoing in the period from 1780 the classic Rostovian 'take-off' into self-sustained economic growth. Against this, the argument runs, the French economy can only seem 'backward' or 'retarded'.[28]

(Cambridge, 1988), esp. ch. 2; and P. McPhee, 'The French Revolution, Peasants and Capitalism', *AmHR*, 94 (1989). Cf. too M. D. Sibalis, 'Corporatism and the Corporations: The Debate on Restoring the Guilds under Napoleon I and the Restoration', *FHS* 15 (1987–8), esp. 720. It is noticeable that even Schama, who espouses most of Furet's arguments on the Revolution, is still often critical of Revisionist stances: *Citizens*, e.g. 188 ff.

[28] Cf. Doyle, *Origins*, 32; id., *Ancien Régime*, 26–8; W. W. Rostow, *The Stages of Economic Growth: A Non-Communist Manifesto* (Cambridge, 1960). The 'backwardness' thesis is stated with great force in the influential D. Landes, *The Unbound Prometheus: Technological Change and Industrial Development in Western Europe from 1750 to the Present* (Cambridge, 1972).

One has only to scratch the surface of this approach today to realize that it lies in tatters. The work of François Crouzet, Nicholas Crafts, Patrick O'Brien and others have pointed up the buoyancy of French economic performance over the eighteenth century, and shown that in many respects it even may have outdistanced Great Britain.[29] Annual averages of both agricultural and industrial growth were higher in France than in Great Britain.[30] If we are to believe Patrick O'Brien and Caglar Keyder, a broad comparability between the British and the French economies continued into the early twentieth century. France's per capita physical product tripled between the early nineteenth and early twentieth centuries, and the authors see this as part of a development which stretches back into the eighteenth century. Perhaps Britain's priority in emergence as First Industrial Nation owed less to her economic performance over the eighteenth century than to factors which predated 1700—the stability of Britain's financial institutions grounded in the establishment of the Bank of England in 1694, and Britain's early switch to mineral fuel, which stimulated the emergence of

---

[29] F. Crouzet's numerous articles around this point are conveniently collected in his *De la supériorité de l'Angleterre sur la France: L'Économique et l'imaginaire (XVIIe–XXe siècle)* (Paris, 1985). See too P. O'Brien and C. Keyder, *Economic Growth in Britain and France, 1780–1914: Two Paths to the Twentieth Century* (London, 1978); id., 'Les Voies de passage vers la société industrielle en Grande-Bretagne et en France (1780–1914)', *AnnESC*, 34 (1979); N. Crafts, 'England and France: Some Thoughts on the Question "Why was England first?" ', *EcHR*, 30 (1977); id., 'British and French Economic Growth, 1700–1831: A Review of the Evidence', *EcHR*, 36 (1983); id., 'British Industrialisation in an International Context', *Journal of Interdisciplinary History*, 19 (1989); R. Roehl, 'French Industrialization: A Reconsideration', *Explorations in Economic History*, 15 (1976); J. L. Goldsmith, 'The Agrarian History of Pre-Industrial France: Where do We Go from here?', *Journal of European Economic History* (henceforth *JEEH*), 13 (1984); R. Aldrich, 'Late-Comer or Early Starter? New Views on French Economic History', *JEEH*, 16 (1987). These are only a sampler from a list which could be considerably extended. The chorus does not sing in unison, there being a number of major differences of opinion between them. However, all are critical of the classic account, as is the wide-ranging C. Sabel and J. Zeitlin, 'Historical Alternatives to Mass Production: Political Markets and Technology in Nineteenth-Century Industrialisation', *P&P*, 108 (1985). Overall it seems a fascinating historiographical paradox that Anglo-Saxon scholarship on Old Regime French society settled into a 'traditionalist', 'backward-orientated' mould just as economic historians of Britain, working comparatively, called into question the economic dynamism of the 'First Industrial Nation'. The edifice of French 'backwardness' is a thus a lot shakier than the confident tone of the Revisionists would suggest.

[30] O'Brien and Keyder, *Economic Growth in Britain and France*, 57.

a coal-fuel technology which would contribute importantly to the industrialization process.[31] But rather than talk in terms of retardation or backwardness, perhaps we should just accept that there is more than one way towards industrialization, and that the British route, though first—or perhaps because it was first—was not necessarily the most appropriate for others. France did not have the sudden spurt in industrial performance which England enjoyed, but her more balanced and drawn-out pathway to industrialization was no less effective in the longer term, and may indeed be particularly deserving of attention in that it avoided many of the direst social costs which accompanied Britain's Industrial Revolution.[32]

Clearly, there are dangers in comparing the economic performance of England and France on the basis of hypothesized aggregate data: not least because the unit of economic growth in the eighteenth century was the region rather than the nation-state.[33] Yet historians such as Herbert Lüthy miss the point when they draw attention to the fact that France's economic performance in the eighteenth century hid a disparity between more progressive port cities and their hinterlands on one hand, and the more backward, traditionalist economies of the remainder of France.[34] For even Britain had its Dorsets and its Rutlands—to say nothing of its Sligos, Denbighshires, and Ross and Cromartys—as well as its Lancashires and Birminghams. Moreover, many regional and urban historians of France now emphasize the extent of rural penetration achieved by dynamic urban centres. The eighteenth century saw an increase in

[31] C. P. Kindleberger, 'Financial Institutions and Economic Development: A Comparison of Great Britain and France in the Eighteenth and Nineteenth Centuries', *Explorations in Economic History*, 23 (1984); J. R. Harris, 'Skills, Coal and British Industry in the Eighteenth Century', *History*, 61 (1976).

[32] O'Brien and Keyder, *Economic Growth in Britain and France*, esp. 186–8, 191–3. Cf. C. Heywood, 'The Role of the Peasantry in French Industrialisation, 1815–80', *EcHR*, 34 (1981).

[33] The consequences of this point, a commonplace in social history, is brought out particularly forcefully for economic history in S. Pollard, *Peaceful Conquest: The Industrialisation of Europe, 1760–1970* (Oxford, 1981). Cf. too, from a quite different perspective, I. Wallerstein, *The Modern World-System*, ii. *Mercantilism and the Consolidation of the European World Economy, 1600–1750* (New York, 1980), 87–90 and *passim*.

[34] H. Lüthy, *La Banque protestante en France de la révocation de l'Édit de Nantes à la Révolution*, 2 vols. (Paris, 1950), esp. 595–7.

intensity of urban domination over surrounding provisioning areas.[35]

If we start to accept that France's industrialization process was not inferior to Britain's, but merely different, then we can acknowledge that much of the French economic performance was a valid response to its situation in terms of resource-levels, geographical configuration, markets, and so on. Although France had achieved by 1789, in global terms, important levels of industrialization and urbanization, it is unhelpful merely to mark these down as a second-best to those of a Britain, whose pattern of industrialization was anyway highly specific. Thus, for example, it is not necessarily a major drawback that France's manufacturing sector was to a considerable degree situated in the countryside and took the form of rural industry rather than factory concentration. Despite the late and startlingly dynamic appearance of cotton production in France in the late eighteenth century, France's industries tended to be traditional, artisanal, and rural-based.[36] Luxury and semi-luxury goods, consumption and production of which were stimulated by the Bourbon court,[37] played a much more important role too in the industrial sector than in Hanoverian England. More concentrated forms of manufacturing—cotton production, coal, minerals—made up a minority of the total output, and it is significant that relatively few of those nobles involved in industry—a small minority, it should be noted, of the total noble order—were engaged in the

[35] For criticism of Lüthy's position, see Crouzet, *De la supériorité*, 462 n. 35; and L. Bergeron's comments in P. Léon (ed.), *Histoire économique et sociale du monde*, iii. *Inerties et révolutions, 1730–1820* (Paris, 1978), 349 ff. For urban/rural relations, see E. Le Roy Ladurie's contribution to G. Duby (ed.), *Histoire de la France urbaine*, iii. *La Ville classique (De la Renaissance aux Révolutions)*, (Paris, 1981); S. L. Kaplan, *Provisioning Paris: Merchants and Millers in the Grain and Flour Trade during the Eighteenth Century* (Ithaca, NY, 1982); and, by way of example, J. P. Bardet, *Rouen aux XVIIᵉ et XVIIIᵉ siècles: Les Mutations d'un espace social* (Paris, 1983).

[36] F. Braudel and E. Labrousse, *Histoire économique et sociale de la France*, ii. *1660–1789* (Paris, 1970), esp. 217–66, 499–528. Cf. too W. Sewell, *Work and Revolution in France: The Language of Labor from the Old Régime to 1848* (London, 1980), which also has a much more positive evaluation of France's economy, 147 ff.

[37] P. Deyon and P. Guignet, 'The Royal Manufactures and Economic and Technological Progress in France before the Industrial Revolution', *JEEH*, 9 (1980); M. Stuermer, 'An Economy of Delight: Court Artisans of the Eighteenth Century', *Business History Review*, 53 (1979).

traditional sector which accounted for the bulk of French
manufacturing production. The prevalence of rural industry,
moreover, helps account for the high rural population density
levels achieved in many regions. Between 80 and 85 per cent of
France's population was still based in the countryside in 1789.[38]
Far from retarding the economy, it may be that the peasant
orientation of the rural economy acted as a kind of holding
operation, circumventing a massive rural exodus which the
urban economy might not have been able to exploit, and which
might have landed France in a classic Malthusian trap.[39]

Clearly, one should not whitewash France's manufacturing
sector in the eighteenth century. Serious problems existed, and
these became particularly acute in the last two decades of the
Old Regime, which saw a recession in all branches of the
economy.[40] Even before British manufactures benefitting from
precocious mechanization had wiped the floor with the more
traditional sectors of textile production after 1786, the woollen
and silk industries were in deep trouble, following the loss of
markets in the Levant and in Spanish possessions. In reviewing
the reasons for this situation, French manufacturers could be
forgiven for not blaming themselves for lack of enterprise so
much as laying the blame at the door of the state, whose fiscal
policy seemed to inhibit growth, whose armed forces were
signally failing to secure French industry the world outlets it
required, and whose economic policies were too erratic, too
favourable to the nobility, and too little attuned to the
commercial interest.[41]

Economic historians are also kinder these days on the agrarian
sector of the Old Regime economy than was that celebrated

[38] J. Dupâcquier, *Histoire de la population française*, ii. *De le Renaissance à 1789*
(Paris, 1988), 86–8; Duby, *Histoire de la France urbaine*, 296.
[39] E. A. Wrigley, *People, Cities and Wealth* (Oxford, 1987), esp. chs. 2 and 3;
Heywood, 'Role of the Peasantry', 360.
[40] The classic account in C. E. Labrousse, *Esquisse du mouvement des prix et des
revenus en France au XVIIIe siècle*, 2 vols. (Paris, 1933) is now updated in Braudel
and Labrousse, *Histoire économique et sociale*, notably 550–4. See too G.
Lemarchand, 'Du féodalisme au capitalisme: A propos des conséquences de la
Révolution française sur l'évolution de l'économie française', *AhRf*, 272 (1988).
[41] An excellent case-study of problems associated with government interventionism in J. K. J. Thomson, *Clermont-de-Lodève, 1633–1789: Fluctuations in the
Prosperity of a Languedocian Cloth-Making Town* (Cambridge, 1982). Cf. Crouzet,
De la supériorité, 88–9.

chauvinist Arthur Young.[42] Young's well-known critique of
French agriculture on the eve of the Revolution has cast a long
shadow. It is not simply that Young constantly disparaged any
rural trait which did not seem to fit into the English ideal type of
agrarian change—hence his attacks on small farms, *métayage*,
absentee landlords, peasant collective practices, and so on. In
addition it has to be borne in mind that he was often comparing
French general practice with English best practice. It would be
fairer to compare, shall we say, the efficiency of a Gascon small
farmer with that of a Scottish crofter, a Welsh hill-farmer, or an
Irish potato-eating peasant than with a prosperous Suffolk
tenant-farmer. Notwithstanding Young's strictures—wholly
predicated on the inherent merits of the 'English way'—we
should not denigrate the overall performance levels of France's
agrarian sector prior to 1789: population grew from 21.5 million
in 1700 to 28.6 million in 1789—an increase of a third.[43] These
extra mouths had to be fed; fed they were, an achievement all
the more remarkable for being made without the kind of
technological breakthroughs current in English farming. If
French peasants in 1789 were hungry and turbulent, at least
they were not starving and comatose as they had been in
1709–10, the last great famine in French history.[44] The additional
food supply did not come to any marked degree from improved
agricultural techniques—although there were some attempts,
particularly on the open-field seigneuries of northern France, to
follow in England's footsteps in technique. In general terms,
food supply to cope with population growth was achieved
through a combination of incremental improvements and
changes: more marginal land brought under the plough, better
storage, more scientific milling, better marketing. Though at
times of bad harvest it might still seem that grain was a prisoner,

[42] A. Young, *Travels in France in 1787, 1788 and 1789*, ed. C. Maxwell
(Cambridge, 1929). It is notable that Young's testimony, a stock-in-trade of the
French backwardness thesis, is cited over a dozen times in Doyle's *Oxford
History*, *passim*. One of Young's sacred cows is attacked in P. O'Brien, 'La
Contribution de l'aristocratie britannique au progrès de l'agriculture', *AnnESC*,
42 (1987); another is critically evaluated in G. Arbellot, 'Arthur Young et la
circulation en France', *Revue d'histoire moderne et contemporaine* (henceforth
RHMC), 28 (1981).
[43] Dupâcquier, *Histoire de la population française*, 64–5.
[44] G. Rudé, *The Crowd in History: A Study of Popular Disturbances in France and
England, 1730–1848* (London, 1964), 20.

as Ernest Labrousse has put it, 'immobilisé sur place faute de moyens d'évasion [et] gardé par des foules anxieuses, pire que geôliers',[45] in fact massive markets in grain operated throughout the course of the eighteenth century.[46] This allowed regions to make a choice of agrarian vocation: areas of more fertile farmland could specialize in grain, while other regions could develop non-subsistence production, whether agrarian or industrial. Languedoc provides a good example of the kind of regional division of labour which might result: in many areas of Upper Languedoc, as Georges Frêche has shown,[47] grain was king, and landowners specialized in its production in the knowledge that surpluses could be marketed via the excellent river basin of the Garonne, extended now by the road system and the Canal du Midi which made even the normally loquacious Arthur Young gasp in admiration. Lower Languedoc, in contrast, its food supply assured, specialized increasingly in wine production and domestic industry. The results were impressive: using only traditional agricultural methods, grain production in the area of the Midi-Pyrénées as a whole studied by Frêche rose by some 15 per cent down to 1789, but population increased by between 45 and 55 per cent on average. Better marketing was the key to this disparity.

There is in fact an increasingly strong-looking case for arguing that the French peasantry overall was more market-orientated than historians have often allowed. Since the times of Marc Bloch and Georges Lefebvre, there has been a virtual consensus among historians that the communal practices of the 'traditionalist' peasantry—common land, grazing rights, gleaning rights, and so on—inhibited that 'agrarian individualism' allegedly integral to rural capitalism.[48] The brilliant work of Olwen Hufton on the poor has helped consolidate this view,[49] for the

---

[45] In Braudel and Labrousse, *Histoire économique et sociale*, 416; Kaplan, *Provisioning Paris*.

[46] Kaplan, *Provisioning Paris*, 380 ff.; D. R. Weir, 'Markets and Mortality in France, 1600–1789', in J. Walter and R. Schofield (eds.), *Famine, Disease and the Social Order in Early Modern Society* (Cambridge, 1989); and cf. L. Tilly, 'The Food Riot as a Form of Political Conflict', *Journal of Interdisciplinary History*, 2 (1971–2).

[47] G. Frêche, *Toulouse et la région Midi-Pyrénées au siècle des Lumières, vers 1670– 1789* (Paris, 1974).

[48] M. Bloch, 'La Lutte pour l'individualisme agraire dans la France du XVIIIe siècle', *AnnESC*, 2 (1930). See too Jones, *Peasantry*.

[49] O. Hufton, *The Poor of Eighteenth-Century France (1750–1789)* (Oxford, 1974).

distinct impression has emerged that the majority of France's population were less concerned with market forces than with crude biological survival. With peasants unwilling or unable to display the required 'modernizing' attitudes, it was left to the domain agriculture of seigneurs in north-eastern France to provide the leading edge of agrarian revolution. The so-called seigneurial reaction, as Cobban originally suggested and as Le Roy Ladurie has documented, should thus be seen, it is generally suggested, as the diffusion of more businesslike, capitalistic methods of estate management. The revival of long-obsolete feudal dues goes hand in hand with encroachment on the commons, more rational surveillance and collection of dues and innovations in farming technology as part of a noble-inspired capitalistic development.[50] Perhaps. A number of recent studies have, however, suggested that this was not the only route to capitalism in the countryside, and that there was a peasant way. Road haulage and marketing provided a valuable supplement for the middling and wealthier peasant. In Pont-Saint-Pierre in Normandy, the subject of a fine recent monograph by Jonathan Dewald, the peasant on the make in the eighteenth century was the peasant with a horse and cart, who could benefit from increased demand for food and higher prices by activities as a haulier as well as a producer.[51] Moreover, the recent work of Hilton Root has shown that the communal practices usually viewed as the bane of rural capitalism could in fact coexist with commercialism: he demonstrates how village communities in Burgundy exploited their communal rights over woodland by marketing firewood, a precious commodity in eighteenth-century France. He also shows how richer peasants upheld the commons on which their large herds—whose produce was also marketed—could graze.[52] Just how far this

[50] Le Roy Ladurie, in his contribution to G. Duby and A. Wallon (eds.), *Histoire de la France rurale*, ii. *1340–1789* (Paris, 1975), esp. 393 ff.; id., 'Pour un modèle de l'économie rurale au XVIIIe siècle', *Cahiers d'histoire*, 20 (1975); Cobban, *Social Interpretation*, 45–52.
[51] J. Dewald, *Pont-Saint-Pierre, 1398–1789: Lordship, Community and Capitalism in Early Modern France* (London, 1987), 74–6, 88–9.
[52] H. Root, *Peasants and King in Burgundy: Agrarian Foundations of French Absolutism* (London, 1987), 117–80; id., 'The Rural Community and the French Revolution', in Baker, *Political Culture of the Old Régime*. Cf. Cobban, *Social Interpretation*, 113–18 on this very point; and M. Agulhon, *La Vie sociale en*

peasant model applies to other regions is open to question. There is a certain amount of supporting evidence from other localities, while the findings of the Soviet scholar Ado on peasant revolts point in much the same direction.[53]

What is particularly interesting about Hilton Root's work is that it allows us to reconceptualize relations between peasants and seigneurs in ways which relate to the specific forms in which commercial capitalism emerged in France. It was not so much that seigneurs were more 'feudalistic' in their demands— though many may have been. Rather, the demands that they did make were now seen through the eyes of a more market-conscious peasantry. The archaic feudal due of *guet et garde*, for example, which had in an earlier age been viewed as some kind of quid pro quo for the seigneur's services of protection, justice, and charity, looked archaic and oppressive in the eighteenth century when peasants preferred royal to seigneurial courts and when the need for protection had long passed—and indeed when fortified *châteaux forts* were being replaced by elegant country houses.[54] The sense of injustice and unfairness which this created in the peasantry seems to have been heightened by the commercial nexus in which they increasingly found themselves. Peasants were not slow, moreover, to take their issues and their arguments to royal courts, where they found lawyers to articulate their grievances in the language of natural rights. The 'moral economy'[55] of the Burgundian peasantry at least

Provence intérieure au lendemain de la Révolution (Paris, 1970), 216–17. See too the interesting discussion, based on France, in H. Meadwell, 'Exchange Relations between Lords and Peasants', *Archives européennes de sociologie*, 27 (1987).

[53] Or so rumour has it, as this major work awaits translation. There is a useful overview on Ado's work in A. Soboul, 'Sur le mouvement paysan dans la Révolution française', *La Pensée*, 1973. See too A. Ado, 'Le Mouvement paysan et le problème de l'égalité (1789–94)', in A. Soboul (ed.), *Contributions à l'histoire paysanne de la Révolution française* (Paris, 1977); and discussion in McPhee, 'The French Revolution, Peasants and Capitalism'. See too the discussion on market vs. subsistence orientation in *History Workshop Journal*, 28 (1989) between Hilton Root, 'The Case against Georges Lefebvre's Peasant Revolution'; and Peter Jones, 'Response to Hilton Root'.

[54] Root, *Peasants and King*, 159–62, 191–6; and M. Gresset, *Gens de justice à Besançon de la conquête par Louis XIV à la Révolution française (1674–1789)* (Paris, 1978), 732 ff. Cf. a similar case regarding attitudes to the *corvée* in O. Hufton, *Bayeux in the Late Eighteenth Century: A Social Study* (Oxford, 1967), 108.

[55] Cf. E. P. Thompson, 'The Moral Economy of the English Crowd in the Eighteenth Century', *P&P*, 50 (1971).

seems less paternalistic and pre-capitalist than it is usually accounted, and more consonant with commercial values. As Peter Jones has demonstrated—contrary to one of the hallowed myths of Revisionism, namely that there was no social crisis prior to 1788–9—a great many rural areas were gripped by severe social conflict in the decades leading up to the Revolution.[56] It is becoming increasingly apparent, moreover, that the last half-century of the Old Regime was in addition a Golden Age of Peasant Litigiousness throughout France.[57] Perhaps, indeed, to misquote Clausewitz, we should see the peasant revolution of 1789 as litigation by other means.

These examples, and the development of regional economic specialization, stand as testimony to a society characterized as much by circulation, mobility, and innovation as by the traditionalism, subsistence farming, and cultural stagnation which feature so strongly on the litany of the New Revisionist Orthodoxy. Perhaps over four million French men, women, and children were dependent for their living on viticulture in 1789, as well as endless hundreds of thousands involved in domestic industry.[58] These individuals had little choice but to embrace the market. They might begrudge it; but they did not flee from it. It is significant in this respect too that road improvements were bringing distance times sharply down in the last decades of the Old Regime: the state road system, now under the care of an increasingly professionalized Ponts et Chaussées service, cut overall distance times from Paris by between 40 and 60 per cent on average.[59] The better articulation of the market was witnessed too by the relative decline of the great periodic regional fairs

[56] Jones, *Peasantry*, ch. 2.
[57] Cf. Y. Castan, *Honnêteté et relations sociales en Languedoc, 1715–80* (Paris, 1974); N. Castan, *Justice et répression en Languedoc à l'époque des Lumières* (Paris, 1980), esp. 136 ff. on 'la sensibilité procédurière'.
[58] Abbé Expilly offers a figure of 4.5 m. for 'vignerons et cultivateurs à bras' and their families in his *Tableau de la population de la France* (1780). For the importance of viticulture, see too the classic study of E. Labrousse, *La Crise de l'économie française à la fin de l'Ancien Régime*, 2 vols. (Paris, 1944).
[59] G. Arbellot, 'La Grande Mutation des routes en France au XVIIIᵉ siècle', *AnnESC*, 28 (1973); id. and B. Lepetit, *Atlas de la Révolution française*, i. *Routes et communications* (Paris, 1987). These same roads were soon to convey the Great Fear: J. Markoff, 'The Social Geography of Rural Revolt and the Beginning of the French Revolution', *American Sociological Review*, 50 (1985); and id., 'Contexts and Forms of Rural Revolt: France in 1789', *Journal of Conflict Resolution*, 29 (1986).

which had lumberingly animated economic life hitherto: regular urban markets now provided the necessary stimuli.[60] The overall volume of French trade quintupled between the death of Louis XIV and the Revolution, and between three-quarters and four-fifths of this took place within the home market.[61] Although the retailing network lacked the sophistication of that of England, a great many localities witnessed 'the rise of the shopkeeper'.[62] The new primacy of exchange and circulation was nicely symbolized by the movement to knock down urban ramparts.[63] Indeed *circulation* (now of goods and persons as well as of the blood) was one of the buzz-words in the general vocabulary of the late Enlightenment, and a host of others related either to transmission and circulation (*commerçant, commercial, baromètre, oscillation, fluctuation, conversion, électriser,* etc.) or to consumption (*consommation, consommateurs, commodité,* etc.).[64] This is the language of an increasingly commercial society. Jean-Claude Perrot, in his study of Caen in the Old Regime, has compared job descriptions as they feature in municipal tax rolls in 1666 and 1792. What is particularly striking is the appearance by the later date of a whole range of terms which characterize a commercial and a consumer-orientated society. Consider for example (running the two fields together): *commissionnaire, directeur de postes, commis des postes, directeur des messageries, banquier, ingénieur des ponts, râpeur de tabac, maître du jeu de boule, maître du jeu de billard, musicien, directeur de spectacles, professeur d'équitation, marchand de modes,* and *marchand de parapluies.*[65]

I would like to stick with *parapluies* a little longer. A good deal of research is going on at the moment on post-mortem inventories. I have been surprised at the extent to which objects

[60] Braudel and Labrousse, *Histoire économique et sociale,* 185–6.
[61] Ibid. 180, 503.
[62] Dewald, *Pont-Saint-Pierre,* 20–1, 37, etc. Dewald cites F. Braudel, *Civilisation and Capitalism,* ii. *The Wheels of Commerce* (London, 1982), esp. 60–75. Cf. H. and L. Mui, *Shops and Shop-Keeping in Eighteenth-Century England* (London, 1989).
[63] Duby, *Histoire de la France urbaine,* 454. Cf. Bardet, *Rouen aux XVIIᵉ et XVIIᵉ siècles,* 164; and G. Viard, *Tradition et lumières au pays de Diderot: Langres au XVIIIᵉ siècle* (Langres, 1985), 143–8.
[64] F. Brunot, *Histoire de la langue française des origines à 1900,* vi (Paris, 1930), *passim.*
[65] J. C. Perrot, *Genèse d'une ville moderne: Caen au XVIIIᵉ siècle,* 2 vols. (Paris, 1975), i. 260–2.

like umbrellas—whose relationship to subsistence, traditionalism, and even popular culture seems obscure or tangential—
are found even in the homes of the relatively humble. Daniel
Roche's work on the *People of Paris* has underlined the extent to
which Parisians underwent a mini-consumer revolution in the
eighteenth century: furnishings and room space in the dwellings
of the popular classes show greater functional differentiation
and more awareness of fashion, with, for example, showy
pieces of furniture such as writing-tables, card-tables and coat-
stands becoming more common; wallpaper, wall-hangings,
mirrors, snuff-boxes, teapots, razors, chamberpots, and clocks
are found in greater abundance; people spend more money on
clothes, and these in turn becomes more showy and more
responsive to changes in fashion; and the humble umbrella
makes its appearance.[66] Recent, unpublished work by Cissie
Fairchilds bears out this general picture.[67] Cheap versions of
cultural artefacts formerly categorized as the luxuries of the
well-to-do—Fairchilds call them 'populuxe products'—are
increasingly widely dispersed: umbrellas, porcelain plates,
clocks, mirrors, and so forth. Books and other reading matter
might also be included in the list. Doubtless servants played a
crucial role in all this as cultural intermediaries between the
élites and the masses.[68] The tendency is very widespread in the
urban milieu—even the poorest immigrant stonecutter from the
Limousin or impoverished Lyonnais weaver had his Sunday
best.[69] It seems to have been disproportionately prevalent

[66] D. Roche, *The People of Paris: An Essay in Popular Culture in the Eighteenth Century* (London, 1987). Cf. A. Pardailhé-Galabrun, *La Naissance de l'intime: 3000 foyers parisiens (XVIIᵉ–XVIIIᵉ siècles)* (Paris, 1988).
[67] C. Fairchilds, 'The Production and Marketing of Populuxe Goods in Eighteenth-Century Paris', unpublished paper delivered at the Clark Library, University of California, Los Angeles, 1988. My thanks to Professor Fairchilds for a copy of this paper. See too Sonenscher, *Work and Wages*, esp. ch. 7 on the luxury trades.
[68] On this theme, see S. Maza, *Servants and Masters in Eighteenth-Century France: The Uses of Loyalty* (Princeton, NJ, 1983), 210–17; C. Fairchilds, *Domestic Enemies: Servants and their Masters in Old Régime France* (Baltimore, 1984); and C. Petitfrère, *L'Œil du maître: Maîtres et serviteurs de l'époque classique au romantisme* (Paris, 1986).
[69] M. A. Moulin, *Les Maçons de la Haute-Marche au XVIIIᵉ siècle* (Clermont-Ferrand, 1986), 211; M. Garden, *Lyon et les Lyonnais au XVIIIᵉ siècle* (Paris, 1975), 418.

among women, who were more attuned to fashion than men and who may also have been seen as objects of conspicuous consumption.[70] In many rural settings, too, pocket-watches and silver, gold, and enamelled buttons increasingly bestudded the Sunday waistcoats of peasant farmers. Perhaps, in her way, Charlotte Corday was trying to bring this new consumerism to the attention of historians, for she took care to murder the hapless Marat in that highly fashionable populuxe product, a zinc bathtub.[71]

The widespread diffusion of populuxe products in late eighteenth-century France is matched by a similar consumerism in diet and in leisure habits. Perhaps historians overemphasize the bipolarity with Old Regime society. A great deal of evidence suggests that between Olwen Hufton's poor and Guy Chaussinand-Nogaret's élite of notables, there were substantial middling and even lower-middling groups who were doing quite nicely for much of the eighteenth century. Bread may have been the major item of the popular budget, but wine used up much family income, as the boom in the drinks trade attested.[72] The consumption of sugar, tea, coffee, and chocolate rose dramatically and this was not simply a reflection of increased élite use; for *café au lait* was well on its way to becoming the breakfast of the urban labouring classes, and was probably penetrating the countryside as well.[73] The fact, for example, that snuff-boxes and hats had become barometers of social status reflects changing social criteria, as does the wide diffusion of tobacco, which had become a prime necessity for many.[74] We should see the mass growth of prostitution in the cities of Old Regime France as another area of burgeoning male consumer

[70] B. Garnot, 'La Culture matérielle du peuple de Chartres au XVIIIᵉ siècle: Méthodes de recherche et résultats', *AB*, 95 (1988), on this point.

[71] For the countryside, A. Babeau, *La Vie rurale dans l'ancienne France* (Paris, 1883) is a decent starting-point. See too J. Nicolas, *La Savoie au XVIIIᵉ siècle: Noblesse et bourgeoise*, 2 vols. (Paris, 1977), ii. 963; Dewald, *Pont-Saint-Pierre*, 44–6. Cf. Garnot, 'Culture matérielle du peuple'.

[72] Brennan, *Public Drinking and Popular Culture*; D. Garrioch, *Neighbourhood and Community in Paris, 1740–1789* (Cambridge, 1986), 180–91.

[73] Nicolas, *Savoie*, ii. 957. A. Babeau, *Les Bourgeois d'autrefois* (Paris, 1886), 204; Braudel and Labrousse, *Histoire économique et sociale*, 196–8.

[74] Garden, *Lyon et les Lyonnais*, 405 ff.; M. Sonenscher, *The Hatters of Eighteenth-Century France* (Los Angeles, 1988).

demand.[75] The emergence of 'red-light districts' in many towns is moreover only part of a general reshaping of urban space which testifies to new cultural tastes: the century saw a boom in pleasure-gardens, coffee-houses, billiard-halls, theatres, libraries, malls. Enthusiasm for urban improvement and 'environmental engineering' (public health measures, drainage, ventilation, etc.), to which J. C. Riley has recently drawn attention, owed much to the wish to open up spaces for pleasure and public consumption.[76]

The consumer market, particularly in the urban setting, then, seems to have been far larger and more buoyant than historians have been usually willing to admit. The tendency has been to write off French towns, in which this new consumerism was centred, as a polarized mixture of, as one contemporary put it, 'richesse et gueuserie, faste et mendicité, magnificence et saleté',[77] which strikes a poor contrast with middle-class England allegedly undergoing the 'first consumer revolution'.[78] Yet while doubtless in consumer terms England led the field— one had only to see those swooning tourists agog in the West End shops—it also had its problems. Living standards of the English working classes were stagnating in the late eighteenth century, a period at which England's rate of economic growth may also have been slowing down.[79] While the intensity of consumerism was probably still more marked in England than in France (if only because a higher proportion of England's population inhabited towns), the actual scale of the market was probably similar. After all, France's population grew by 7.1 million in the eighteenth century—twice England's population

---

[75] E. M. Bénabou, *La Prostitution et la police de mœurs au XVIIIᵉ siècle* (1987); C. Jones, 'The Montpellier Bon Pasteur and the Repression of Prostitution in the Ancien Régime', in id., *The Charitable Imperative: Hospitals and Nursing in Ancien Régime and Revolutionary France* (London, 1989), 263–4.

[76] J. C. Riley, *The Eighteenth-Century Campaign to Avoid Disease* (London, 1987). Cf. Bardet, *Rouen aux XVIIᵉ et XVIIIᵉ siècles*, esp. ch. 3, 'Changer la ville'.

[77] Citation from Marchand, 1769, quoted by Le Roy Ladurie in Duby, *Histoire de la France urbaine*, 289.

[78] N. McKendrick, J. Brewer, and J. H. Plumb, *The Birth of a Consumer Society: The Commercialization of Eighteenth-Century England* (London, 1982) is the classic formulation, and it informs the fine synthesis of R. Porter, *England in the Eighteenth Century* (London, 1982).

[79] P. H. Lindert and J. G. Williamson, 'English Workers' Living Standards during the Industrial Revolution: A New Look', and Crafts, 'British Economic Growth', both in *EcHR*, 43 (1983).

increase of 3.6 million.[80] London, with nearly a million inhabitants, clearly outgunned Paris, with its 650,000. But the number of city-dwellers in France as a whole rose by over 40 per cent between 1725 and 1789, and the 5.3 million French town-dwellers in 1789 comfortably exceeded Britain's urban population of 2.3 million by the later date.[81] Even were we to accept that per capita disposable income was much higher in England than in France, the total demand generated by a very large number of even quite poor people is considerable, so that the scale of demand on France's colossal home market was still pretty impressive.[82]

In urban centres in both France and England, moreover, one of the liveliest and most dynamic of periodical publications was the advertiser, the branch of the media most attuned to a consumerist society. For too long overlooked by cultural historians, who have concentrated their interest on the enlightened culture of the élite on one hand and the purportedly timeless demotic escapism of the *Bibliothèque bleue* on the other, advertiser-like *Affiches* were established in most major French cities over the eighteenth century. In 1789, there were forty-four in existence, and they tended to prosper in administrative centres where the liberal professions and the tertiary sector were particularly strong.[83] Aimed at providing for 'le plaisir . . . et l'utilité du public',[84] and filled to the brim with small-ads and advertisements for every conceivable need from cosmetics to piano-tuners, these periodicals testify not only to the existence of a sizeable audience of consumers, but also to the lively spirit of exchange and consumerism which animated them.

Every society makes its cultural heroes in its own image, and it therefore seems particularly significant that one of the great popular heroes of eighteenth-century France was the smuggler Mandrin, usually portrayed Robin Hood-like distributing consumer goods (tobacco, light textiles, salt) at a fair price to the

[80] Wrigley, *Peoples, Cities and Wealth*, 170.

[81] Dupâcquier, *Histoire de la population française*, 296; Wrigley, *People, Cities and Wealth*, 170.

[82] A point made in a different context by C. Dyer, 'The Consumer and the Market in the Later Middle Ages', *EcHR*, 49 (1989), 325.

[83] G. Feyel, 'La Presse provinciale au XVIIIᵉ siècle: Géographie d'un réseau', *Revue historique*, 272 (1984), esp. 365–8.

[84] Ibid. 368.

poor and needy.[85] If Mandrin was a consumerist hero for a consumerist and increasingly materialistic age, by the same token the century's hate figures were the officials of the General Farm, the collectors of indirect taxes who were widely viewed as leeches, privileged bloodsuckers on the body social.[86] The state perhaps attracted a certain amount of flak from popular consumers. No one took the old sumptuary legislation seriously: the last measure, in 1720, had forbidden commoners wearing of jewellery save with the written permission of the king.[87] But government tolls and taxes inhibited consumerism—and perhaps a certain amount of naked consumer envy was canalized away from the wealthy towards the state, which could be blamed for conspiring to put populuxe products and new consumer needs out of the reach of many.[88] If this was a 'moral economy', it was one attuned to novelty and individualistic materialism as well as subsistence and community values.

I have thus far portrayed eighteenth-century France as a more and more commercial society, increasingly sensitive to the market, very different from the stagnating, traditionalist society encountered in the New Revisionist Orthodoxy. Seen from this viewpoint, it seems clear that the main intermediaries and beneficiaries of this growing commercialization were the allegedly 'traditional' bourgeoisie. Merchants, artisans, shop-keepers, and the *paysannerie marchande* were in the fore, with only a sprinkling of the nobility. The size of the bourgeoisie grew over the century from 700,000 or 800,000 individuals in

[85] E. Esmonin, 'Comment naît une légende, ou la véritable figure de Mandrin', in his *Études sur la France des XVIIᵉ et XVIIIᵉ siècles* (Paris, 1964); F. Funck-Brentano, *Mandrin, capitaine général des contrebandiers de France* (Paris, 1908); M. H. Bourquin, 'Le Procès de Mandrin et la contrebande au XVIIIᵉ siècle' in id. and E. Hepp, *Aspects de la contrebande au XVIIIᵉ siècle* (Paris, 1969).
[86] Y. Durand, *Les Fermiers généraux au XVIIIᵉ siècle* (Paris, 1971); F. Hincker, *Les Français devant l'impôt sous l'Ancien Régime* (Paris, 1971); and the sources at n. 85.
[87] P. Perrot, *Les Dessus et les dessous de la bourgeoisie: Une histoire du vêtement au XIXᵉ siècle* (Paris, 1981), 38 ff.
[88] Thomson, *Clermont-de-Lodève*, passim; J. F. Bosher, *The Single-Duty Project: A Study of the Movement for a French Customs Union in the Eighteenth Century* (Roudon, 1964), esp. 129 ff.; S. L. Kaplan, *The Famine Plot Persuasion of Eighteenth-Century France* (Philadelphia, 1982). Anti-fiscal feeling by 1789 was doubtless amplified by the very low tax levels which had obtained at mid-century: J. C. Riley, 'French Finances, 1727–68', *Journal of Modern History* (henceforth *JMH*), 59 (1987).

1700 to perhaps 2.3 million in 1789—getting on for 10 per cent of the global population.[89] The New Revisionist Orthodoxy that bourgeoisie and nobility were somehow identical in economic terms thus seems rather wide of the mark: even were we to take all of the 120,000 nobles Chaussinand-Nogaret claims to have been in existence in 1789 as engaged in entrepreneurial activity—a hypothesis very far from the mark, as Chaussinand-Nogaret would admit—they would still be sinking without trace in a bourgeois sea.[90] Entrepreneurial nobles were anyway more likely to be involved in monopoly capitalist ventures or financial dealing than in the more humdrum bread-and-butter mercantile and manufacturing activities which were the staple of French commercial capitalism.

The exact timing and the character of the commercialization of French society inevitably varied from region to region and from class to class. But it may well be feasible to link it with the great change in *mentalités* observable from roughly the middle of the century.[91] I do not wish to get embroiled in the religious significance of the move away from baroque piety which Michel Vovelle, Pierre Chaunu, Philippe Ariès, and others have detected in wills and other socio-religious documents: was it dechristianization or anticlericalism? was it a shift towards a more sincere, internalized spirituality? Yet however the mutation is interpreted, it is clear that something important was happening from that time to the most basic attitudes towards death, life, and material possessions.[92] Evidence from wills also suggests that the comportment of nobles and bourgeois was relatively distinct.[93] The diffusion of coitus interruptus—'le toboggan

[89] These figures are from Pierre Léon's contribution to Braudel and Labrousse, *Histoire économique et sociale* are accepted by Doyle, who suggests they might even be revised upwards: *Origins*, 129, 231.

[90] Chaussinand-Nogaret, *French Nobility*, 28–30, 87–8.

[91] For an overview, cf. M. Vovelle, 'Le Grand Tournant des Mentalités en France, 1750–89: La "Sensibilité" pré-révolutionnaire', *Social History*, 2 (1977).

[92] M. Vovelle, *Piété baroque et déchristianisation en Provence au XVIIIᵉ siècle: Les Attitudes devant la mort d'après les clauses des testaments* (Paris, 1978); P. Chaunu, *La Mort à Paris, XVIᵉ–XVIIᵉ–XVIIIᵉ siècles* (Paris, 1978); P. Ariès, *The Hour of Our Death* (London, 1981), 470–1. For more recent contributions to the debate, see P. Hoffman, *Church and Community in the Diocese of Lyon, 1500–1789* (London, 1984); K. Norberg, *Rich and Poor in Grenoble, 1600–1814* (London, 1985); C. Jones, *Charity and 'Bienfaisance': The Treatment of the Poor in the Montpellier Region, 1740–1815* (Cambridge, 1982).

[93] M. Vovelle, 'L'Élite, ou le mensonge des mots', *AnnESC*, 29 (1974).

contraceptif', as Jean-Pierre Bardet has picturesquely put it—even in rural areas also supports the view that a seismic shift in *mentalités* was in process in the latter half of the eighteenth century.[94] Overall, it thus seems fair at least to hypothesize that changes in *mentalités* and the commercialization of society are connected phenomena.

This hypothesis is strengthened by the fact that the commercialization of Old Regime society did not simply relate to the provision of material goods, but covered the provision of services more generally and was indeed tantamount to the development of a more consumerist outlook on everyday life. The service sector of the French economy—in social terms overwhelmingly in non-noble hands—remains the great unknown for economic historians, who usually leave it out of their aggregate calculations.[95] It seems likely that it was doing extremely well, and that the mercantile developments of the century had stimulated a concomitant expansion in both the numbers and the wealth of individuals involved in transport, domestic service, the provision of legal, medical, and other general services. The range of what we might loosely call the 'professions' also rose: to the 'profession of arms', and the three classical liberal careers of theology, law, and medicine, were added over the course of the century a host of related or analogous occupations: schoolteacher, estate manager or *feudiste*, scientist, and civil engineer are just a few that spring to mind.[96]

---

[94] Bardet, *Rouen aux XVIIe et XVIIIe siècles*, 269. Cf. Dupâcquier, *Histoire de la population française*, 373 ff.; and G. Gullickson, *Spinners and Weavers of Auffay: Rural Industry and the Sexual Division of Labor in a French Village, 1750–1850* (Cambridge, 1986), 154–61.

[95] See, for example, O'Brien and Keyder, *Economic Growth in Britain and France*, 29–32; and Riley, 'French Finances', 234. Yet the importance of the service sector is seen by many economists as a key aspect of industrialization. See, for examples unfortunately more focused on the nineteenth century than the eighteenth, R. M. Hartwell, 'The Service Revolution: The Growth of Services in Modern Economy'; and W. Minchinton, 'Patterns of Demand, 1750–1914', both in C. M. Cipolla (ed.), *Fontana Economic History of Europe*, iii. *The Industrial Revolution* (London, 1971).

[96] A general overview, with articles covering the eighteenth century on doctors (M. Ramsey), psychiatry (J. Goldstein) and surgeons (T. Gelfand), in G. Geison (ed.), *Professions and the French State, 1700–1900* (Philadelphia, 1984). For *feudiste*, see A. Soboul, 'De la pratique des terriers', in his *Paysans, sans-culottes et Jacobins* (Paris, 1966), and J. Q. C. Mackrell, *The Attack on 'Feudalism' in Eighteenth-Century France* (London, 1973), 72. On scientists, R. Hahn, 'Changing Patterns for the Support of Scientists from Louis XIV to Napoleon', *History and*

In the New Revisionist Orthodoxy, the professions are usually patronizingly labelled the 'traditional élites', the assumption being that they remained locked in the rigidities of the Society of Orders until 4 August 1789. In fact they were in a state of institutional and intellectual ferment in the eighteenth century. Each seems to have undergone important institutional changes over the century, and developed in self-esteem, self-definition, and commitment. This was accompanied by a certain consumerism—one might say a bourgeoisification—in their lifestyles which reflects the extent to which they were adjusting to the inroads and the potentialities of commercial capitalism.

To look at any one of the professions in the late eighteenth century is to uncover a welter of ongoing debates—grounded, I would contend, in the changing size and nature of demand—on the nature of professionalism. In these debates, issues fundamental to the role of the service sector in a capitalist economy— the provision of services, rational organization, public accountability, market forces, quality control, and so on—were addressed. These are matters which we can as yet glimpse only darkly, and on whose exact nature we can at this stage only hazard guesses. To make an outrageously bald generalization, however, it seems helpful to classify the arguments utilized into two broad camps. On the one hand there were arguments for professionalization which adopted a corporative framework, and which sought changes on a 'vertical', internalist, and hierarchical basis. Expertise, internal discipline, and segregation from the wider society was the key. On the other hand, there were arguments which adopted a civic dimension, where the framework for professionalism was transcorporative, egalitarian, 'horizontal'. The profession should be opened up on to the wider society. Both sets of arguments utilized the same kinds of language, though if proponents of the corporative professionalism tended to think in terms of 'subjects' of the 'state'

Technology, 4 (1987); id., 'Scientific Careers in Eighteenth-Century France', in M. P. Crosland, *The Emergence of Science in Western Europe* (London, 1975); and C. C. Gillispie, *Science and Polity in France at the End of the Old Régime* (Princeton, NJ, 1980). For naval engineers, J. Pritchard, 'From Shipwright to Naval Constructor: The professionalisation of eighteenth-century naval shipbuilding', *Technology and Culture*, 28 (1987). For naval officers, M. Vergé-Franceschi, 'Les Officiers généraux de la marine royale (1669–1774)', *Revue historique*, 276 (1987). Cf. for actors even, A. Goodden, *'Actio' and Persuasion: Dramatic Performance in Eighteenth-Century France* (Oxford, 1986), esp. 138 ff.

(sometimes even personalized still as 'the king') the civic professionalizers referred to 'citizens' and the 'Nation' or, sometimes, 'the public'.[97] It is a language which in its most democratic and egalitarian formulations prefigured the debates in the National Assembly in the summer of 1789.

Let us take the profession of arms as an example. David Bien, in a brilliant Revisionist article, has familiarized us with the notion of the professionalization of the army officer corps.[98] This took the form of measures aimed to produce an effective army, Spartan in its virtues (though Prussia was the real blueprint), operating within more bureaucratic and hierarchical structures, and enjoying more efficient training and a more articulated career structure. Even the infamous Ségur ordinance of 1781 which limited high command to officers enjoying four quarters of nobility can be regarded as a professionalizing measure.[99] The aim of the ordinance was to exclude not commoners so much as recently ennobled bourgeois who had bought their way into the corps through the system of venal office and were thought to lack the sense of inbred honour which only dynasties of military nobility could produce in young recruits. What has tended to be seen as a flagrant instance of feudal reaction thus takes on the more anodyne colours of military professionalization; privilege is legitimized by service, high birth by social utility. Unfortunately, this is only half of the story. Though Bien does not tell us so, in fact there was more than one way of

[97] J. Merrick, 'Conscience and Citizenship in Eighteenth-Century France', *Eighteenth-Century Studies*, 4 (1987); R. Robin, *La Société française en 1789: Semur-en-Auxois* (Paris, 1970); and cf. J. Revel, 'Les Corps et communautés', in Baker, *Political Culture of the Old Régime*, 539–41. Those who have read W. Sewell, *Work and Revolution in France* will know how much I owe on some of what follows to this marvellous book (for a helpful, if critical review of which, see L. Hunt and G. Sheridan, 'Corporatism, Association and the Language of Labor in France, 1750–1850', *JMH*, 58 (1986)). There remains a whole area of socio-cultural linguistic study to be done on the shifting meanings of key terms in these debates.

[98] Bien, 'Réaction aristocratique' (see above, n. 9). Cf. id., 'The Army in the French Enlightenment: Reform, Reaction and Revolution', *P&P*, 85 (1979). Incidentally, as Bien admits, the artillery was both one of the most highly professional of all sectors of the armed forces in the late eighteenth century and one sector in which noble dominance was least marked. See too S. F. Scott, 'The French Revolution and the Professionalisation of the French Officer Corps', in M. Janowitz and J. van Doorn, *On Military Ideology* (London, 1971).

[99] Bien, 'Réaction aristocratique', 519–22; E. C. Léonard, *L'Armée et ses problèmes au XVIIIᵉ siècle* (Paris, 1958), 286 ff.

construing professionalization. The corporative model of the old nobility was matched by a very different, civic model, reflected and furthered by the writings of Rousseau, but transcending any narrow lineages of literary influences.[100] Embraced by many younger officers, this model was grounded in the belief that professionalism could best be achieved through opening up the army on the wider society. The military man was a citizen before he was a soldier: this basic message comes through in a whole host of writings from the 1770s onwards, rising in a crescendo, as one might expect, with the American War of Independence. Guibert's *Essai de tactique* (dedicated *A ma patrie*) (1772) and Joseph Servan's *Le Soldat citoyen* (1780) may serve as instances of the genre.[101] Consider in this respect too the early career of Lazare Carnot, the 'Organizer of Victory' in Year II, and a military engineer in the last years of the Old Regime. Carnot's prize-winning 'Éloge de Vauban' (1784) is a fine example of civic professionalism. Writing self-proclaimedly as a *militaire philosophe et citoyen*, Carnot praises the technical skills of Vauban as a servant, but he also sees him as a friend of the people, whose professional artistry was intended to defend *la Nation* from the sufferings of war. In this civic version, the professional ethic was combined with a critique of Ségur-style privilege, and the corporative professionalism which camouflaged it.[102]

   Antagonistic strands of civic and corporative professionalism are to be found in the secular clergy prior to 1789 too, as Timothy Tackett has shown.[103] The corporative model owed

---

[100] See Léonard, *Armée*, chs. 12–14. There is relevant material too in J. Chagniot, *Paris et l'armée au XVIIIe siècle: Etude politique et sociale* (Paris, 1985), particularly useful for not being orientated around the rural nobility. Chagniot also emphasizes the importance of lower non-noble officers in entrepreneurial activity (moneylending, petty trading, etc.).

[101] J. A. H. de Guibert, *Essai général de tactique*; J. Servan de Gerbay, *Le Soldat citoyen*; and others discussed in Léonard, *Armée*, 251 ff.

[102] L. Carnot, 'Éloge de Vauban', discussed in M. Reinhard, *Le Grand Carnot*, 2 vols. (Paris, 1950–2), i. 76–86. See too ch. 16, entitled 'Le civisme du militaire'.

[103] T. Tackett, 'The Citizen-Priest: Politics and Ideology among the Parish Clergy of Eighteenth-Century Dauphiné', *Studies in Eighteenth-Century Culture*, 7 (1978); B. Plongeron, *La Vie quotidienne du clergé français au XVIIIe siècle* (Paris, 1974). See also Tackett's *Priest and Parish in Eighteenth-Century France: A Social and Political Study of the Curé in a Diocese of Dauphiné, 1750–91* (Princeton, NJ, 1977); and his *Religion, Revolution and Regional Culture in Eighteenth-Century France: The Ecclesiastical Oath of 1791* (Princeton, NJ, 1986); D. Julia, 'Les Deux Puissances: Chronique d'une séparation de corps', in Baker, *Political Culture of the Old Régime*.

much to the continuing post-Tridentine reforms of the Catholic hierarchy, which aimed to make of parish priests spiritual gendarmes working obediently under their bishops. Intensive training, through seminaries and apprenticeship as *vicaires*, bade fair to make the Catholic clergy a force quite as disciplined, quite as *pur et dur* as the professionalized army corps. The equation of professionalism with the wearing of the clerical cassock highlighted the congruity.[104] This conception of the parish priest had increasingly to compete, however, with a more civic view which stressed the duties the clergy owed to the Nation. The citizen-clergy, often fuelled by Richerist ideas, resented the overly hierarchical and disciplinarian character of the Church, as well as its social dominance by the high nobility; practised the virtues of charity and consolation to their fellow citizens; and invoked the rights of the Nation. Their lifestyle as well as their outlook became increasingly bourgeois: the watches, clocks, mirrors, books, and other decorative bric-à-brac found in their homes revealed them as very much part of the new consumer culture.[105] The large number of civic-minded lower clergy elected to the Estates-General were to play a crucial role in helping to win the political initiative for their bourgeois fellow deputies in the Third Estate.[106]

Schoolteachers—very largely within the aegis of the church— were a group amongst which this civic ideology made a particular mark.[107] The pedagogy of the last decades of the Old Regime was thoroughly infused with civic values. Schoolteachers included some of the most eloquent and persuasive members of the revolutionary assemblies: Lanjuinais, Fouché, Billaud-Varenne, Daunou, François de Neufchâteau, Manuel, and Lakanal are a representative crop.

---

[104] Plongeron, *Vie quotidienne du clergé*, 75.

[105] Supporting older, anecdotal scholarship on this point, are recent studies based on post-mortem inventories: e.g. A. Pardailhé-Galabrun, 'L'Habitat et le cadre de vie des prêtres à Paris au XVIIIe siècle' and R. Plessix, 'Les Inventaires après décès: Une piste d'approche de la culture matérielle des curés du Haut-Maine au XVIIIe siècle', both *AB*, 95 (1988).

[106] R. F. Necheles, 'The Curés in the Estates General of 1789', *JMH*, 46 (1974); M. G. Hutt, 'The Role of the Curés in the Estates General', *Journal of Ecclesiastical History*, 6 (1955).

[107] A great deal on schoolteachers and civic values in this classic work of D. Mornet, *Les Origines intellectuelles de la Révolution française* (Paris, 1933), esp. 319 ff. and 419 ff.

There was to be a good admixture of medical men among the deputies of the revolutionary assemblies too, the good doctor Guillotin not least.[108] Debates over professionalism in the world of medicine were complicated by the traditional split between university-trained physicians and the more artisanal surgeons. Medicine was a jungle: the physicians cordially despised the surgeons, and the major medical faculties were perennially at daggers drawn. Over the course of the century, however, important changes took place. Surgeons hoisted up their prestige, wealth, and status: a liberal education came to be required for a surgical career.[109] A growing professionalization on their part, grounded in their highly centralized organiza- tion—the King's First Surgeon was effectively 'King of Surgery' throughout France—was helped by their proven utility in their service of the royal armies.[110] As the century wore on, many physicians also tried to transcend the corporative petty- mindedness for which they were famous, and to stress the public benefits of medical professionalism.[111] The foundation of the Royal Society of Medicine in 1776 was viewed as an attempt to give some corporative structure to the straggling bands of physicians throughout France; but it also made a great play of its mission as recorder and diagnostician of epidemics and as information network on disease and the environment.[112] Above all, it stood as the scourge of medical 'charlatanism', and argued

[108] G. Saucerotte, *Les Médecins pendant la Révolution* (Paris, 1887).

[109] T. Gelfand, *Professionalizing Modern Medicine: Paris Surgeons and Medical Science and Institutions in the Eighteenth Century* (Westport, Conn., 1980).

[110] Ibid. 43–4; and J. Guillermaud (ed.), *Histoire de la médecine aux armées; De l'Antiquité à Révolution* (Paris, 1982).

[111] The history of medical practice is marvellously illuminated in M. Ramsey, *Professional and Popular Medicine in France, 1770–1830: The Social World of Medical Practice* (Cambridge, 1988). See too 'La Médicalisation en France du XVIIIᵉ au début du XXᵉ siècle', *AB*, 86 (1979); J. P. Goubert (ed.), *La Médicalisation de la société française, 1770–1830* (Waterloo, Ontario, 1982); and C. Jones, 'The Medicalisation of Eighteenth-Century France', in R. Porter and A. Weare (eds.), *Problems and Methods in the History of Medicine* (London, 1987). For medical training, see L. W. B. Brockliss, *French Higher Education in the Seventeenth and Eighteenth Centuries: A Cultural Study* (Oxford, 1987).

[112] C. Hannaway, *Medicine, Public Welfare and the State of Eighteenth-Century France: The Société Royale de Médecine (1776–93)*, University Microfilms edn. (1975) of Johns Hopkins Ph.D. thesis (1974). See id., 'The Société Royale de Médecine and Epidemics in Ancien Régime France', *Bulletin of the History of Medicine*, 40 (1972); and J. Meyer, 'L'Enquête de l'Académie de médecine sur les epidémies, 1774–94', *Études rurales*, 9 (1969).

that social utility and public health required the enforcement of a monopoly of medical services by trained physicians.[113] Even before 1789, medical eulogists were portraying the dedicated physician as a bastion of citizenship, a cross between an altruistic notable and a secular saint devoted to his ailing flock.[114]

The legal profession seems in many respects to have been the least professionalized of the traditional professions prior to 1789. The training of lawyers was almost scandalously routine, and though there was an insistence that graduates should do an apprenticeship before they practised independently—four years in Paris after 1751—the profession had little hierarchical and disciplined character.[115] Yet, as Bailey Stone has argued, the magistrates of the Parlement held a highly elevated conception of their professional competence, and this led them strongly to support not only the corporative rights of their caste and the 'fundamental laws of the kingdom' but also the prerogatives of the Nation.[116] A highly vocal minority of barristers and attorneys, moreover, generated many of the ideas of civic professionalism we have noted in the other professions. Free legal advice centres established by Boucher d'Argis in Paris in 1783 and in Toulouse by Bertrand Barère in 1787 exemplified

[113] Ramsey, *Professional and Popular Medicine*; id., 'Traditional Medicine and Medical Enlightenment: The Regulation of Secret Remedies in the Ancien Régime', in Goubert, *Médicalisation*; and T. Gelfand, 'Medical Professionals and Charlatans: The *Comité de salubrité enquête*, 1790–1', *Histoire sociale/Social History*, 8 (1978).

[114] D. Roche, 'Talents, raison et sacrifice: L'Image du médecin des Lumières d'après les Éloges de la Société Royale de Médecine (1776–89)', *AnnESC*, 32 (1977); J. P. Goubert and D. Lorillot, *1789, le corps médical et le changement: Cahiers de doléances (médecins, chirurgiens et apothicaires)* (Toulouse, 1984), 25–6.

[115] For the legal profession, see L. Berlanstein, 'Lawyers in Pre-Revolutionary France', in W. Prest (ed.), *Lawyers in Early Modern Europe and America* (London, 1981); id., *The Barristers of Toulouse in the Eighteenth Century (1740–93)* (London, 1975); Fitzsimmons, *Parisian Order of Barristers*; F. Delbèke, *L'Action politique et sociale des avocats au XVIIIᵉ siècle* (Louvain, 1927); J. Carey, *Judicial Reform in France Before the Revolution of 1789* (Cambridge, Mass., 1981); and the excellent M. Gresset, *Gens de justice*. For lawyers' education, see also Brockliss, *French Higher Education*, 276–330. There is valuable information to be gleaned too from institutional studies of the Parlements: see esp. W. Doyle, *The Parlement of Bordeaux and the end of the Old Régime, 1771–90* (London, 1970). What we lack— with the honourable exception of Gresset—are local studies of the whole community of law, including magistrates, barristers, attorneys, the *basoche*, etc.

[116] B. Stone, *The French Parlements and the Crisis of the Old Régime* (London, 1986), esp. 223 ff.

this.[117] Lawyers in a number of jurisdictions in eastern France—and possibly elsewhere—also developed a new style of argument over seigneurial dues heavily impregnated with civic values.[118] Responding to peasant feelings that seigneurial dues were effectively unfair exchange—as I suggested earlier—lawyers argued that archaic feudal dues infringed natural freedom and justice. It was a dispute over *guet et garde*, plus the Parlement of Besançon's refusal to register the royal decree of 1780 abolishing mortmain, which detached many lawyers in the region from their formerly emphatic solidarity with their parlementary colleagues.[119] These civic values thus articulated the anti-seigneurial grievances of the peasantry as well as the professional ethic of the law, and laid the foundations of the cultural hegemony of Natural Rights in 1789.[120]

Though riddled with corruption and the object of tremendous popular hostility, as the *cahiers* were to make clear in 1789, legal practitioners still maintained a high estimation of their constitutional importance. They sometimes claimed to comprise a kind of Fourth Estate, for example, a position which clearly chimed in with the constitutional pretensions of the Parlements.[121] As Sarah Maza and Keith Baker have shown, many legal practitioners came to exploit civil and criminal cases so as to develop significant civic and political arguments, which were widely followed by the literate public—as well as by others not so literate.[122] The Calas affair is only one example—there are many—in which a contentious lawsuit led to an outpouring of pamphlets and polemical writings, normally the work of lawyers or attorneys, which invoked *l'opinion publique* as a kind

---

[117] Fitzsimmons, *Parisian Order of Barristers*, 17; Berlanstein, *Barristers*, 100–1.

[118] See above, p. 86.

[119] Gresset, *Gens de justice*, 730 ff.; Root, *Peasants and King*, 159–62, 183–93.

[120] I emphasize these links, as Revisionist accounts normally see peasant revolt, political ideas and financial crisis in 1789 as connected only adventitiously. See, for example, Doyle, *Origins*, 158; and P. R. Campbell, *The Ancien Régime in France* (Oxford, 1987), 72. Cf. Gresset, *Gens de justice*, 761 ff.

[121] Berlanstein, 'Lawyers', 164 ff.

[122] S. Maza, 'Le Tribunal de la Nation: Les Mémoires judiciaries et l'opinion publique à la fin de l'Ancien Régime', and K. Baker, 'Politique et opinion publique sous l'Ancien Régime', both *AnnESC*, 42 (1987). Cf. M. Ozouf, 'L'Opinion publique', in Baker, *Political Culture of the Old Régime*; and W. Doyle, 'Dupaty (1746–88): A Career in the Late Enlightenment', *Studies in Voltaire and the Eighteenth Century*, 230 (1985), esp. 82 ff.

of supreme arbiter.[123] The sociological supports of this powerful concept clearly lay in the growing market for cultural products and services over the eighteenth century which I have already described.[124] Be that as it may, 'public concern' in the mouths of prerevolutionary lawyers and polemicists predicated a feel for natural justice soon to receive more famous embodiment in the Rights of Man and the Nation, promulgated by a National Assembly in which were to sit some 151 lawyers.[125] The 'tas de bavards, avocats, procureurs, notaires, huissiers et d'autres semblables vermines' who, in the charmingly unlovely language of the *Père Duchesne*,[126] dominated every subsequent revolutionary assembly owed much to their exposure before 1789 to the problems inherent in exercising their profession in a fast-changing commercial society whose service sector was being transformed.

The debate over professionalism, civic and corporative, is particularly interesting to follow in the state bureaucracy, where it is complicated by the system of venal office. Classic Weberian reforms were increasingly introduced over the last decades of the Old Regime, to limit the rampant patrimonialism which characterized the service generally. The most hated branch of the service, the General Farm, was most advanced in its corporative professionalism, having introduced a wide range of rational bureaucratic procedures, and also having installed a career structure for employees which included a contributory pensions fund.[127] Elsewhere, there was a reaction against the

[123] For Calas, see D. Bien, *The Calas Affair: Persecution, Toleration and Heresy in Eighteenth-Century Toulouse* (Princeton, NJ, 1961).

[124] Maza, Baker, and Ozouf (see references at note 122) draw heavily on J. Habermas, *L'Espace public: Archéologie de la publicité comme dimension constitutive de la société bourgeoise* (Paris, 1978). It is symptomatic of the Revisionist approach that they neglect the aspects of Habermas's work which deal with the infrastructural aspects of the growth of a public, and also its bourgeois dimension, both of which are directly related to the present essay.

[125] E. H. Lemay, 'La Composition de l'Assemblée nationale constituante: Les Hommes de la continuité', *RHMC*, 24 (1977). The assembly also contained 315 office-holders, a great many of whom had legal training too.

[126] Cited in F. Brunot, *Histoire de la langue française des origines à nos jours*, ix (1967), 944–5.

[127] G. Matthews, *The Royal General Farms in the Eighteenth Century* (New York, 1958); and V. Azimi, *Un modèle administratif de l'Ancien Régime: Les Commis de la ferme générale et de la régie des aides* (Paris, 1987). On the bureaucracy in general, see too C. Church, *Revolution and Red Tape: The French Ministerial Bureaucracy, 1770–1850* (Oxford, 1981); Doyle, 'Price of Offices'; M. Antoine, 'La Monarchie

prevalence of venal office. The latter was widely blamed for, as one critic put it, 'cette séparation injurieuse qui règne entre l'administration et la Nation'.[128] Venality was in fact reduced or abolished in a number of services in the last decades of the Old Regime, including the *maréchaussée*, the postal system, and the saltpetre service.[129] Necker attempted to centralize the multiple treasuries of the financial bureaucracy.[130] There were some valiantly civic-minded administrators who endeavoured to move the popular imagination into believing them citizens as well as Crown servants. But bureaucrats continued to be seen essentially as *vendeurs d'espérance et de protection, de petits despotes, d'insolents roitelets*, the very embodiment of privilege, without any social utility or public benefit.[131] One can understand why the revolutionary assemblies would desire to debureaucratize French society—a familiar phantasm.[132]

Showing an awareness of the interpenetration of political and economic factors which is in itself an object-lesson to historians, many critics of venal office in the late Old Regime attacked the way in which such posts could entail what might be seen as unfair market advantage. This whole question of venal office has been reopened in recent years by a number of important Revisionist articles. In an article in the *Historical Journal* in 1984, for example, William Doyle demonstrated that the market for venal office was more buoyant than Marxists and indeed many Revisionists had held. The price of some offices falls, but far more rise, and Doyle concludes in general that overall the price of office was rising; he ascribes this to the traditionalism of the Old Regime bourgeoisie, who were failing to give up their secular preference for status over profit.[133]

Before this view finds its niche within the canon of the New

---

absolue', in Baker, *Political Culture of the Old Régime*; J. F. Bosher, *French Finances, 1770–1795: From Business to Bureaucracy* (Cambridge, 1970); and G. Bossenga, 'From Corps to Citizenship: The *Bureau des Finances* before the French Revolution', *JMH*, 58 (1986).

[128] V. Azimi, '1789: L'Echo des employés, ou le nouveau discours administratif', *XVIIIe Siècle*, 21 (1989), 134.

[129] Church, *Revolution and Red Tape*, 28.

[130] Bosher, *French Finances*, 142–65; R. D. Harris, *Necker, Reform Statesman of the Ancien Régime* (Berkeley, Calif., 1979); Bossenga, 'From Corps to Citizenship', *passim*.   [131] Azimi, '1789', 134.

[132] Church, *Revolution and Red Tape*, 46.

[133] Doyle, 'Price of Offices', 844.

Revisionist Orthodoxy, however, let us consider how this rise in the value of venal office might relate to the growth of the market for services. The post of court physician (*médecin du roi*), on which I have done some research, is an interesting starting-point. In 1720, only seventeen physicians could claim this title, while in 1789, eighty-eight, to whom might be added quite as many *chirurgiens du roi* and *apothecaires du roi*.[134] The price of these posts seems to have been pretty buoyant. As only a handful of the individuals who could style themselves *médecin du roi* came near the person of the monarch, or even resided at Versailles, it might be concluded that here was a title that meant prestige and little else. In fact, this was far from the case. The purchase of a post was a means of circumventing the monopoly which the Paris Medical Faculty had on medical services within the capital. One has only to remember the wild enthusiasm of Parisians for every medical fad and fancy in the eighteenth century to see how valuable that access could be: Paris rocked to, and *médecins du roi* made money out of, the crazes for vapours, male *accoucheurs*, smallpox inoculation, Mesmerism, and a good many forms of treatment for venereal disease—the most exotic of which must surely have been Lefebvre de Saint-Ildephont's anti-venereal chocolate drops. This particular court physician claimed that one could medicate one's wife against venereal infection by providing her with an unending supply of boxes of chocolates.[135]

Crudely put, purchase of a post within the royal medical Household was a means of cashing in on medical consumerism. It represented a headlong rush towards a market—even an entrepreneurial interest in stimulating it—rather than a flight from it. One wonders whether there are similar stories to tell about many of the other venal offices. Indeed, if we turn again to William Doyle's list of venal offices for which prices were rising, we find that a good number of them—attorneys, notaries, legal clerks, auctioneers, and wigmakers—do indeed

---

[134] C. Jones, 'The *Médecins du Roi* at the End of the Ancien Régime and in the French Revolution', in V. Nutton (ed.), *Medicine at Court, 1500–1800* (London, 1989).

[135] Ibid., plus P. Delaunay, *Le Monde médical parisien au XVIIIᵉ siècle* (1906) (p. 100 for Lefebvre), and R. Darnton's classic *Mesmerism and the End of the Enlightenment in France* (Cambridge, Mass., 1968), for insights into the general atmosphere.

relate to expanding markets for professional services or fashionable lifestyle.[136] Venal office (and perhaps a similar case might be mounted for land purchase) begins to look less like an option for status than a shrewd investment aimed to give the purchaser access to a market or edge within it.[137] Money bought privilege within this market as well as within the polity and within the social hierarchy.

Attacked by their co-professionals as the embodiment of privilege and social inutility, many venal officers themselves grew progressively disenchanted by their posts. The advantages of market edge plus the returns on the initial investment palled as the monarchy, increasingly beset by financial problems, came to interfere with the venal office market in a number of ways. The value of the investment was reduced by a series of injudicious decisions by the monarch to levy forced loans, for example (on the *corps* of financial officials in particular), to increase the number of offices in a particular *corps*, or to reduce wages.[138] The downturn in the economy from the 1770s may also have diminished the buoyancy of many markets for services. Economies in the state bureaucracy—pursued by all controllers-general in the last years of the Old Regime, but with no greater vigour than by Loménie de Brienne in 1787–8—must have helped venal officers to see the writing on the wall.[139] In any event, with state bankruptcy on the horizon, it was a pretty shrewd move, on the Night of 4 August 1789, to agree to the abolition of all venal offices. For the abolition was agreed on the basis of compensation which, it was hoped, would be financially more advantageous than forcible expropriation or sale in depressed market conditions.[140] So much for the 'patriotic rhapsodies' of altruism!

[132] Doyle, 'Price of Offices', 852–4, 856–7. See R. Giesey, 'State-Building in Early Modern France: The Role of Royal Officialdom', *JMH*, 55 (1983) for some interesting ideas on office and markets.

[137] Cf. in this respect the arguments of R. C. Allen on the economic rationality behind land purchase, allegedly for status reasons, in eighteenth-century England: 'The Price of Freehold Land and the Interest Rate in the Seventeenth and Eighteenth Centuries', *EcHR*, 41 (1988).

[138] Bossenga, 'From *Corps* to Citizenship'; and D. Bien, 'Office, Corps and a System of State Credit: The Uses of Privilege under the Old Régime', in Baker, *Political Culture of Old Régime*.

[139] Bosher, *French Finances*; J. Egret, *The French Pre-Revolution, 1787–8* (Chicago, 1977), 43–61, 95–9; Harris, *Necker*, 107–15.

[140] Carey, *Judicial Reform*, 105.

In the question of venal office were encapsulated many of the problems of the absolute monarchy. The state operated the most extraordinarily ornate system whereby it sold offices which thereby became the private property of their owners. The holders could not be bought out *en bloc*—the expense was too colossal; so kings turned disadvantage to advantage by levying forced loans on the main bodies of venal office-holders to help it in its financial difficulties. The king was thereby to a certain extent digging his own grave, in that these loans ran up the National Debt to colossal proportions. In addition, the royal demands amplified the corporate awareness of the bodies of venal office-holders. This was particularly marked in the case of the towns, as Gail Bossenga has recently shown.[141] Venal municipal offices, constantly chopped and changed over the course of the century, bred discontent both within the charmed circle of municipal officials, and outside in sectional groups wanting to get in. This provided a seed-plot in which—over all sorts of issues, from street lighting to local taxes—could grow a civic awareness quite as cogent as that developing within the professions.

A growing sensitivity to civic issues is found elsewhere in Old Regime society too. Even at village level, Hilton Root finds Burgundian peasants deciding on local matters utilizing, in pretty sophisticated fashion, the concept of the General Will long before the latter term was dreamed up by Jean-Jacques Rousseau.[142] Urban guilds were often too the micro-sites for similar exercises in political education and the exercise of political democracy. They too, like Hilton Root's peasants, utilized the courts as means of redress, with lawyers playing the part of cultural intermediary between legal form and social issues.[143] If we suspend the New Revisionist Orthodoxy's certainty that modern political culture was born in 1789, we can glimpse within Old Regime society, even at these lowly levels

---

[141] G. Bossenga, 'City and State: An Urban Perspective on the Origins of the French Revolution', in Baker, *Political Culture of the Old Régime*.

[142] Root, *Peasants and King*, esp. ch. 3. Cf. K. Tonnesson, 'La Démocratie directe sous la Révolution française: Le Cas des districts et sections de Paris', in Lucas, *Political Culture of the Revolution*, 295–6.

[143] The outstanding work of Michael Sonenscher is especially illuminating of this theme: besides his *Work and Wages*, see too his article 'Journeymen, the Courts and the French Trades, 1781–91', *P&P*, 114 (1987). Cf. Revel, 'Corps et comunautés', 239–41.

supposedly locked away into the bromides of a 'popular culture', a vibrant and developing political sensibility which cries out to be inventoried, classified, and understood.

Although what came to be at issue often had far wider ramifications, these burgeoning debates within the professions and other corporative cells of the Society of Orders were at first often localized and sectional. The courts and, by way of the press, the notion of 'public opinion' provided a conduit along which civic sensibilities could penetrate the body social, as we have seen. A number of other institutions came to act as a crucible in which these fragmented disputes were fused into a supra-corporative consciousness. The Enlightenment Academies were a case in point.[144] Their internally democratic practices favoured such fusion, for the niceties of the social hierarchy were normally not observed within them, and bourgeois rubbed shoulders with noble, as well as doctor with lawyer. To be frank, the Academies were often dominated by local nobles and dignitaries, and consequently stuffy, if worthy, in their procedures. The egalitarian, meritocratic sharing of experience which they embodied was doubtless important for some. Even more important, however, the Masonic lodges.[145] The cult of Masonry had its adepts throughout the social pyramid; yet the numerical predominance among the body of 50,000 French Masons was clearly with the professional classes and with their social equivalents. Businessmen—often excluded from Academies for being lacking in tone and breeding—were here in massive numbers: they represented 36 per cent of members in major cities, and the proportion was often well over 50 per cent in numerous localities. Soldiers were the main professional category, although lawyers, administrators, and doctors—if few

---

[144] D. Roche, *Le Siècle des Lumières en province: Académies et académiciens provinciaux, 1680–1789*, 2 vols. (Paris, 1978); id., 'Académies et politique au siècle des Lumières: Les Enjeux pratiques de l'immortalité', in Baker, *Political Culture of the Old Régime*.

[145] Roche, *Siècle des Lumières en province*, i. 257 ff.; R. Halévi, *Les Loges maçonniques dans la France d'Ancien Régime: Aux origines de la sociabilité démocratique* (Paris, 1984); D. Roche, 'Négoce et culture dans la France du XVIIIᵉ siècle', *RHMC*, 25 (1978); Hunt, *Politics, Class and Culture*, 198–200; and the classic M. Agulhon, *Pénitent et franc-maçons dans l'ancienne Provence* (Paris, 1965). Cf. too the general overview of E. François and R. Reichhardt, 'Les Formes de sociabilité en France du milieu du XVIIIᵉ siècle au milieu du XIXᵉ siècle', *RHMC*, 34 (1987).

priests—were also there in bulk.[146] The same elements—in a slightly different mix—were found in *sociétés de lecture, chambres littéraires* and their like.[147]

These new forums for egalitarian mixing and discussion were as much organs of sociability as anything else. In his recent work on Masonry, Ran Halévi has dubbed this a 'democratic sociability'.[148] Halévi, like his close collaborator François Furet, is in fact particularly interested in the lodges as lineal ancestors of the Jacobin Clubs, and so chooses a narrowly political term. I prefer the term 'civic sociability', which I think expresses rather better the urban and wider cultural implications of this form of social mixing, and has the additional merit of making explicit the clear affinities it has with the civic ideologies and practices exuded by the professional and corporative institutions of the Old Regime.

In the light of the previous discussion, we can now revisit the debate on the social origins of the Revolution of 1789. Given the development of commercial capitalism in eighteenth-century France, the spread of a consumer society, the development of professionalization within the service sector of the economy which this helped to spawn, and the appearance of associated forms of civic sociability, it no longer looks realistic to disparage the vitality nor indeed the ideological autonomy of the Old Regime bourgeoisie. Far from the social structure of Old Regime France being locked remorselessly into 'traditional' 'pre-capitalist', 'archaic' forms, the progress of commercialization and the spread of a consumer society suggests a relative 'bourgeoisification' of Old Regime society. Far from an élite of 'notables' melding harmoniously and cosily together in the last years of the Old Regime, moreover, conflict over the role of privilege and the implications of citizenship was endemic and established an explosive agenda beneath the surface calm of the Society of Orders. Yet though civic sociability had achieved much, it had signally failed to capture control of the state

---

[146] Roche, *Le Siècle des Lumières en province*, ii. 419–24; and cf. François and Reichhardt, 'Formes de sociabilité', 465 ff.

[147] For a general overview, see M. Agulhon, 'Les Sociétés de pensée', in M. Vovelle (ed.), *État de la France pendant la Révolution, 1789–99* (Paris, 1988), 44–8.

[148] Halévi, *Les Loges maçonniques*. Cf. Furet, *Interpreting the French Revolution*, 37 ff.

apparatus. This was to be the achievement of the men of 1789.

Who, then, were the 'revolutionary bourgeoisie' (if we can now assume there was one)?[149] Alfred Cobban characterized it as a mixture of landowners, venal officers, and professional men. To a certain degree he was correct. Yet he saw both the professions and the venal office-holders as declining, inferiority-complexed classes, so many shrinking violets easily written off as 'traditional élites'. What I have argued here is that the professions and indeed a great many venal office-holders, far from being sectional and 'traditionalist' in their orientation and outlook, were in fact responding to and very much part of the development of capitalism in the Old Regime. These groups were more genuinely bourgeois than ever before, and exuded a new civic professionalism which had its roots in a developing 'market-consciousness' and which clashed with the corporative values espoused by many of their fellows. They shared the vision and the reflexes of the commercial bourgeoisie of the Old Regime in a far more direct way than has hitherto been recognized. Moreover, although they thought through these problems at first perhaps largely through the corporative framework, the ongoing debts on professionalization nurtured widening perspectives. Masonic lodges, *sociétés de pensée*, and the like further elaborated and refined the debate and also opened it up so that it included sections of the economic bourgeoisie in the years leading up to 1789. Professionalization was thus not simply a part of the noble reaction, as David Bien might have us believe. In its civic form, professionalism legitimated the attack on privilege, even when the latter was defended by corporative values. It stimulated a conception of the state as something which was not so much embodied in the dynast as present in the 'Nation', an ideological construct which developed *pari passu* with the growth and elaboration of the market. The organs of civic sociability, finally, provided forums in which new ideas of equality, democracy, and civic concern could take material form among an increasingly homogeneous bourgeoisie and their allies among the liberal aristocracy.

In his notorious *Qu'est-ce que le Tiers État?*, Sieyès showed himself very much the apologist for this new civic consciousness.

[149] Cf. W. Reddy, *Money and Liberty in Western Europe: A Critique of Historical Understanding* (Cambridge, 1987), 5: 'There was no revolutionary bourgeoisie.'

He argued that the 'Nation' was composed of useful classes and groups which with great lucidity he itemized as including agriculture, industry, the mercantile interest, services 'pleasant to the person', and the public services of the army, the law, the Church, and the bureaucracy.[150] His thinking was not as much the early appearance of a revolutionary ideology which sprang out fully developed from the political context, as the Revisionists are prone to argue. Rather, as the list of groups suggests, the new ideology of the Third Estate was in essence the ideology of prerevolutionary civic professionalism. Its presence in one of the cardinal texts of the Revolution of 1789 indicates something of the contribution this new and increasingly aggressive civic ideology made to the downfall of the Old Regime. The civic sociability which had developed among this fraction of the bourgeoisie in the last decades of the Old Regime was corrosive of the deferentialism and hierarchical structures of the Society of Orders.

The ability of the Old Regime state to provide social and political conditions free from privilege and corporatism was in question long before its financial shipwreck in 1787–8. In the decades which preceded 1789, successive ministers had found themselves trying to float public loans by appeals to a general public increasingly impregnated with civic consciousness. The mercantile and professional bourgeoisie—together with the liberal fraction of the noble class—were, however, loath to go on extending moral or financial credit to a state which continued to conjugate public interest with the entrenched privileges of the aristocracy. As a social force, public opinion stretched out and reached every corner of this increasingly commercialized society. As an intellectual construct, moreover, 'public opinion' was too closely tied into the cultural hegemony established by the professions and the new organs of civic sociability to be plausibly invoked by a monarch who seemed to be indissolubly wedded to the maintenance of the institutions of privilege.[151]

---

[150] E. J. Sieyès, *Qu'est-ce que le Tiers État?*, ed. S. E. Finer (Chicago, 1963), 63–4. Cf. Sewell, *Work and Revolution*, 79.

[151] See e.g. the highly illuminating recent study of D. R. Weir, 'Tontines, Public Finance and Revolution in France and England, 1688–1789', *Journal of Economic History*, 49 (1989). On a different tack, see too the interesting perspective on the problem opened up in J. de Viguerie, 'Le Roi, le "public" et l'exemple de Louis XV', *Revue historique*, 278 (1987).

The Nation, credit, public opinion, professionalism, and civic sociability had become woven into a spider's web in which privilege became helplessly stuck—and was then devoured. Far from the financial crisis of 1789 being, as the Revisionists contend, somehow extrinsic to earlier social developments,[152] it was in many ways the apotheosis of the social, political, and cultural developments I have been outlining.

The influence of the professional classes upon the Revolution was not only at the level of cultural hegemony. When one looks at political participation in 1789 and in the following revolutionary decade, what strikes one at once is the importance of the professional classes at every level and their interpenetration with other branches of the bourgeoisie. Cobban's original perception that declining venal officers and liberal professions dominated the Constituent Assembly is at least a starting-point,[153] though his analysis is misguided: venal officer-holders were not necessarily a declining group; and anyway further research has shown that their representation in later revolutionary assemblies fell drastically, while that of professional men (including, increasingly, what one might call career or professional politicians) stayed consistently high. Moreover, as Lynn Hunt has brilliantly shown, local administration was very much in the hands of lawyers, physicians, notaries, and local bureaucrats, often with a good admixture of the merchants and manufacturers found only rather rarely at national level. In 1793 and 1794, a bigger input of petty bourgeois elements—shopkeepers, artisans, and minor clerks—is often visible, and in the countryside wealthier peasants got a look in.[154] But this really only underlines the bourgeois and professional orientation. Recent work on Parisian local politics confirms the general picture: the districts of 1789–90, as R. B. Rose has shown, were a fairly representative bourgeois cross-section; while incisive work on the Parisian sansculottes of Year II, conducted by Richard Cobb and others in his wake, has revealed the more solidly bourgeois backgrounds of many militants who, for

---

[152] Reddy, *Money and Liberty*, 128–9, for arguments along the same lines as here.   [153] Cobban, *Aspects*, 109–11.
[154] Hunt, *Politics, Class and Culture*, ch. 5; and L. Hunt, P. Hansen, and D. Lansky, 'The Failure of the Liberal Republic in France, 1795–9: The Road to Brumaire', *JMH*, 51 (1979).

reasons of political expediency, deflated their social rank in the democratic atmosphere of the Terror.[155]

The analysis of Edmund Burke, cited by Lynn Hunt, that the Revolution was the work of 'moneyed men, merchants, principal tradesmen and men of letters' thus seems pretty accurate, as a description of both the key participants in the political process after 1789 and many of the major proponents of 'civic sociability' before that date.[156] It is important, in the light of my earlier arguments, however, to view Burke's 'men of letters' not as an autonomous, free-standing group, but rather as the vocal representatives of the professions. This interpretation clashes, I am aware, with Robert Darnton's fine studies of men of letters as a significant influence on the revolutionary process.[157] However, to classify men of letters as an autonomous group seems to distort and to underplay the professional and corporative framework within which such men had done—and maybe continued to do—their thinking. Clearly the concept had an important role in revolutionary ideology and myth-making. In particular, there is a brand of counter-revolutionary interpretation which rejoices at seeing the Revolution allegedly in the hands of an anomic pack of Grub Street low-life, seedy intellectuals cut off from any experience of real-life political problems, and consequently wild and utopian in their aims. The professional prism puts quite a different, more solid, more pragmatic, more market-orientated view on the revolutionary bourgeoisie. The latter is no more synonymous with Darnton's riff-raff intelligentsia than Old Regime professionals are with David Bien's reactionary army officers.

I have suggested that there was a far closer, organic link between the development of capitalism in the eighteenth

---

[155] R. B. Rose, *The Making of the Sans-Culottes* (Manchester, 1983); R. Cobb, *The Police and the People: French Popular Protest, 1789–1820* (Oxford, 1970), 178–9; R. Andrews, 'Social Structures, Political Elites and Ideology in Revolutionary Paris', *Journal of Social History*, 19 (1985); M. Sonenscher, 'The Sans-Culottes of the Year II: Rethinking the Language of Labour in Revolutionary France', *Social History*, 9 (1984).

[156] Hunt, *Politics, Culture and Class*, 161, citing E. Burke, 'Thoughts on French Affairs', in R. A. Smith (ed.), *Burke on Revolution* (New York, 1968), 190.

[157] Most famously in R. Darnton, 'The High Enlightenment and the Low Life of Literature in pre-Revolutionary France', *P&P*, 51 (1971); and more recently in 'The Facts of Literary Life in Eighteenth-Century France', in Baker, *Political Culture of the Old Régime*. Cf. too Furet, *Interpreting the French Revolution*, 36–7.

century and the emergence of more 'market-conscious', and public-spirited intellectual élites than historians have normally allowed. The attractiveness of this hypothesis is amplified when we look at much of the social and economic legislation carried out by successive revolutionary assemblies which would do so much to shape nineteenth-century France. If one assumes that the liberal professionals who made up such an important constitutive part of the assemblies are socially autonomous from the economic bourgeoisie, then reforms as classically capitalistic in their character as the formation of a national market, the abolition of guilds, the introduction of uniform weights and measures, the removal of seigneurial excrescences, the re-definition of property rights come to be seen as the product of conspiracy, accident, or a hidden hand. The impregnation of the bourgeoisie with market values, the 'bourgeoisification' of the professions, and the organic links developing between the professions and mercantile groups prior to 1789, on the other hand, help to provide a more viable political and cultural framework for understanding why such reforms were introduced. These phenomena constitute a 'silent bourgeois revolution' which was the essential precursor of the noisier, messier, and better-known events of 1789.[158] They also help to explain why one of the most durable and toughest legislative legacies of the revolutionary years should be the so-called 'career open to talents', a principle which was indeed tailored to the career interests and civic sense of the liberal professions by, precisely, the members of the liberal professions who dominated the assemblies.

A great deal more work still needs to be done on relations between the different branches of the bourgeoisie—the different types of professionals, the landed and commercial bourgeoisie, and so on—as well as what Colin Lucas has called the 'stress zones' between them. These relationships, moreover, shifted, sometimes radically as a result of the revolutionary experience. The quotation by Barère with which I began is symptomatic of

---

[158] The phrase 'silent bourgeois revolution' comes from D. Blackbourn and G. Eley, *The Peculiarities of German History: Bourgeois Society and Politics in Nineteenth-Century Germany* (Oxford, 1982), a work which has a number of similarities of approach to those outlined here, but which I unfortunately encountered only when writing the final draft of this essay.

the problem: Barère attacks commerce and speculation from a political viewpoint; yet, on the other hand, his rhetoric connives in a good commercial operation. We need to know more about how the Revolution affected the professions, and the arguments about professional standards, quality control, educational requirements, and public interest which had percolated within them throughout the late Enlightenment. The events of 1789 moved these debates which had gripped the professions under the Old Regime on to a new level, and their subsequent history highlighted the mixed and sometimes contradictory legacy of the revolutionary experience.

There was to be, it seems, no single trajectory for the professions in the 1790s, nor any common destiny for their members. The abolition of venal office on 4 August and the enunciation of the principle of the career open to talent in the Declaration of the Rights of Man on 26 August 1789 left a great deal of room for debate and disagreement of how professionalism should be conjugated with the exigencies of citizenship. The response of each of the professions differed, and new fault-lines emerged out of the process. The furore within the army is relatively well-known.[159] How far did the rights of soldiers as citizens entitle them to political activities which, in the opinion of many of their supporters, nullified professional *esprit de corps*? The path towards the patriotic citizen-soldier of Year II passed by way of the Nancy mutiny and its repression and the emigration of 60 per cent of the putatively 'professional' noble officer corps. The late 1790s and the napoleonic period were to see the reassertion of a more corporative version of professionalism, with the sacrifice of many of the more democratic procedures of Year II, such as election of officers.

The experience of the clergy was rather different.[160] The Civil Constitution of the Clergy may in many respects be viewed as the charter of a professionalized secular clergy, establishing as it

---

[159] S. Scott, *The Response of the Royal Army to the French Revolution: The Role and Development of the Line Army, 1787–1793* (Oxford, 1978); J. P. Bertaud, *The Army of the French Revolution: From Citizen Soldiers to Instrument of Power* (Princeton, NJ, 1989). Cf. too J. Godechot, *Les Institutions de la France sous la Révolution et l'Empire* (Paris, 1968), 113–38, 353–74, 494–5.

[160] Tackett, *Religion, Revolution and Regional Culture*; and J. McManners, *The French Revolution and the Church* (London, 1969) for introductions to this massive topic.

did democratic procedures, rational hierarchies, and a well-founded career structure. Yet civic professionalism fell foul of corporative professionalism: many priests found it difficult to accept the loss of their monopoly of spiritual services consequent on the enunciation of the principle of freedom of conscience, and jibbed at National Assembly's failure to consult either the Church as a corporate entity or its hierarchical head, the Pope. The 1790s was to prove an often tragic backcloth against which the clergy rethought their attitudes towards ecclesiastical hierarchy, conscience, and civic responsibility.

A similar reassessment was necessary for the medical and legal professions and for the state bureaucracy.[161] The career open to talents and the attack on privilege within corporate hierarchies justified the attack on the Old Regime bureaucracy, the abolition of many of its services (such as the General Farm, probably the most corporatively professionalized of all state services), the closure of legal and medical faculties, and the dissolution of first attorneys, then barristers. By the late 1790s, however, a barrage of complaints emerged from all quarters which highlighted how the opening up of a free field for medical and legal practice had damaged public interest and (so it was said) standards of professional competence. The public was, it was argued, prey to medical charlatans, legal sharks, and corrupt and ill-trained clerks. The reassertion of a corporative hierarchy and the reintroduction of better training methods under the Thermidorian Convention, the Directory, and the Consulate attested to a reworking of the relationship between profession, state, and public.

There is much about the civic-inspired deregulation of many of the professions in the 1790s and their corporative re-professionalization later in the decade which remains obscure. Certainly the professions were transformed in the Revolutionary decade—a fact palpable in the disappearance of many pre-revolutionary titles such as *procureur, avocat, chirurgien,* and so

---

[161] D. M. Vess, *Medical Revolution in France, 1789–96* (Gainesville, Fla., 1975) and D. B. Weiner, 'French Doctors Face the War, 1792–1815' in C. K. Warner (ed.), *From the Ancien Régime to the Popular Front: Essays in the History of Modern France in Honor of S. B. Clough* (New York, 1969); Fitzsimmons, *Parisian Order of Barristers,* esp. 116 ff.; I. Woloch, 'The Fall and Resurrection of the Civil Bar, 1789–1820s', *FHS,* 15 (1987–8). See too Godechot, *Institutions,* 154–5, 449–53, 704–5 and *passim.*

on. After the perils of the 'free field' had been exposed, it looked as though for most the best guarantee of professional success after 1789 was state utility. Hence the unrivalled prestige of the armed forces from the late 1790s; hence the formidable strengthening of the state bureaucracy; hence the emergence of a prestigious scientific profession, very much under the wing of the state; hence too the arguments of state utility advanced by doctors and lawyers in their attempts to win government support.[162] The civic and corporative models of professionalisation which had emerged in the Ancien Régime were transformed by the experience of the 1790s; but in broad terms, it was something akin to the corporative model which often prevailed, while maintaining the career open to talent which the civic model had required. The Revolution had changed both the context of and the protagonists in the debate over professionalism. And the transformed professions were to make a massive and well-documented contribution to the character of nineteenth-century France.

The professions remained after 1800, finally, still very much tributary to the market for their services. Though the state was often a valued client, most depended very considerably on the overall situation of the economy. As the Revisionists have pointed out with an often wearisome frequency, the Revolution did not mark a transition to industrialism in the French economy. (Actually, Georges Lefebvre and Albert Soboul seem to have been pretty much aware of that fact too, as their balanced assessments of the sometimes contradictory social and economic legacy of the Revolution should make clear.)[163] France's economy was still in the commercial mould, and the professions inevitably reflected that fact.[164] *Pace* many

---

[162] C. C. Gillispie, 'Politics and Science, with Special Reference to Revolutionary and Napoleonic France', *History and Technology*, 4 (1987); Bosher, *French Finances*; Church, *Revolution and Red Tape*; M. Brugière, *Gestionnaires et profiteurs de la Révolution* (Paris, 1986); id., 'Les Finances et l'Etat', in Lucas, *Political Culture of the French Revolution*.

[163] See, for example, G. Lefebvre, *The French Revolution*, 2 vols. (New York, 1962, 1964), ii. 303 ff.; and A. Soboul, *The French Revolution, 1787–1799* (London, 1974), 553 ff. Cf. Edmonds, 'Successes and Excesses', 198–200.

[164] See generally the works cited above, n. 29, by O'Brien and Keyder, Crafts, Roehl, Goldsmith, and Aldrich, plus Heywood, 'Role of the peasantry' and Lemarchand, 'Du féodalisme au capitalisme'. See too M. Lévy-Leboyer, 'La

Revisionists, however, the French economy was not irredeemably traditionalist nor stagnatingly precapitalist. France continued its measured and balanced way towards industrialization. Indeed growth in the early nineteenth century, even before the creation of a national rail network, is now being recognized as having been far stronger than has often been thought. In that progress, the Revolution had been perhaps a less heroic and dramatic episode than the Old Marxist Orthodoxy would maintain; though it certainly had far more importance, and positive influence, than the New Revolutionist Orthodoxy would allow. The legislative achievement of successive Revolutionary assemblies and the eradication of Old Regime privilege provided a more appropriate environment for commercial capitalism in general to develop, and the bourgeoisie in particular to prosper. France moved slowly towards its industrializing goal at the end of a bourgeois nineteenth century for which the stage had been set by a bourgeois revolution, Revisionist reports of whose sad demise I persist in finding greatly exaggerated.

Croissance économique en France au xixᵉ siècle', *AnnESC*, 28 (1973); W. H. Newell, 'The Agrarian Revolution in Nineteenth-Century France', *Journal of Economic History*, 33 (1973); and J. Marczewski, 'Economic Fluctuations in France, 1815–1938', *JEEH*, 17 (1988).

5

The Revolution: Catastrophe or New Dawn for the French Economy?

LOUIS BERGERON

THE very fact of choosing this topic and of expressing it in the form of this question testifies to the survival of recurrent polemics about the long-term effects of the 1789 Revolution. These polemics continue to mark even the most recent developments in French historiography.

To be sure, in past but not so very remote times, great French historians belonging to the Jacobin or Marxist traditions argued in oversimplified terms and predicated the opening of a new era of economic progress with 1789, as if it were a kind of 'natural consequence' of a political and social revolution which itself appeared as a sort of prerequisite for such progress. According to this logic, the abolition of feudalism in all its aspects was to be followed by the blossoming of individual initiative and the multiplication of wealth. The same historians tended also to glorify the various aspects of state interventionism which, for a while, were enforced by the revolutionary government and assemblies, and which they depicted as a magic weapon ensuring military success and greater social justice in general.

Recently, a critical current—a rightist one, which obviously can be traced all the way back to the time of counter-revolution itself—has frequently used arguments drawn from the economic history of the Revolution in order to blacken the picture further. It takes for granted, of course, that the whole revolutionary episode was above all a disaster in its ideas, its politics, and also its economic consequences. This current further insists on long-term negative effects of the Revolution. These authors accuse it of having unquestionably destroyed the impetus to business and the prosperity which characterized the late Old Regime. In other words, they accuse it of having broken the nascent industrial revolution, thus leaving France on the roadside, handicapped and condemned to backwardness. In this perspective, the French Revolution becomes the scapegoat which has been sought by generations of theoreticians of the so-called decline of France.[1]

At the same time, one cannot but be struck by how slow progress has been during recent decades in research into both the conjunctural and structural economic aspects of the Revolution, as well as by the inadequacy of the limits—chronological, geographical or, mainly, political and institutional—within which that research has generally been conducted, with the exception of some excellent material in the recent work of Denis Woronoff, Serge Chassagne, and Jean-Pierre Hirsch.[2] Indeed, we may pose the question of whether the revolutionary decade and its years of warfare are amenable to any pertinent analysis, even if we extend it to the napoleonic era and to the whole period of the wars.

Let me state as a premiss that I do not by any means favour the pessimistic interpretation over the optimistic, or vice versa. I must confess to being bored by this kind of debate. It simply offers a pretext for a few economic facts or arguments (always the same ones, moreover) to be used as ammunition in a combat with quite different real objectives. I prefer to try to pose correctly the problems of periodizing French growth over two centuries and, by that means, to evaluate as reasonably as possible the impact of the events of the Revolution. Such an evaluation should, moreover, make a careful distinction between short-term economic consequences, between damage easy to repair quickly, and long-term ones, which were beyond repair. Finally, the French Revolution was something greater than an earthquake. Basically, it was a reconstruction of social institutions, a reconstruction of society itself, which, right up to the

---

[1] See e.g. Florin Aftalion, *L'Économie de la Révolution française* (Paris, 1987), very aggressive even if poorly argued.

[2] Jean-Pierre Hirsch, 'Les Deux Rêves du commerce: Entreprise et institution dans la région lilloise (1780–1860 environ)' (thèse d'état, University of Lille III, 1989).

present day, continues to demand commentary in terms well beyond the usual attempts to draw up a balance sheet. We should rid ourselves of the typical obsession of the statistical agents of the Consulate and the Empire: by this, I mean the constantly repeated enquiry into how people, animals, and things were doing in Year VIII when compared with the eve of the Revolution. Of course, historians certainly do have some excuse for remaining so preoccupied with this question. The mountain of surviving documents from these years, directed as they are to that question, inevitably shapes the pattern of their research and determines the shape of their conclusions.[3]

We should begin our discussion here with the immediate effects of the Revolution. Although years-long agreement about these effects has not necessarily been accompanied by improved analysis, it has acquired the status of a classic description and we need not spend a great deal of time on repeating that here. None the less, we can try to sketch out a hierarchy of effects, to propose a classification, to suggest a better equilibrium between them. Undoubtedly, special emphasis has to be laid on financial and monetary difficulties. The *assignats* hold no more secrets for us; we know about their origins, how the system worked, and its practical efficiency, given the lack of a sound tax system. However, we must also remember that there were some dreadful effects. In the first place, we should stress the disappearance of specie. Metallic currency, gold and silver, fled abroad in the bags of the émigrés and bankers; or else, it was hoarded by people refusing to circulate it. As a consequence, there was further recourse to the printing-press; a double rate for prices appeared, as did a parallel market for all goods, and hence a bitter opposition between those who were living exclusively on paper and those who had opportunities to get rid of it. When the Directory, squeezing the monetary system like an accordion, imposed a return to metal because of the total loss of value of paper, it

---

[3] Recent literature on statistics (its practice, contents, and representations): *La Statistique en France à l'époque napoléonienne: journée d'étude à l'École des Hautes Études en Sciences Sociales, 1980* (Paris, 1981); Jean-Claude Perrot and Stuart J. Woolf, *State and Statistics in France, 1789–1815* (New York, 1984); Marie-Noelle Bourguet, *Déchiffrer la France: La Statistique départementale à l'époque napoléonienne* (Paris, 1988).

turned out to be a very painful process. Metal remained rare, only emerging slowly from its hiding-places, so that in some regions people had to practise a barter economy. In the second place, and in the long-term, the experience of a badly managed issue of paper money twice in one century destroyed any confidence among French people in that kind of money. As a result, Banque de France notes only very slowly came into general use during the nineteenth century and they were confined for a long time to big notes for specific uses or specific clienteles. We should stress also some other durable aspects of the experience, such as the deterioration in credit practices and trade habits. At the end of the Old Regime, creditors used to allow their debtors to clear their debts over a period such that it might sometimes transform a credit term into a real participation or investment. However, it is noticeable that, when trade relationships resumed their normal rhythm after the post-revolutionary internal pacification of France, terms tended henceforth to be much shorter, generally no longer than six months.[4]

Politics and wars during the Revolution were, no less clearly, responsible for major disruptions in production and trade. However, here again, we should distinguish temporary damage from that which unquestionably brought about a loss of power for France.

Let us begin with the question of agricultural production. It is not easy to arrive at an adequate evaluation. To be sure, cyclical events, such as the extremely bad harvest of Year III, generated spectacular disparities in the distribution of available supply, which led in turn to tension between the producing countryside and the consuming cities, to the enforcement of more stringent regulations on the movement and sale of grain, to monetary disorder, to the instant politicization of disputes, to vigorous resistance to requisitioning, and so on. Did the countryside run short of labour from the moment when volunteers, and then the military levies, robbed the villages of hundreds of thousands of male workers? It is certainly true that Napoleon's prefects were to emphasize the noticeable increase in the wages of day-labourers as a consequence of a scarcity of labour. However,

---

[4] See Guy Thuillier, *La Monnaie en France au début du XIXᵉ siècle* (Paris, 1983).

some areas were affected at a time of high demographic pressure, whilst the flexibility in the distribution of tasks within the peasant family probably permitted some compensations through the more extensive use of female labour or that of younger or older people.

Another subject for debate, and a much broader one, is the division of large units of production into smaller ones at the time of the sale of national lands. Did the reduction in the average size of these units open the way to a stagnation or even a recession in productivity? We can expect to find no clear answer to that question, if it is examined only in the short-term context. The same may be said on the question of the survival of communal rights. Furthermore, the Revolution is often accused of having authorized a veritable plunder of woodland, especially coppices, as a result of ill-judged sales, lack of adequate supervision, and the excessive appetite of peasants for claims over woodland and for sales of wood. In this domain, the risk clearly lay in the potential impoverishment of a heritage over which all kinds of interests (most specifically, industrial ones) were in competition, whilst extending cultivation to bad soils or to mountainous land of low economic value. However, it is not easy to draw the frontier here between myth and reality, especially when we are dealing with the complaints of owners or iron-masters, all experts at getting their voices heard.[5] Moreover, the napoleonic era inaugurated a century of regulation, supervision, and reafforestation which resulted in an impressive upgrading of woodland. Finally, the Revolution caught the French rural economy in the process of a century-long upturn in agricultural productivity, achieved by means of small advances (not all so small, indeed), and there is no evidence that the Revolution caused a reversal of that trend.

As for the effects of the Revolution on industrialization, caution should once again be the historian's watchword. To be sure, there were powerful inhibitors to patterns of consumption: alternating inflation and deflation, periods of civil war, foreign invasion, and occupation (albeit brief) of parts of France, a deteriorating road network and sometimes downright insecurity for those using it. None the less, this was balanced by

---

[5] See Denis Woronoff, 'La "Dévastation révolutionnaire" des forêts', in *Révolution et espaces forestiers* (Paris, 1988).

phenomena of delayed consumption as the situation returned to
the norm. What appear much more dramatic are a number of
cases of deindustrialization, mostly in the hinterland of ports
which fell victim to the decline in trade with Europe and colonial
countries. This was the starting-point for a profound reshaping
of the economic map of France. However, should we ascribe this
exclusively to the circumstances of the Revolution? We should
also take into account other factors: the effects of the napoleonic
wars, the differing capacity to react and adapt (or not, as the
case may be) demonstrated by businessmen, and even the
decline of some facets of the French Atlantic and colonial
economy as early as ten to fifteen years prior to the wars.

On the other hand, for my part, I find it equally significant
and of equally far-reaching consequence that the Revolution,
however great an upheaval it may have been, did not alter the
various structures of industrial production which coexisted at
that time in France. Proto-industrial forms of the organization of
work emerged from the troubles reinforced rather than weakened.
The Revolution does not seem to have had a damaging effect on
the beginnings of new concentrated and mechanized forms of
industrial production, such as had started in the cotton industry
in the 1780s. Recent research demonstrates that the French
Revolution neither destroyed the spirit of enterprise and
innovation, nor completely wiped out the transfer of technology
from Britain.[6] Certainly, some of the new-born modern enter-
prises vanished and others were short-lived. The Terror and
galloping inflation acted as deterrents. Yet, with the passage of
time, it is noticeable that new generations of manufacturer–
adventurers were budding, portents of blooming new plants in
the years of the Consulate and the Empire. As for the
millwrights and skilled workers from Britain, some of whom
evolved into entrepreneurs, they stayed on in France, even after
1793 when they were considered to be prisoners of war.
Naturally, their minds and pockets were not filled with the
plans of the most recent types of machinery; but they did ensure
a continued transfer of technology by building and adapting
machines—not to mention the inventiveness of native-born

[6] See Serge Chassagne, 'Naissance de l'industrie cotonnière en France: Trois
générations d'entrepreneurs (1760–1840)' (thèse d'état, University of Paris I,
Paris, 1986).

French mechanics, nor continued industrial espionage. We may go further. The reforms and legislation of the Revolution had positively beneficial consequences for industrial development. Whether as purchasers or as tenants, cotton spinners and printers seized the opportunity to transform into manufactures at low cost dozens of spacious, conveniently located and sturdy buildings confiscated from the Church, which were perfectly suited to industrial activity. As for the recruitment of the labour force, employment was deregulated and thus employers felt free to take on very large numbers of such poorly paid people as women or very young children.

As a critique of the thesis which is still employed to assert that the French Revolution abruptly aborted the take-off of a type of capitalism that had the support of the king and the aristocracy, we should examine afresh the three principal examples used to buttress this theory. They prove to be singularly ill-chosen. The first is the celebrated experimental furnace at Le Creusot, in operation from 1785. In reality, its product was still in need of further perfection. Indeed, the majority of French ironmasters were far from ready to follow De Wendel's or Wilkinson's innovations, notwithstanding the noticeable renewal in the recruitment of ironmasters at the time of the Revolution.[7] The second example is the coal-mining company at Anzin. Historians, eager to stress the part played by the old aristocracy in its foundation, seem all too ready to forget that the confiscation and sale of the Compagnie d'Anzin allowed it to achieve a fresh take-off, under the guidance of Claude Perier and his sons. As a matter of fact, of all the provincial merchant and manufacturing families, the Perier family showed itself to be one of the most adept at brilliantly taking advantage of the springboard offered by the Revolution for access to a higher class and wider range of business.[8] The third example is furnished by their namesake, Jacques-Constantin Perier. He had introduced James Watt's steam-engine to France and had been building it in Paris since the 1770s. His business in this field slowed down after 1789 and he shifted towards other kinds of manufacture. He was never to

---

[7] See Denis Woronoff, *L'Industrie sidérurgique en France pendant la Révolution et l'Empire* (Paris, 1984).
[8] See *Une Dynastie bourgeoise dans la Révolution: Les Perier* (Vizille, 1984); *Bourgeoisies de province et Révolution: Colloque de Vizille 1984* (Grenoble, 1987).

resume production of steam-engines again. The truth of the matter is that Perier's difficulties began before 1789 and stemmed from the effect on his business of the Compagnie des Eaux, which controlled the supply of water to Paris. The fact that the first phase of France's industrialization was marked by the decision to operate textile plants by water-power rather than steam-power should not be attributed exclusively to the history of Perier's business. That choice was determined by a much wider and more complex balance of forces, even if we accept that Jacques-Constantin Perier never ceased to be a fierce, though largely ignored, advocate of types of power generation inspired by the model of England.[9]

Finally, we should look once again at the arguments behind the thesis which we may entitle 'Revolution versus Trade' (that is, both maritime and continental trade), even though few surprises can be expected on this topic. As far as internal trade is concerned, there is no denying that the Revolution abandoned all plans to endow France with a consistent transportation network. The system of royal roads was left incomplete; the system of local roads was not begun, despite a general demand for what seemed a precondition for a serious development of the rural economy; and last but not least, the general plan for waterways was deferred. In this manner, the Revolution and later Napoleon displayed an incredible indifference to the technical instruments necessary for a unified internal market of the future—a future which was delayed by over fifty years. Indeed, if we are to point to some major discrepancy between the English and French experiences, this must certainly be the one.

In the case of foreign trade, the problem seems to centre not so much in the collapse of the former pattern of Atlantic growth, but rather on what did or did not replace it. Thirty years after the Fall of the Bastille, Chaptal could write in the opening pages of his *De l'industrie française* (published in 1819), under the heading 'Plan et motifs de l'ouvrage':

Le monde commerçant se présente sous une face nouvelle: il s'agit moins aujourd'hui de chercher à rétablir ce qui existoit, que de bien

---

[9] See Jacques Payen, *Capital et machine à vapeur au XVIIIe siècle: Les Frères Perier et l'introduction en France de la machine à vapeur de Watt* (Paris, 1969).

étudier notre position actuelle pour reconstituer des relations commerciales d'après les changemens survenus. Pour arriver à ce but, il faut savoir ce que nous étions et ce que nous sommes; calculer nos pertes en commerce, et apprécier nos progrès en agriculture et en industrie; comparer nos productions agricoles et manufacturières avec celles des pays étrangers . . . pour y adapter nos produits.

As for Chaptal's idea of not restoring what had existed in the good old days of colonial trade, it is true that British or American commerce quickly overwhelmed a few attempts by French businessmen to recreate prosperity, by basing themselves either on the eastern seaboard of the United States or else on the islands of the Indian Ocean. As for the reconstruction of the commercial network along new lines, the only outlet was towards continental Europe. Whatever the appearances, France was in no position to take advantage of this. It is true, on the one hand, that Imperial France enjoyed a real superiority over most of Europe, except for Belgium, in the domain of industrial technology; yet, on the other hand, its manufacturing capacity lagged far behind the volume of European demand and it was thus incapable of supplanting British goods. Moreover, the transport system did not provide the long-distance connections that such a hypothetical international trade would have required, despite Napoleon's launching of the first attempts to provide Paris–Hamburg and transalpine links. As for the cities which housed the great fairs (Frankfurt-on-Main, Leipzig), Eastern Europe, the Balkans, British smuggling or Swiss traders were in an even better position to offer a challenge. Ultimately, the only solution available was to withdraw inside the national frontiers, behind the solid defences of a strong tariff policy initiated by the revolutionary assemblies themselves.

What, specifically, were the prospects for a new prosperity based primarily upon the internal market? At this point, we find ourselves face to face with another far-reaching consequence of the Revolution: the unprecedented transfer of property initiated by the sale of Church lands and, to a much lesser extent, of émigré estates. It is not my intention to get involved in the debate about the abolition of feudalism—this subject has been abundantly explored by a range of Soboulian and post-Soboulian historians, who have examined the burden of dues and obligations on the eve of 1789, the details of their cancellation, and the degree to which that contributed to an improvement in the living standards of the poorer end of peasant society. My preoccupation here is with the economic criticisms levied against the sale of the national lands. These criticisms are principally three: that the sale neutralized huge amounts of capital, of which later industrial growth was consequently deprived; that is reinforced the percentage of small and medium-sized units of property and agricultural enterprise, thus inhibiting a capitalist, productivity-driven evolution of French agriculture; that, more generally, it pushed France irremediably into economic, social, and mental immobility and transformed the French into a people clinging desperately to the land and to its values. In this way, alone among the powers, France was to be deprived of the benefits of a massive shift from a predominantly rural to a predominantly urban society.

D'Holbach wrote in his *Système social* that a man who owns nothing in a state will be tied by no links to society. In point of fact, more than one *philosophe* expressed the same idea in different words. By the time of the fall of the Old Regime, the men who were to redefine the state had learned the lesson perfectly. They replaced privilege with property as a basic principle of society and they delegated to future generations (despite some theoretical statements which found very few applications in practice) the task of recognizing formally the rights of merit, talent, and education. Seen from this perspective, the attitudes of the supporters of the Revolution should be interpreted primarily as manifestations of their will to hold on to their rank in the new socio-political order.

Does this mean that real estate investments by merchants and manufacturers in the following years do not deserve an economic interpretation? Far from it; but once again, it may well be that the classic interpretation is not the right one. If the great figures in shipping and trade at Le Havre or Bordeaux found it convenient to invest in vineyards and lush meadows or good arable land, is it right to accuse them of some kind of mismanagement of their affairs? Rather, we may see it as a shelter for accumulated capital, ready for a new start with the return to peace. That need not necessarily mean a start in new patterns of trade; it could equally well be in commercialized agriculture, banking, and so forth. At the same time, we should also conceive of these purchases as the creation of reserves, of security for credit on mortgage which later proved to be of considerable assistance in the take-off of many industries. Of course, such purchases may also have resulted in such men being absorbed into landed society and being lost to trade and industry; but this phenomenon was far from being general.

The other aspect of the issue concerning the sales of national lands is that they undoubtedly favoured a particular kind of property structure by dividing the largest blocks, increasing the number of medium-sized properties or farms, and encouraging the development of smaller ones. Recent research in France and Britain appears to point clearly towards a revision of some ideas which, only a few years ago, seemed unassailable: for example, the belief in the decisive role played by aristocratic estates in the English agricultural revolution, or the credence given to an unavoidable connection between economic backwardness and the small size of agricultural holdings in nineteenth-century France.[10] Indeed, the history of the structural link between type and size of units of production and agricultural progress in France remains to be written. We can already be certain, however, that in many instances and regions French peasant democracy in the nineteenth century cannot be evaluated properly, if it is not envisaged as a micro-undertaking in mixed economy in which agriculture was bound in with many other activities, principally but not exclusively of an industrial nature.[11] Rural multi-activity was the source of subtle economic and social equilibria. The agrarian structures consolidated by the

[10] Michel Morineau, 'Trois contributions au Colloque de Göttingen', in *Pour une Histoire économique vraie* (Lille, 1985) deals with the question of the comparative advantages of capitalist or family farming (p. 382) and, more generally, with the problem of the English industrial revolution as 'unique', compared with the French and other continental *Sonderwege*. See also, Ronald Hubscher, 'La Petite Exploitation en France: Reproduction et compétitivité (fin xixe–début xxe siècle)', *Annales: Économies, sociétés, civilisations*, 40 (1985), 3–34, and Patrick O'Brien, 'Quelle a été exactement la contribution de l'aristocratie britannique au progrès de l'agriculture entre 1688 et 1789?', ibid. 42 (1987), 1391–409. The author emphasizes the fact that the big landlords spent more on consumption than on investment and that one would be wrong to consider the British aristocracy as exceptionally progressive.

[11] See Gilbert Garrier and Ronald Hubscher (eds.), *Entre faucilles et marteaux: Pluriactivités et stratégies paysannes* (Lyon, 1988).

1789 revolution did not prevent economic progress in French agriculture.

Two conclusions can be drawn from this reading of the economic history of the Revolution. First, there can be no doubt that revolutionary France lost control over and thus the benefit of a system in which growth had been stimulated for as long as France remained integrated into a world-wide network of rapidly expanding trade relations. By contrast, the Revolution determined the rules of the game in a different manner: France embarked on an industrialization at two different speeds, the slower one having its pace reduced by checking the migration from the countryside to urbanized areas. It is from this that derives the image of nineteenth-century, and to some extent twentieth-century, France as standing in sharp contrast to the English, German, or American patterns of growth, since its periodization and rhythm were quite different. However, it would misrepresent matters if this were taken to be synonymous with attitudes that were either backward-looking or hostile to industry, as denoting a perception of growth as something alien: that is to say, a situation in which the gains made by a rural and/or urban society during the Revolution were seen for many decades as more precious than any incentive to accelerate capitalist concentration, including the elimination of industries in some regions.

The second conclusion concerns liberty, a theme which would have required more space than is available here but one which, none the less, can provide one more key to the problems of the Revolution and its relationship to economic growth. It seems that the revolutionary legislators settled a somewhat cumbersome gift upon French businessmen: thoroughgoing freedom in production, trade, work, and circulation of goods. To be sure, this gift had been long expected, since the monarchy had begun to encroach upon the old-fashioned institutions which constrained economic life. The abolition of tolls or of the privileged companies, the imposition of absolute freedom of contract between masters and wage-earners could only be welcome. The 1786 treaty with England, on the other hand, or the removal of all constraints on entry to the ranks of entrepreneurs or on the ways in which products were processed, were often perceived as threats of a new kind, just as was the abolition of all representative chambers of commerce. No doubt, the greatest fears were generated by the prospect of an unlimited challenge from anyone who aspired or was able to settle as an independent producer—a dream as potent among the artisans and *compagnons* as the obsession with land was among the rural poor. Part, at least, of the business class was not prepared to take advantage of the stimulants of liberty, and another part—consisting of merchants and new industrial entrepreneurs—favoured a style of development which would avoid displacing and uprooting rural populations and the consequent destruction of the traditional framework of rural society. Revolution was liberty, certainly; but businessmen were what they were, that is to say a class undergoing slow modernization but no tremendous change in composition. That class probably refused the opportunity to experience the full potential of a liberal economy. Revolution was proceeding faster than society. Had it entrusted government to the philosophers of the Enlightenment, then fresh air would have blown much more strongly through the doors and windows of French workshops and warehouses. But then that wind might possibly have blown away the philosophers themselves as well. To some extent, it is possible in this context to talk of a revolution betrayed by some of its children.

6

The Adventures of Reason, or From Reason to the Supreme Being

MICHEL VOVELLE

ARE we certain that we know what the Cult of Reason in Year II really was? Put as bluntly as this, the question appears paradoxical.

Received ideas and clichés have been well preserved: the memory of the 20 Brumaire ceremony at the cathedral in Paris has come down to us, as has that of the similar events at Strasbourg, Nevers, Nancy, Bordeaux, and elsewhere. Late nineteenth-century local historians provided detailed descriptions of what happened in various places. But for many of them, even to the present day, the prevailing image has been of the triumphant atheism of a handful of extremists, illustrated by the presence of living goddesses, traditionally believed to have been prostitutes or girls from the Opéra. To remain at this level would be to ignore all the historical writing devoted to this subject with such good effect at the turn of the century. In his seminal 1892 article, Alphonse Aulard discussed the Cult of Reason and the Cult of the Supreme Being; in 1895 the Abbé Sicard published 'In Search of a Civil Religion'; in 1905 Albert Mathiez dealt with the origins of the revolutionary cults.

We are not, therefore, without serious references or established hypotheses; but these are far from having raised all the problems. What did this Reason, conceived in the form of a goddess, really represent? This question may be posed on several levels—that of the promoters of the cult (were they atheists or deists, heirs to Helvétius or to Jean-Jacques?); that of the receivers, influential people who assured the movement's diffusion; and, above all, that of the masses. The masses are said to have been restive; none the less, they were not massively indifferent or hostile to this new message. The magnitude of the phenomenon makes that abundantly clear. Yet, what was it that the masses perceived, or better, what did they do about it?

This cluster of problems gives rise to another set of questions. Robespierre and the Committee of Public Safety, in common with the majority in the Convention, disavowed the Cult of Reason. They were the first to give credence to the identification of reason with atheism. As a response, in his report of 18 Floréal (7 May 1794), Robespierre secured acceptance for an affirmation of belief in the Supreme Being and the immortality of the soul. This was a preamble to the great celebrations of 20 Prairial (8 June 1794) in honour of the Supreme Being, which took place both in Paris and in the provinces. How had this transition from Reason to the Supreme Being come out? Should we believe, like several of the authors to whom we have referred, that a lot of people saw no great difference between the two and that therefore the transition was easily achieved? In short, was the Supreme Being already contained within the Cult of Reason? Yet a flood of addresses did congratulate the Convention on having banned atheism and on laying the foundations of a new civil religion. Similarly, to what extent were the masses touched by the Supreme Being? Did the success and scope of the 20 Prairial celebrations reflect simply an ephemeral act of civil conformism, subsequently reduced to nothing by the fall of Robespierre?

Today, we have access to a much more considerable body of information than was available to our predecessors. Over the past twenty years, the comprehensive study of dechristianization in Year II has prompted monographs and works of synthesis. The continuing publication of the *Archives parlementaires* (currently dealing with the records of the Convention) has made more than 5,000 dechristianization addresses available to researchers, allowing the enquiry to be pursued well beyond the impressionistic vision possible for Aulard and Mathiez. The problematic too has evolved: we are now in a position to abandon presuppositions in the investigation of a subject long encumbered by prejudices and taboos.

Michel Vovelle

The Cult of Reason held an essential place in the complex set of phenomena collectively designated as dechristianization from the winter of 1793 to the spring of 1794. It was the counterpoint to everything which derived from the degradation of 'fanaticism' and 'superstition', to use the terminology of the time. The Church's material resources were attacked—through the closure or even destruction of places of worship, *autos-da-fé* of sacred objects, and seizures of bells and silverware. The Church's human capital suffered, too, through renunciations of the priesthood or the marriage of priests. In compensation, the Cult of Reason was instituted in an encompassing framework of events which brought together elements of a festive system, sometimes initiated by the government (for instance, the celebrations for the recapture of Toulon or the *décadaire* ceremonies) but more often spontaneous (such as the celebrations for the 'martyrs of liberty'—Marat, Lepeletier, and Chalier—which developed into the Cult of the Martyrs of Liberty). The celebration of festivals of Reason and, less ephemeral, the transformation of churches into temples of Reason achieved a special prominence among these events, beginning with the example given in the former cathedral of Paris on 20 Brumaire (10 November 1793). These events have long fed a particular image into collective memory and bequeathed to an often hostile historiography the cliché of goddesses of Reason as living incarnations of the new religion in its processions and civil ceremonies. The movement was both imposed and created, mixing spontaneity with constraint, combining conformity with disregard for state directives, and this caused it to develop slowly over a total of ten months. The Cult of the Supreme Being was superimposed on this phenomenon, but in very different terms. It came from on high, the truth being imposed brutally in the course of a very short period—three months in all, with the month of Prairial being pivotal.

How was the transition from Reason to the Supreme Being achieved? In what manner did repudiation of the former produce a turn-around? We can follow the course of this if we start with the documents gathered from the sources: the addresses and reports printed in the *Archives parlementaires* which deal with the inauguration of the temples, the practice of the cult, and the festivals of Reason—three elements which often combined, as the account of the inaugural celebrations indicates.

Parisian sections and towns close to the capital were the first to announce the cult towards the end of Brumaire and into Frimaire Year II (mid-November to December 1793):

L'erreur qui, d'âge en âge, s'était propagée jusqu'à nos jours, vient de s'évanouir . . . les préjugés du fanatisme ont disparu . . . nous ne connaîtrons désormais d'autre culte que celui de la raison et de la liberté. (Villemomble, 4 Frimaire)

Nous nous mettons au niveau de la raison et nous consolidons son empire. Qu'elle seule désormais règne sur nous, et soyez-en toujours les infatigables ministres. (Commune of Issy, 4 Frimaire)

Une députation de la section de Brutus . . . renonce au culte de l'erreur . . . Ils ne reconnaissent d'autre Dieu que la nature, d'autre culte que celui de la vérité. (Brutus, 5 Frimaire)

A flow of addresses and reports developed rapidly from the provinces, even very distant ones, reflecting the spread of the movement from its initial epicentres such as, in the centre of France, the Allier and the Nièvre, or the Paris region.

The progress of what I have called the 'Adventures of Reason' is documented by a thousand addresses (984, to be more precise) to the Convention. The Cult of Reason assumed real importance (27 per cent of the addresses) both in relation to the general movement of dechristianization addresses and also in comparison to other acts that we can measure (such as iconoclasm or abdications), although it was less than expressions of adherence to the Supreme Being (33 per cent). Above all, the movement continued for a long time, not being limited to a sudden outburst in the winter as was the case of the majority of the acts of destruction. It is true that the first push came in Frimaire (November–December 1793); but there was a much more powerful one in the spring of 1794 between Pluviôse and Germinal (from late January to early April), peaking in Ventôse (February–March) when one-fifth of these addresses of homage to Reason were sent. Finally, it was only after Prairial (May–June) that a marked decline was registered, though Reason was not completely eclipsed by the Supreme Being since, despite all the filtering, one can still count about sixty addresses up to

Thermidor. We can understand this persistence by plotting the origin of the addresses on the map. This reveals that in Brumaire, with a few exceptions, they were confined to the Paris region and some places in the centre and the north of France, but that they then exploded into central France in Frimaire, reaching peripheral areas of France like the Midi and the west in the spring, when they also experienced a marked resurgence in the departments around Paris from Normandy to the Yonne. The overall picture demonstrates a contrast between zones strongly affected (the Paris basin, the centre of France, the Lyon area and the Rhône valley, part of the Mediterranean Midi, and some places in the south-west) and zones of rejection (the Atlantic west defined in broad terms, the north-east, the heart of the Massif Central, the interior of the Alps, and the Pyrenees).

Obviously, the thousand addresses from which we are extrapolating here represent only the tip of the iceberg, only what was visible from Paris. We can measure the true magnitude of the movement by using (where they exist) in-depth departmental monographs in order to compare this image to reality. Thus, we know that the Gard, which sent twenty-one letters, witnessed the opening of 233 temples of Reason, which is ten times as many. If this proportion were adopted for the whole of France, one could suppose that roughly one-quarter of French towns opened a temple of Reason. This may be an inflated proportion because the Gard is not a truly average example to use, but we can retain this order of magnitude as an overall image of the spread of the new religion.

It is often difficult to make a distinction between the inauguration of temples and the celebration of festivals because in many cases the two ceremonies coincided. The festivals of Reason held an important place in the festive complex which we can see deployed principally during the winter of 1793–4, forming a movement which did not entirely coincide with the outburst of dechristianization. In fact, the peak was not registered in Frimaire (the crucial month in more ways than one), but came two months later in Pluviôse, that is to say from the end of January to 20 February. The curve climbed noticeably in Nivôse, culminated in Pluviôse, maintained that high level in Ventôse, and began to decline distinctly in Germinal. Although it was to be spectacularly, but only temporarily, relaunched in

Prairial, the movement had by now collapsed, stifled by the Festival of the Supreme Being at the beginning of the summer. Granted, there was a time-lag from one zone to another, as for example in the south-east. The movement was confirmed in the majority of the most northern departments by Nivôse, with a few more in Ventôse. In contrast, the Midi concentrated its festive season in Pluviôse. However, one does not have the impression that the movement was disseminated slowly. This is easily explained: an important segment of the festivals—at least in so far as the recorded events are concerned—were festivals for the 'martyrs of liberty' and festivals to celebrate the retaking of Toulon. Since these were the subject of official prompting, they were celebrated everywhere at nearly the same time, usually during Nivôse in the north and Pluviôse in the south. Therefore, the Festival of Reason formed part of an ensemble which, with some simplification, may be divided into three categories: celebration of the Republic's victories (40 per cent of the festivals in the south-east, 50 per cent in the south-west); festivals of Reason or *décadaire* celebrations (40 per cent in the south-east, 32 per cent in the south-west); celebrations for the 'martyrs of liberty' (20 per cent in the south-east, 15 per cent in the south-west).

Generally, these ceremonies were held in towns of some importance. Their celebration came in two major waves, the one in winter beginning in Brumaire but above all during Frimaire, and the other in early spring, beginning sometimes in Pluviôse but in the majority of cases culminating in Ventôse and Germinal. It depended on the region which was the more important of the waves—the earlier in the north-east quarter of France, the later in the two halves of the south and in the north-west. Thus, in the north-east, the first festivals of Reason were urban phenomena, originating in an epicentre in the Meurthe. Nancy and Toul held celebrations on 20 Brumaire, with a repeat at Nancy ten days later. The influence of the deputy Faure in this area is noticeable; similarly, the celebration at Strasbourg on 20 Brumaire took place in the presence of the deputy Baudot. Besançon, an equally isolated location, was penetrated by the light of Reason on 30 Brumaire. These individual manifestations of the phenomenon occurred before the movement appeared in a number of towns closer to Paris, such as Reims, which waited until 30 Frimaire to celebrate its first festival. In general, however, the peak in this area was registered in Pluviôse, with about forty addresses from the north-east; although the movement fell off at this point, it continued until Ventôse and Germinal. A comparable pattern can be demonstrated for the area running from the epicentre in central France to the Mediterranean south. In Frimaire, the centre and the Lyon region joined the movement (Bourges, Lyon, Saint-Étienne, Feurs, Yssingeaux, Grenoble, and so on, as well as Montpellier and Béziers, which was the earliest location in the Midi). The lead given by the towns was sometimes followed without delay by villages or hamlets (thus, La Guillotière, Neuville, Anse in the Rhône). In Nivôse, the Ain was affected and then, in Pluviôse, the Alps (Chambéry, Saint-Marcellin, Gap, Digne, and so on); by that time, the movement had reached the Midi, with cases at Aix-en-Provence and in the Gard. However, in this region, the great festivals of Reason took place only later: in Ventôse at Arles, Draguignan, and Manosque and not before Germinal at Marseille, which was particularly late. The influx of addresses from hamlets and villages can be added to the chronology of the movement in important towns, revealed by monographs. We have, thus, considerable and incontrovertible proof that the rural world, or at least the world of villages and hamlets, did not miss out on these celebrations. However, although the inauguration of temples of Reason appears from the sources to be no insignificant phenomenon, the celebration of festivals and the personification of the goddess of Reason in one of the grand liturgies that left a lasting impression seems to have been characteristic of a minority of gatherings. Possibly, this is a false impression, due to the accounts of the witnesses. Certainly, Maillane was not a large hamlet when Riquelle, the old woman whom Frédéric Mistral was to tell us about much later, played the role of the goddess of Reason in the splendour of her seventeen years of age. The same may be said of Renaison in the Loire, an example of a different type where a woman over 100 years old was chosen to incarnate the goddess, fully alert none the less, since she displayed much eagerness in crying several times, 'Vive la République, vive la Montagne'.

Using this body of material on temple inaugurations and Festivals of Reason, we can try to conclude on the remaining issues raised by our central concern here: what was this goddess of Reason? We should say that this is a belated object of concern. It must be admitted that, with the exception of the great national festivals in Brumaire (from Paris to Strasbourg), the accounts used here provide few descriptions of the personification of Reason. Evidently, these references were quite quickly found to be rather unwelcome. However, what the *Archives parlementaires* do not reveal can often be discovered in local archives. Let us limit ourselves to the case of Provence, where the richness of the documentation is perhaps exceptional in the examples that it supplies.

The most common case is that of a woman as living statue— goddess of Liberty, goddess of Reason, or Victory. In the celebration of the recapture of Toulon held at Entrevaux on 25 January 1794, Victory, with the features of a young female citizen, was promenaded on a cart, whilst the goddess of Liberty walked under the church's processional canopy which had certainly never before been put to such use. At Nice, it was the goddess of Liberty who triumphed in Nivôse; at Digne, Madeleine, a patriotic young woman from the club, served as the image of a new divinity in the Temple of Reason (formerly Saint-Jérôme's Church), half-reclining under a canopy of red velvet and draped in a linen dress. At Fréjus on 30 Nivôse, citizenness Franc acted as Reason, whilst citizenness Laget sang appropriate couplets as the goddess of Liberty. Liberty or Reason? Could the popular eye discern a difference? Coulet, an Avignon weaver who kept a most useful diary, thought he was looking at the 'mère de la patrie', and this could well be what the popular eye perceived them to be, until the Marseille goddesses of Reason (the celebrated 'Cavale' and 'Fessy') paid the price for having been goddesses for a day, a ghastly death in Year III under the blows of royalist killers.

Therefore, the descriptions of the celebrations provide an ambiguous image where Reason, Victory, or Liberty appear as interchangeable deities. Would an analysis of the daily corres- pondence sent to the Convention reveal a more precise discourse? In an attempt to discover what Reason represented, I have analysed several dozen revealing addresses selected from a group of addresses received at the Convention at the height of the campaign, that is, between Frimaire and Pluviôse. I examined the names and concepts invoked in the speeches and addresses, as well as the decoration and scenery of the festivals. One cannot fail to be struck by the great diversity of forms and language. This explains the note of perplexity in Romme's speech on *décadaire* festivals, delivered to the Convention on 29 Nivôse: 'Ici on célèbre des fêtes à la raison, là c'est la mémoire des grands hommes et des martyrs de la liberté qu'on veut honorer. Par-tout on s'évertue pour embellir ces fêtes, mais il en est peu de régulières.'

Even leaving aside the 'martyrs of liberty' (though we may well encounter them again somewhere along the route of the procession), our analysis seems to make quite clear that whenever Reason was present, which, self-evidently, was nearly always (though replaced in 10 per cent of the cases by Liberty or Nature), it was rarely alone. A veritable pantheon took shape as Reason's retinue. Indeed, we can produce a kind of ranking honours list according to the number of times each appeared for every ten recorded festivals:

Reason	9.0	Fraternity	1.0	Republic	0.3
Liberty	6.0	Philosophy	1.0	*Patrie*	0.3
Supreme Being	4.0	Truth	0.5	*Humanité*	0.3
Equality	3.5	Unity	0.5		
Nature	2.0	Martyrs	0.5		

Reason's companions, usually female beings, occupied various places, depending on the case, in a gathering that sometimes attained the dimensions of a full constellation of deities. Often they figured as auxiliaries, but sometimes also as equal companions or even rivals. An ambiguous relationship developed between them, sometimes complementary, sometimes subordinate.

Before we turn to analysing the different types of figures, we should note that some occasionally surprising features are immediately visible, such as the infrequent appearance of Republic or *Patrie*. Was Alphonse Aulard wrong to see the Cult of Reason as an expression of patriotic feeling in the specific conditions of the revolutionary struggle during Year II, or was Reason the mask which allowed this sentiment to be expressed? It is less surprising to see the prominence achieved by Liberty (two-thirds of cases) in association with Reason. The hierarchy of Liberty (six out of ten cases), Equality (three cases) and Fraternity (one case) holds no surprises for those who have studied discourse or engravings. This was generally the ordering that prevailed in what we may term the 'hit parade' of the newly proclaimed values, where Fraternity in particular never made much progress up the 'charts'. Nature occupied a specific place in this structure. It was apparently limited yet complementary, as we shall see when we turn to studying the relationships which hold these different elements together. When Nature appeared, it was not in a walk-on part or a supporting role, as was the case of Truth and Philosophy, but as the supreme reference. As such, we should evaluate its role in comparison to that of the Supreme Being, whose perhaps unexpectedly large number of appearances (four out of ten cases) makes it second in importance. In reality, Reason, Nature, and the Supreme Being soon defined themselves by means of a complex interplay. Sometimes, Reason was the voice of the Supreme Being in a system which excluded Nature; sometimes, Reason was the expression of Nature, a configuration that had no need of a reference to the Supreme Being. However, a third type of arrangement also existed, in which Reason was made into the daughter of Nature, herself created by the Supreme Being.

At this point, let us move this somewhat sterile and reductionist breakdown of our information to the reconstruction of a system—if, indeed, one existed. This is a difficult enterprise, for the formulations were far from simple since they reflected a period which we are still a long way from having mastered.

If this was a religion, who was the divinity? Temples were inaugurated, but for whom? The use of words was marked by a real ambiguity. Rare were those who went straight to the point: for example, the members of the club at Chevry who declared, on 29 Nivôse, that their only religion was that of Reason, or the youth of the Section des Piques in Paris who recited, on 26 Nivôse,

> Désormais la saine raison
> Fera notre religion.

Others praised Reason—'consolidons son empire . . . elle seule règne' (Commune of Issy, 4 Frimaire)—even if this did lead in

Michel Vovelle

the end to phrases of the sort: 'La raison, cette souveraine de l'Univers, cette véritable et unique divinité des nations, établit enfin son empire' (Department of the Charente, 30 Frimaire). Religion, empire, homage, reign: the haziness of the terminology expressed the real-life contradictions and the differing perceptions in play, as truth sought to discover itself.

If we attempt a classification, we find that Reason really only appeared alone, as the unique goddess, in one out of ten cases. In a primary variant, it was associated with Truth and/or Philosophy, which opened the way for it: 'la vérité s'est fait entendre; toutes les communes s'empressent de rendre hommage à la Raison' (Marcigny, Saône-et-Loire, 29 Nivôse). However, the most frequent situation was the one where, without calling into question its pre-eminence, Reason had Liberty and Equality alongside, usually in an imprecise relationship, but occasionally subordinated as in 'la raison qui toujours s'appuya sur la liberté et l'égalité, établit donc enfin son règne parmi les Français' (Cosne-sur-Loire, 27 Nivôse). But an inverted relationship also occurred, which made Reason only the emissary of Liberty. Thus, in a festival of this type held in the Nièvre on 1 Nivôse, a sign clearly proclaimed that 'La raison est éternelle'. This was carried in front of a cart on which was seated Liberty, who then got down in order to enter the Temple of Reason. Occasionally, it was *Patrie* and not Liberty which acted as the supreme reference point, so that at Tours, on 20 Frimaire, the people sang, 'Raison sois notre guide unique!' but none the less concluded that

le salut de la République
Est le culte que veut ta loi.

However, the most frequent situation, visible in a quarter of the cases, was where the Cult of Reason was constructed through the authority given to the Supreme Being, which remained the ultimate recourse.

Therefore, even with all the nuances we have just introduced, the goddess of Reason was really a goddess in only two-thirds of the cases. Liberty might be her direct rival, but more often it was *Patrie*. However, the real debate took place between Nature and the Supreme Being, the advantage going to the latter.

It is certainly true that Nature was sometimes presented in a dominant or even an exclusive position. On 5 Frimaire, the citizens of the Section de Brutus said that they recognized no other god than Nature, no other religion than Truth. The citizens of Lucenay in the Nièvre were more cautious or less certain, throwing their disgusting idols on to the pyre and purifying their temple 'en attendant que le culte de la Raison ou de la Nature s'y professe'. And the people of Tours, quoted above, made Nature subordinate to Reason:

> Fille aimable de la nature,
> Compagne de l'égalité,
> Ce n'est point avec l'imposture
> Que peut vivre la liberté!

They were close to the spirit that inspired Hollier in his 'Ode to Reason', presented to the Convention on 20 Nivôse:

> Raison, fille de la Nature,
> Et mère de la Vérité,
> Des rayons de ta clarté pure
> Environne la Liberté
> .   .   .   .   .
> Et que sa compagne fidelle
> L'Egalité fixe auprès d'elle
> Et le bonheur et les vertus.

Indeed, some complex systems took shape, which amounted to veritable genealogies. Perhaps the most fully developed example of these commendable attempts to combine and reconcile various beliefs was the one produced by a youth from the Section de Lazowsky in Paris, who declared to the Convention on 20 Pluviôse that his companions would be

en garde contre les insinuations perfides de ceux qui tenteroient de nous faire croire à d'autre bonheur qu'à celui de la République une et indivisible et à d'autre divinité qu'à l'Être suprême, dont le culte est la Raison, et en présence duquel l'inébranlable Montagne rend ses décrets salutaires et dont les martyrs sont Marat, Peletier, Chalier, les amis de Lazowsky, et les braves défenseurs des droits du peuple. Vive la République, Vive la Montagne.

However, the Supreme Being was already present in this

discourse, as the last example makes clear. In more than two-thirds of the addresses, it had a prominent place as the one without which Nature and Reason would be nothing. In Paris, citizen Mirbeck paid homage to Reason, underlining the hierarchy of causes: 'Raison divine, émanation pure de l'Être suprême, qui règle, à sa volonté, la destinée des hommes et des empires' (30 Frimaire). Another inspired citizen opted for the metaphor of the blind man: in such circumstances, the creator, 'cet être bon, nous fournit une canne du moins pour nous diriger, et ce guide c'est la raison'. On the same day, at the other end of France, the deputy Milhaud at Béziers, though paying homage to Reason and Universal Morality, turned to 'l'Être suprême [qui] n'a d'autre Temple que l'univers' and who is the 'juge incorruptible et suprême, infaillible et souverainement bon'. His colleague Dartigoeyte, notwithstanding his activities as an ardent dechristianizer, used the same language at Montagne-Marat in the Gers, when he proclaimed that 'le soleil de la vérité se lève. Dieu, cet être incompréhensible mais nécessaire, ce principe de tout bien, cette source de toutes délices exquises'. Reason and Nature submitted themselves, therefore, to the great architect, even if they participated in his grandeur and his eternity.

It was through homage to Reason that many people re-discovered the Supreme Being. Pastoret, in his speech at Montauban on 23 Nivôse, made the process clear: 'il faut un culte à l'homme, mais un culte que la raison puisse avouer, et qui soit digne de l'intelligence souveraine dont elle est une émanation sacrée . . . Il n'y a qu'un Être suprême . . . Rempli de toi, mon cœur t'adore.' However, can we say that the debate was already settled? Can we conclude that, between Nature and the Supreme Being (in the guise of Reason), the consensus tilted decisively in favour of the great architect? In fact, there was visibly some hesitation, indeed a bit of impatience concerning the great arranger, whose usurped authority 'couvrit les crimes du fanatisme et de la superstition', concerning this 'être incomprehénsible mais nécessaire', as we earlier saw him defined. People did at least take some precautions. On 10 Frimaire, the Soissons club warned citizens:

> Ne souffrez pas que sous un joug nouveau,
> Notre raison demeure assujettie

concluding

> Auteur du monde! Être juste et puissant
> Nous t'adorons dans toute la nature,
> Mais rejetant toute croyance obscure
> Pour remonter à toi plus dignement
> Nous te voulons invoquer librement.

That was a sentiment which the citizens of La Châtre echoed:

> Être ordonnateur des mondes
> De vains soins, des chants confus
> Dans tes demeures profondes,
> Ne te fatigueront plus.

It was not these isolated spokesmen who were to have the last word.

In successive strokes, the addresses sketched out the elements of a system which, from Paris to the provinces, was developed by collective experience. If we allow the texts themselves to be our guide, we can see no obvious breakpoint between Reason and the Supreme Being. That rupture only becomes visible when viewed from above, through the clues to the great collective options which, from Frimaire to Floréal, were to steer the new course of events, which began with the proclamation of the immortality of the soul and the Supreme Being. It was already present in the majority of explicit speeches, biding its time. Perhaps that explains why the new Cult of the Supreme Being received such a massive welcome, judging by the evidence that has come down to us. In less than four months, from Floréal to Thermidor, there were 1,235 addresses of approval after the decree of 18 Floréal on the soul's immortality and after the proclamation of the Supreme Being. This is a considerable number, and this massive collection of documents is the most important one that we have to take into account. The tally of approving addresses demonstrates that the Supreme Being garnered in a brief span of time more votes than Reason had gathered in ten months. A critical reader will of course object that most of these letters of support were no more than proclamations which carried no further obligation, and that a true evaluation of the situation would require a comparison with the number of celebrations for the Supreme Being. However, such an assessment cannot be undertaken because matters were interrupted by 9 Thermidor. Instead, we can compare the circumstances surrounding the establishment of the Cult of Reason (at one and the same time imposed and spontaneous, official and marginal) to the grand gesture of reassuring conformity which adherence to the Supreme Being represented. This comparison makes the apparently abundant success of the latter cult much less surprising. Even so, conformity is not the whole explanation: we have seen that when Reason was triumphant, the Supreme Being was not absent.

The new religion was less tolerant. We can follow the way in which everything shifted by using the addresses received at the Convention after the great speech of 18 Floréal. On 24 Floréal, the town councillors of Chagny in the Saône-et-Loire were still stating that their town had renounced the Catholic faith and had established the Cult of Reason; the small popular society at Dornecy in the Nièvre used similar terms on 25 Floréal. However, on that same day, the General Council of the Paris Commune, better placed to sense which way the wind was blowing and eager to take advantage of it, announced that it was going to erase the inscriptions on the 'temples de la Raison' in order to replace them with 'temple de l'Être Suprême'. The Paris sections followed this lead in the next few days, but not without noticeable reluctance. On 26 Floréal, approval was voiced for the 'principes religieux' without further precision, and on 6 Prairial the Section de l'Observatoire announced a reading on the Supreme Being in the 'temple de la Raison'. The new habit was not established in addresses until Messidor and henceforth, from Choisy-sur-Seine (5 Messidor) to Sommerwiller in the Meurthe (7 Messidor), all confusion of genres was avoided. Some places went further and made efforts to demonstrate that they had received the message loud and clear. To take some examples from the south, people in the Hérault retrospectively repudiated persecution and intolerance; in the Vaucluse or the Bouches-du-Rhône, atheism was bitterly denounced; in the Basses-Alpes, the club at Entrevaux emphatically affirmed its horror of atheism, 'destructeur de tout ordre et de toute morale' (1 Thermidor). These arguments hastening to support the victory of authority are perhaps less convincing than the private discourse which we were earlier able on occasion to apprehend.

The magnitude of the flood of addresses testifies beyond any doubt to the fact that the impulse had had real effect, even though it was recorded by only 3 per cent of localities, which was a poor showing. Mobilization had been swift, concentrated essentially in the period from the end of Floréal to Messidor and Prairial (with about 500 announcements a month). The slackening-off in Thermidor does require some exploration because, after 10 Thermidor, these addresses and letters were no longer reported but were consigned directly to the waste-paper basket. Indeed, this happened to such an extent that any map which we might draw up of the distribution of the Cult of the Supreme Being would necessarily be incomplete. Incomplete though it is, however, it is suggestive and interesting. Most of the early addresses (in Floréal and Prairial) came from north of the Loire, including the Paris basin, the north and the north-east, together with some extension towards the west where the movement encountered a first barrier of refusal in the Celtic fringe of Brittany. The Midi was late, apart from a few specific cases found especially in the Rhône valley and Provence. However, alongside these specific cases we also find several departments (exceptions which prove the rule) where the presence of dynamic Robespierrist deputies accelerated the movement (Ariège, Pyrénées-Orientales). These nuances or modulations do not affect the overall picture, whose significance becomes fully apparent when we compare this distribution map with that of the Cult of Reason. Even if we make due allowance for the important role of Paris, the Cult of Reason was the product of a poly-epicentric explosion followed by diffusion from these centres. The Cult of the Supreme Being, on the other hand, was a Paris-commanded movement and the manner of its propagation beyond the northern area first affected is to be explained by the constraints on progress and transmission characteristic of a centralized national impulse.

This does not mean that the Cult of the Supreme Being was received in the same fashion everywhere. A comparison of the places of origin of the addresses to the Convention on the two cults is a sound test of their national dimension because of the contrasts that become apparent. At first glance, one is tempted to see a real continuity between Reason and the Supreme Being in geographical terms since only fifteen departments show a contrast in the two movements. The overall picture is similar, with the emphasis on the Paris basin, on the Paris–Lyon–Marseille axis through Burgundy and the Rhône valley to Languedoc and Provence, and also on a portion of the south-west along the Garonne valley. Correspondingly, the zones rejecting innovation, whether in the name of Reason or of the Supreme Being, were to be found in both cases in the west, the north-east, and the heart of the Massif Central.

Upon closer examination, however, some significant changes became evident. A number of loquacious departments fell silent once they had been visited by the Cult of the Supreme Being; others, which had previously stubbornly resisted religious innovation, found themselves to be more hospitable to the Supreme Being. It left traces in several places: in part of the west (Calvados, Manche, Orne, Ille-et-Vilaine) and in the north-east (Côte-d'Or, Haute-Marne, Meurthe), as well as in the alpine and Provençal south-east (Hautes-Alpes, Basses-Alpes, Var). Thus, about twenty departments were affected by this progression—areas of mild dechristianization (the alpine region) or lands of ethnic minorities (the Celtic fringe) where such a re-establish-ment of religion seems to have been welcome, even if it was something quite different from the old religion. By contrast, a number of homogenous regions appear (certainly not by chance) as zones where the incidence of Reason remained higher than that of the Supreme Being. Whereas the immediate vicinity of Paris (Seine, Seine-et-Oise, Seine-et-Marne) toed the line with respect to the new religion, certain important zones persisted in drawing back from their earlier involvement, notably in the north and to the south-west of Paris as far as the centre of France. A similar situation prevailed in the centre-east stretching from the Saône-et-Loire to Mont Blanc via the Ain and the Isère, as well as in certain departments of the Midi (Gard, Vaucluse).

What are we to make of this contrasting behaviour? Occasion-ally, it is possible to identify here the manifestation of some deep-seated phenomenon of resistance which could express itself equally well in quite contradictory ways, either by deep attachment to the Cult of Reason and rejection of the Supreme Being or else by a warmer welcome to an appeal less traumatizing than that of the previous initiative. It is also possible to detect in the apathy of some regions, formerly sympathetic to religious innovation, the indifference of populations too powerfully affected during preceding months now to throw themselves into a new adventure. This could be the case for the centre and the Lyon area, or the northern Alps. At all events, it is certainly not without significance that a department like the Gard (even allowing for its specific confessional situation) sent thirty-six addresses on Reason but only fourteen in honour of the Supreme Being. This is all the more striking when one considers that nearby areas of Provence and the Comtat, where de-christianization had been tardy and mild, rallied in a relatively massive manner to the Supreme Being, whose success there was as real as it was unexpected.

If we are to sketch a conclusion on this theme, whose complexity this essay has sought to reveal, it seems necessary to look again at one or two established notions. Between Frimaire and Floréal Year II, Robespierre (although he was not alone in this) helped to establish the notion that atheism and the Cult of Reason were bedfellows. It was the statue of atheism that burned on the pyre of the auto-da-fé on 20 Prairial. Historical paradox though it is, this excessively simplistic cliché has been adopted and reiterated by an entire conservative or clerical historiographical tradition, which has contented itself with this image. Today, extending rather than refuting Alphonse Aulard's analysis, our greater documentary base enables us to get closer to the truth about the complete practice of the Cult of Reason, which developed at grass-roots level and was composed of a number of syncretisms linking Reason, Liberty, *Patrie*, and the Cult of the 'Martyrs of Liberty'. The materialist naturalism of the Enlightenment did have a part in it, visible certainly but only in a minor way. In reality, the Supreme Being was already present, as has been evident from more than one example. We are better able to understand how the transition from Reason to the Supreme Being was effected and to realize that it was a much less traumatic process than we might think. Rather than being predominantly a patriotic attitude or one of civil defence in response to invasion, as Alphonse Aulard saw it in his time, it seems to me that this change of heart or this shift took place within the framework of a natural religion that did not yet know how to dispense with the comforting presence of the Supreme

Being. Still, not everyone was fooled. The significant differences in the distribution of the recorded reception of the two cults reveal that even the lesser combatants in this battle in the clouds were not as naïve as we might think; they sensed malice aforethought. Even in its failure, the episode of the Cult of Reason remains one of the most significant and durable aspects of the cultural revolution of 1793–4.

7

Regionalism and Counter-Revolution in France

ALAN FORREST

IN the vast literature of counter-revolution regional identity is often subsumed or alluded to, but it is rarely investigated in depth, and the significance of regional loyalties is seldom analysed. This is not hard to understand. Regionalism is a rather imprecise concept, a sense of belonging or of mutual identity which defies quantification, a gut feeling of pride in the past and in a shared experience. Like nineteenth-century nationalism, it has diffuse cultural, linguistic, and literary inspirations. It is certainly more deeply implanted in some regions than in others. And, like nationalism again, it may be stronger in times of conflict, when there is a common enemy to be fought or a common threat to be fended off. That threat, in an eighteenth-century context, was clearly to be found in the advancing pretensions of the centralist state, whether of the Bourbon monarchy or, more dramatically, of the Revolution. The enemy could easily become the revolutionary administration itself.

Yet the term remains vague and ill-defined. Regionalism can seem terribly nostalgic and backward-looking—at best a vehicle for the defence of a traditional way of life, at worst an excuse for mawkish sentimentality. Historians have preferred to search for more structured explanations for acts of collective defiance of revolutionary government—economic or class interpretations, for example, or the struggles of tenant against landowner, of outworker against textile merchant, of country against town.[1]

---

[1] A recent historiographical essay is C. Petitfrère, 'The Origins of the Civil War in the Vendée', *French History*, 2 (1988), 187–207.

Such interests have a clear logic about them which notions of regional identity lack. Or they have offered religious faith as the motor of revolt against authority, or hidden behind plot theories, the sorts of theory which the revolutionary leaders themselves liked to propose and which dominated the thinking of the Republic and of its deputies on mission. Others again have pointed to local political circumstances which plunged communities into internecine strife—the struggle between leading families in a town or village, the seizure of power by one faction within city politics, the extreme and uncompromising behaviour of patriots or clubists or royalists in the early years of the Revolution.[2] In their different ways and in differing circumstances all these interpretations can be richly sustained, and it is in no sense my objective here to cast doubt upon them. Economic reasons, political reasons, and sociological reasons all played a significant part in spreading and kindling animosity. But must we in consequence dismiss out of hand any idea of regional identity in sparking local discontent or in providing a focus for resistance? Did such a sense of identity exist at all, and did it play any part in directing feelings of defiance?

What is not in doubt is the regional incidence of the various counter-revolutionary movements that threatened the unity of revolutionary France. Though the Revolution was viewed with a marked lack of enthusiasm throughout large swathes of rural France, counter-revolution never achieved the status of a national movement. Despite the best efforts of émigré nobles and refractory clergy, despite foreign intrigues and the promise of English gold, insurrectionary movements remained stubbornly localized. Ideology played a relatively limited role, and royalism among the rank and file was not a major force in the counter-revolution. There were always local circumstances, local leaders, local issues. *Chouannerie* was particular to Brittany, the Vendean insurrection limited to five or six departments of the West, and the rural revolt of Year VII restricted to Languedoc and Gascony; while royalist *brigandage* during the Directory flourished mainly in the Rhône valley and in the bandit country of the south-west. Elsewhere there were fears and scares rather than serious outbreaks of insurrection. Similarly the series of urban revolts of

[2] H. Johnson, *The Midi in Revolution: A Study of Regional Political Diversity, 1789–1793* (Princeton, 1986), 249.

1793—the so-called federalist revolts which threatened to cut vital communications with the armies during that most volatile of summers—was largely confined to a number of large provincial cities whose leaders withdrew their part of national sovereignty and defied the authority of the Jacobin Convention. Lyon, Marseille, Bordeaux, Caen, and a number of other cities hurled abuse and defiance at the government, even daring to arm themselves with departmental battalions which they talked of sending against the capital. Toulon, rather unwisely, went so far as to hand over the French fleet and the dockyards to the English and Spanish navies. From Normandy a federalist army advanced falteringly towards Paris. But suggestions that this was in any sense a national movement were quickly refuted. It is true that urban defiance threatened to spread as delegates were sent to neighbouring departments to whip up support. There was excited talk of sixty-six, sixty-nine, even seventy-two departments which had expressed open sympathy or which were on the point of declaring themselves in a state of insurrection. But they never did so. At most thirteen departments became seriously embroiled with federalism: like rural counter-revolution, it remained the preserve of a few well-defined centres.[3] It never lost its clear regional character.

But does this regional incidence imply any sense of regional identity, any collective response as parts of the same regional whole? On one level, the assertion that counter-revolution has a strongly regional profile may simply be a statement of the blindingly obvious. For provincial history almost inevitably has connotations of regionalism. Geography ensured that it could not be otherwise. As the atlas of the French Revolution currently appearing in thematic fascicules under the imprint of the École des Hautes Études en Sciences Sociales tellingly shows, the social, economic, and cultural history of the period is effectively the history of different and contrasting regional models, not the history of a single whole.[4] Indeed, the extent of these internal contrasts is such that we may legitimately ask if we are dealing

[3] P. Hanson, 'The Federalist Revolt of 1793: A Comparative Study of Caen and Limoges', unpublished Ph.D. thesis, University of California, Berkeley, 1981, 14.

[4] G. Arbellot and B. Lepetit, *Atlas de la Révolution française*, 5 vols. published to date (Paris, 1987–9).

with a single country at all. There was little shared experience
between the men and women of different provinces or different
areas of France. Their diet, the climatic conditions in which they
lived and worked, even their life expectancy were widely at
variance. So were patterns of settlement. Whereas some parts of
the country had been opened up to a wider market by a network
of roads and rivers, others remained sealed in an almost
primeval autarky. If dispersed habitation was the norm in much
of Brittany and the north, in large parts of the Auvergne and the
southern Massif peasant society was organized around the *mas*,
the form of household settlement characteristic of the Cévennes
and the *ségala*.[5] And the countryside of the Midi was already
urbanized, in the sense that the peasants and farm-workers
clustered in villages and in small towns from where they fanned
out into the fields. Here was the homeland of the village bar
and the political *cercle*, of tenacious family and clan loyalties, of
concepts of honour and vendetta.[6] The patterns of habitation
and settlement, in other words, were not only important in
geographical and economic terms: they were also central to
popular culture and popular psychology.

The nature of farming also had important cultural repercussions for rural communities, with different sorts of farming
producing very different social mores. Life was very different in
areas of cereal production and areas of pasture; in regions of
grain and regions of wine; in *pays de grande culture* and *pays de
petite culture*. But differences were far more than simply
economic and affected more than the nexus which evolved
between the producer and the market. Eighteenth-century
France was a country of contrasting laws and legal traditions, a
country of several religions and none. In some regions religious
faith was deeply and even passionately defended as integral
part of the culture of the people: that was true, for instance, in
Brittany and Normandy, in Alsace and the east, in the Pays
Basque and in Flanders. In others, as in the parts of rural
Provence studied by Michel Vovelle, faith had been largely lost
and custom laicized, to the extent that he can talk, long before

[5] P. M. Jones, *Politics and Rural Society: The Southern Massif Central c. 1750–1880*
(Cambridge, 1985), 18–25.
[6] C. Lucas, 'The Problem of the Midi in the French Revolution', *Transactions of
the Royal Historical Society*, 28 (1978).

the intervention of the Jacobins, of a countryside that was effectively dechristianized, where God and religious observance had little relevance for the everyday lives of the people.[7] Theirs was a completely different world from that of shrines and wayside crosses, pilgrimages and *pardons*, which characterized so much of rural Brittany.

The system of administration and local government in Old Regime France helped accentuate these regional distinctions. It was not that it imposed clear geographical limits which helped identify each province: that would imply a level of sophistication of which eighteenth-century France was not yet capable. Administrative and juridical boundaries overlapped rather chaotically, and royal government was not universally effective. But these very inconsistencies helped to break down any sense of national identity: as Calonne explained, most succinctly, to Louis XVI in 1787, France was not in any real sense a single nation or a unified state; it was united by its common loyalty to the person of the king, but by very little else:

La France est un royaume composé de pays d'états, de pays d'administrations mixtes, dont les provinces sont étrangères les unes aux autres, où les barrières multipliées dans l'intérieur séparent et divisent les sujets d'un même souverain, où certaines contrées sont affranchies totalement des charges dont les autres supportent tout le poids, où la classe la plus riche est la moins contribuante, où les privilèges rompent tout équilibre: c'est nécessairement un royaume très imparfait, très rempli d'abus et tel qu'il est impossible de le bien gouverner.[8]

Under such a system power was unavoidably devolved from the centre, whatever the theory of absolutism might suggest. Major provincial cities were given a myriad of responsibilities which had the effect of building them into regional capitals and which focused loyalties on the regional unit rather than on the nation as a whole. Eighteenth-century Frenchmen were Bretons and Burgundians before they were French, and Rennes and

[7] M. Vovelle, *Religion et révolution* (Paris, 1976); T. Tackett, *Religion, Revolution and Regional Culture in Eighteenth-Century France: The Ecclesiastical Oath of 1791* (Princeton, 1986).

[8] An excellent discussion of ideas of centralization in the late Old Regime is to be found in Y. Fauchois, 'Centralisation', in F. Furet and M. Ozouf (eds.), *Dictionnaire critique de la Révolution française* (Paris, 1988), 653–64.

Dijon were more their capital cities than was Paris. In a country where the sense of the nation was weak, where authority was personal rather than national, and where royal power was devolved to governors and provincial nobles, local people identified primarily with their regional centres and with the bodies which provided justice and law—with the *sénéchaussées*, Parlements, and provincial estates. Governments needed local hierarchies to provide an administrative solidity which they themselves lacked; and it was in the localities that a natural hierarchy of noble administrators was evolved. But regionalism was not the sole creation of the State. The Church, too, contributed to regional awareness and regional pride by the implantation of abbeys and cathedrals, by the pomp and ceremonial which surrounded its sees, and by the presence of ecclesiastical courts with their own judges and ecclesiastical lawyers. Cultural life centred on Academies, *sociétés de pensée*, *cercles*, and Masonic lodges. And the military organization of France in the Old Regime added further to regional identity in the provinces, since the king depended very heavily for his troops on provincial regiments commanded by members of the leading aristocratic families of the region. In almost every sphere of local life there was a strong element of localism, while regional identity and regional loyalty were used to win popular support and to maintain the authority of the regime.

The policy clearly enjoyed more than a germ of success. Soldiers, in particular, came to see themselves as fighting in the service of the local duke or count, or took pride in identifying with the Regiment of the Auxerrois or the Bourbonnais, with that of Armagnac or Navarre.[9] But civilians, too, often saw their local Parlement as a defender of their traditional rights against incursions from the outside. The Fronde had proved a timely warning in this respect, but it was a warning that was barely heeded. In eighteenth-century food riots crowds still looked to the Parlement for a degree of protection, not to the Crown. The Parlements were often seen as repositories of regional political liberties, too, as in the Brittany Affair of the 1760s or in the continued battles between the Parlement of Grenoble and royal

[9] S. F. Scott, *The Response of the Royal Army to the French Revolution: The Role and Development of the Line Army, 1787–1793* (Oxford, 1978), 217–24.

government in the 1770s and 1780s.[10] Of course the local Parlements had played the regionalist card with great skill over the centuries, but there was an element of deference in the attitude of both peasants and urban crowds which the revolutionaries found disturbing. It was for this reason that many of them were so distrustful of local government, so intolerant of provincial differences. In their eyes, provincialism could not be other than a focus for social privilege and an impediment to the implementation of any genuine concept of citizenship. The very distinctions between provinces seemed to encourage a sense of superiority and to direct pride and consciousness away from the legislative revolution in Paris. The revolutionaries therefore demanded that local government be reformed, that its personnel be purged, and that political decision-making be centralized. Even in the first, supposedly devolutionist phase they were suspicious of local initiative. The anti-noble prejudice of the Revolution demanded it, since the provinces had for too long been privileged and hierarchical, the tool of aristocratic power.[11]

And yet we must be wary of the assumption that the province was a political entity capable of any real hold over the minds and hearts of the people. Albert Soboul, in a sensitive essay on the nature of the regional problem, warns against any facile identification between the population and their province. For, he notes, whatever focused and directed regional loyalties it could not be the province. Even the term 'province' was not widely used in the eighteenth century. Men referred to their 'pays', or their 'nation': 'La province au sens propre, en effet, n'existait pas sous l'Ancien Régime. Le mot fut employé pour la première fois, avec sa valeur administrative rigoureuse, dans le règlement de juin 1787 qui créa les assemblées provinciales dans les pays d'élections.'[12] Only in the administration of the Church

---

[10] W. Doyle, 'The Parlements', in K. M. Baker (ed.), *The French Revolution and the Creation of Modern Political Culture*, i. *The Political Culture of the Old Regime* (Oxford, 1987), 160–1; G. Chianéa, 'Institutions dauphinoises, pré-révolution et identité provinciale', in V. Chomel (ed.), *Les Débuts de la Révolution française en Dauphiné, 1788–1789* (Grenoble, 1988), 33–49.

[11] A. Patrick, 'French Revolutionary Local Government, 1789–1792', in C. Lucas (ed.), *The Political Culture of the French Revolution* (Oxford, 1988), 399–420.

[12] A. Soboul, 'De l'Ancien Régime à la Révolution: Problème régional et réalitiés sociales', in C. Gras and G. Livet (eds.), *Régions et régionalisme en France du dix-huitième siècle à nos jours* (Paris, 1977), 26.

were there provinces, and these had little emotive power. Where there was a strong element of regional loyalty, Soboul suggests that it was derived from language and from a shared history which together had 'façonné une mentalité spécifique'— and this last element was the vital one. Common language alone did not suffice. For whereas Brittany, Flanders, and Roussillon all showed signs of regionalist sentiment based on their linguistic inheritance, other areas which shared a common language or patois did not. Gascony, for instance, enjoyed linguistic particularism without any suggestion of a strong provincial identity.[13]

Such identity was aided by common history, by the sheer habit of sharing common administrative, governmental, and judicial traditions. But again, the simple fact of being administered in common did not necessarily create a common mentality. The degree of respect that was shown for the institutions of local administration varied considerably from region to region. This was especially true of rural areas of isolated pasture and difficult terrain, and of frontier regions where the writ of central government had always run with great difficulty, boundaries between provinces or between tax farms. All such regions traditionally presented particularly acute problems of governability, and all posed a challenge to the strained resources of the *maréchaussée*.[14] For if there were areas of France that were traditionally obedient to government, so there were regions where law and order had always presented special difficulties and where local people connived openly with thieves and bandits, smugglers and army deserters. The famous Bande d'Orgères in the Beauce might be particularly notorious among eighteenth-century robber bands, but it was not unique, and its marginal lifestyle was emulated on a more modest scale up and down the kingdom.[15] During the Revolution, too, it was not just political counter-revolution which was regional in character. So were other forms of community resistance against the pretensions of the state. Agrarian insurrection, for instance, often

[13] M. Bordes, 'La Gascogne à la fin de l'Ancien Régime: Une province?', in Gras and Livet (eds.), *Régions et régionalisme en France*, 139.
[14] I. Cameron, *Crime and Repression in the Auvergne and the Guyenne, 1720–1790* (Cambridge, 1981), 60–1.
[15] R. C. Cobb, 'The Bande d'Orgères', in *Reactions to the French Revolution* (Oxford, 1972), 181–211.

directed against the remaining vestiges of feudalism or the need
to redeem seigneurial dues, was restricted to well-defined
regions. Like the Great Fear of 1789, peasant revolution was a
localized phenomenon, but one which often fed off established
traditions of insurrection.[16] Thus between 1790 and 1792, while
other regions remained largely quiescent, there were risings,
and sometimes repeated bouts of rioting, in Normandy, in parts
of the west, in the southern Massif, in Provence, and in areas of
the rural South-west.[17] In some cases, as in the Périgord, the
insurgents could be said to be continuing an honourable
tradition of revolt, that of the Croquants in the previous
century. In others, and most notably in the Cantal, the peasant
movement rapidly became subsumed into revolutionary politics:
here local Jacobins succeeded in wooing the peasant insurgents
and in linking the demands of the peasantry to their own
political platform.[18]

But such co-operation could not be assumed in rural areas.
Peasants who had resisted the intrusion of the state during the
Old Regime might easily continue to resist the revolutionary
state and to view its legislative record on peasant questions with
suspicion, not to say with antipathy. As Peter Jones has shown,
the record of the revolutionaries was not one that was
guaranteed to win peasant approval.[19] If the abolition of Old
Regime dues and the removal of the former tax burden could
not but adduce general enthusiasm, the steps subsequently
taken to bind the peasantry to the newly created nation were
more divisive. The politicians remained committed to the
defence of property rights—but these tended to favour some
peasants and disadvantage others, which could in turn create a
form of class conflict inside the rural community. The insistence
that certain rights and dues could only be redeemed by high
money payments similarly divided the peasantry between those
who could afford to benefit from the law—in many parts of

[16] Y.-M. Bercé, 'Le Phénomène contestataire saisi dans la longue durée à
travers la mémoire et l'imaginaire', in J. Nicolas (ed.), *Mouvements populaires et
conscience, 16ᵉ au 19ᵉ siècles* (Paris, 1985), 713–17.
[17] A. Ado, *Les Paysans et la Révolution française: Le Mouvement paysan en 1789–
1794* (Moscow, 1987).
[18] J. R. Dalby, *Les Paysans cantaliens et la Révolution française, 1789–1794*
(Clermont-Ferrand, 1989), 60–2.
[19] P. M. Jones, *The Peasantry in the French Revolution* (Cambridge, 1988).

France a derisory proportion of the local population—and those who could not. Laws that favoured proprietors could not but disadvantage tenants, a fact which created new tensions inside rural society and which, as Donald Sutherland has demonstrated in the case of the Ille-et-Vilaine, could drive sections of the rural population into support for counter-revolution.[20] Similarly the abolition of old taxes was far more welcome than the introduction of a new revolutionary tax on land; the ending of seigneurial jurisdictions more popular than the imposition of new decrees and new tribunals. And the selling-off of the lands of others, whereas of the Church or of émigré nobles, proved less difficult than any reform of peasant land use. When, under the Jacobins, the state presumed to reform landholding by offering to divide up the common lands and distribute them among peasant proprietors, a measure that was intended to please the peasantry was met with a very mixed response. Though undoubtedly popular in the open plains of the north and east—both Georges Lefebvre and Florence Gauthier acknowledge its importance in the Nord and in Picardy[21]—*partage* had little appeal in the Massif Central or among the smallholders of the south-west. For them common land was not an archaic luxury but a necessary supplement to their livelihood, the difference between making do and facing starvation. In the valleys of the Pyrenees the commons could even constitute the largest part of the land of the community. In the Béarn, for instance, it was only the spread of viticulture during the eighteenth century that had begun to undermine collective traditions.[22]

In peasant France, indeed, the intervention of the state could easily be interpreted as unwarranted intrusion, as interference with custom and with a lifestyle that had been largely self-regulating over many centuries. Legislative solutions were often neither welcome nor terribly relevant, especially, perhaps, the highly interventionist solutions adopted in Year II by the Jacobins. When revolutionary government tried to insist that peasants part with their grain to feed the troops or supply the

[20] D. M. G. Sutherland, *The Chouans: The Social Origins of Popular Counter-Revolution in Upper Brittany, 1770–1796* (Oxford, 1982), 127–66.

[21] G. Lefebvre, *Questions agraires au temps de la Terreur* (Paris, 1955); F. Gauthier, *La Voie paysanne dans la Révolution française* (Paris, 1977).

[22] P. Tucoo-Chala and C. Desplat, *La Principauté de Béarn* (Pau, 1980), i. 25.

cities, it was greeted with sullen resentment and with rumours of a new famine pact. The units of the *armées révolutionnaires* sent in from the Paris sections to persuade villagers to part with their corn could easily be mistaken for urban bully-boys and their mission for simple theft. The state's insistence that peasants sell through established markets at the prices laid down by the *maximum* only added to the general sense of grievance, that their interests were being once again sacrificed to the greater good of the capital. Market forces were lauded when they benefited the towns, yet they were being abandoned when it was the villagers who stood to gain. Not that market forces themselves enjoyed universal popularity in the countryside. Among the poorer peasantry, in particular, the Revolution's capitalist ethic was itself a source of grievance, and one which had alienated peasant opinion long before the months of the Jacobin Dictatorship.[23]

A number of questions must be asked. What was the relevance of a free market to subsistence peasants who had no experience of using money? What could be the justification for the free movement of grain when the villagers knew that they faced dearth the following spring? And did not the market ethic leave the poor and underemployed even more at the mercy of charity, even more dependent on the economy of makeshifts which had so often been their lot in the Old Regime? In many parts of France, especially in the poorer agricultural areas where subsistence farming was the norm, the Revolution's commitment to free trade and the market economy led to rapid disillusionment. The revolutionaries took no account of their traditional cultural patterns, patterns which had sustained them through years of famine and shortage. The market economy was quite foreign to most subsistence peasants. It belonged elsewhere: to Paris, to the towns, to the rich. Theirs, as Edward Thompson has reminded us in the English context, remained essentially a moral economy, where social justice and tradition played a large part in popular perceptions.

If rural areas were often alienated from the Revolution by the actions of others, what of provincial towns and cities? They, at least, shared with Paris a common urban culture of clubs and

---

[23] Jones, *Politics and Rural Society*, 48–61.

popular societies, pamphlets and newspapers; they had an educated élite which followed very closely the twists and turns of national policy; their deputies made revolutionary laws in their name and often kept in regular contact with their constituents. And with the municipal revolution of 1790, they were encouraged to take an active political role which their citizens had never previously enjoyed—a role which, it might be assumed, would serve to attach a substantial part of their population to the cause of the Revolution. The early enthusiasm shown in provincial cities seemed to sustain this belief. They supported the Third Estate in the Estates-General and pressed for the abolition of privilege, even accepting that their own municipal privileges would have to be sacrificed. They demanded more representative government and were strong advocates of the Rights of Man. To counter the rural unrest of the Great Fear and the outbreak of popular violence against granaries and arsenals, they raised battalions of the National Guard and reimposed order where disorder had threatened.[24] It might seem that unanimity had been created on which a solid revolutionary achievement could be built. But that unanimity was deceptive. By1790, with the first elections, the extent of local divergence became apparent: some towns opted for radical patriots, others for staunch conservatives. In Montauban the council was so conservative as to form, in Daniel Ligou's words, 'a bastion of the Old Regime'.[25] In contrast, Marseille already enjoyed a reputation throughout the Midi for its radicalism and revolutionary enthusiasm.[26] Unanimity had already been sacrificed to political ambition and economic interest.

Nor should it be assumed that all provincial cities were happy with the role which they were assigned. For the Revolution, even in 1790, was more concerned with administrative control than with any genuine spirit of devolution. The law which abolished the administrative privileges of the Old Regime quite

[24] For a detailed discussion of the formation of the National Guard in Rennes see R. Dupuy, *La Garde nationale et les débuts de la Révolution en Ille-et-Vilaine* (Paris, 1972).

[25] D. Ligou, *Montauban à la fin de l'Ancien Régime et aux débuts de la Révolution* (Paris, 1958), 205.

[26] J. B. Cameron, Jun., 'The Revolution in the Sections of Marseille—Federalism in the Department of the Bouches-du-Rhône in 1793', unpublished Ph.D. thesis, University of North Carolina, 1971, 29–37.

explicitly attacked their privileges, too. 'Tous les privilèges particuliers des provinces, principautés, pays, cantons, villes, et communautés d'habitants', it declared, 'soit pécuniaires soit de toute autre nature, sont abolis sans retour.'[27] In the administrative reforms that followed, the old provinces were replaced by a new structure of *départements*, *districts*, and *municipalités*; local justice was to be dispensed at the level of the *canton*. Justice and administration were brought closer to the people, and towns were chosen as administrative or judicial centres on the understanding that they could be accessible to the population. Whereas smaller and medium-sized towns might stand to benefit from this arrangement, many larger towns lost their historic claim to greatness as well as some of the prosperity which lavish Old Regime administration had bestowed.[28] For it was not just the provinces and *intendances* that were abolished; so were guilds and *corporations*, economic monopolies and toll revenues. The ending of trading concessions and company privileges clearly helped the economies of some cities, but it was to prove near-fatal to the prosperity of others, most notably, perhaps, of Bayonne.[29] And for regional capitals like Rennes, Rouen, Aix, or Grenoble the loss of a Parlement, of an *intendance*, of a cathedral chapter and a chamber of commerce, was hardly compensated for by the honour of being nominated *chef-lieu de département* under the new administrative dispensations. As such, they enjoyed no more legal influence than such meagre towns as Foix and Digne, Privas and Vesoul. Already they could be counted among the losers in the revolutionary lottery. Their pride and dignity suffered as well as their economy, since what was being denied them was their aspiration to play a regional rather than a purely local role in government. Some among them would still harbour that resentment during the federalist crisis of 1793.

But if feelings were hurt by the administrative reallocations of 1790, there was as yet no evidence of counter-revolutionary intent among the provincial cities of France. Indeed, all seemed

[27] Law of 4 Aug. 1789.
[28] L. Hunt, *Revolution and Urban Politics in Provincial France: Troyes and Reims, 1786–1790* (Stanford, Calif., 1978), 2–5.
[29] H. Léon, *Étude historique sur la Chambre de Commerce de Bayonne* (Paris, 1869), 47–50.

eager to present their candidates for the honours that were on offer, vying with one another in central location, accessibility, patriotism, virtue, and any other quality that seemed worthy of recompense. The Comité de Division had laid down the basic criterion of equality: that departments should be of roughly equal size, that the towns chosen as *chefs-lieux* should be easily accessible to all the people of the locality, that in the best of all worlds the principle of division would be that of the *cadastre*.[30] The reality, of course, was very different, with a chaotic scramble for honours, a stream of indignant petitions and representations, and a marked tendency to run down one's neighbours and rivals. More than a hundred petitioners arrived in person in Paris to make sure that their case was not overlooked, for the urgency of the question was not lost on local communities. Hotels, bars, businesses, and meeting-rooms all depended for their prosperity on the Committee's largesse, and woe betide the elector who overlooked to make the best possible case for his corner of the *hexagone*. The result was less a tribute to Reason than a somewhat undignified carve-up, with each town seeking as much as it could for its own citizens. Towns could point to their prosperity as market centres or could plead dire poverty; either might seem a good reason for the siting of a *tribunal* or a *collège*. They might argue that they were already equipped with the public buildings they would require, or they might point to a suitably sited church property that was ripe for secularization. They often emphasized their utility to the peasant community of the surrounding area, adding, wherever possible, the supporting voices of compliant villagers. Or they painted a heart-rending picture of the losses they had suffered in the cause of the Revolution, arguing that the extent of their sacrifices should be taken as a reflection of their political virtue.[31]

In the final allocation—and especially the decisions about which towns should serve as departmental *chefs-lieux*—tradition was generally favoured over wealth. The seats of the former Parlements (Rennes, Rouen, Douai, Dijon, Besançon, Metz,

[30] M.-V. Ozouf-Marignier, *La Formation des départements: La Représentation du territoire français à la fin du dix-huitième siècle* (Paris, 1989), esp. 35–42.
[31] These documents are to be found in Archives Nationales, series DIV[bis] (Comité de Division de la Constituante).

Nancy, Grenoble, Aix, Toulouse, Bordeaux, and Pau, as well, of course, as Paris) were all allocated one of the new departments to administer; and cities which had been the seats of *bailliages* or of *sénéchaussées* in the Old Regime rarely went unrewarded. By way of contrast, the great commercial ports did rather badly: if Bordeaux became capital of the Gironde, Le Havre, Dunkerque, Bayonne, and Marseille all had to make do with less. Bayonne, indeed, was placed in the District of Ustaritz and Le Havre gave way to the claims of Montivilliers. These decisions did not go uncontested, and they do in part result from a very unequal distribution of electors. But they also reflected the weight of rural opinion, which was almost unanimously against the concentration of too much power and wealth in a merchant community with which they had few commercial links. Take, for instance, the long and often acrimonious debate between Aix and Marseille for the *chef-lieu* of the Bouches-du-Rhône. The attitudes of the people of the hinterland showed both respect for tradition and intense hostility to the mercantile élite. 'Aix', claimed the citizens of Aubagne with evident approval, 'est la capitale de la Provence, et à ce titre il n'est pas un Provençal dont le vœu ne soit qu'on fasse exception à la règle en faveur de cette ville.'[32] But there was no such sympathy for Marseille. The deputies of Provence poured scorn on the suggestion that a city whose economy was so completely orientated towards trade could adequately perform the functions of *chef-lieu*. Their language concealed animosity as well as distrust. 'Plus Marseille est riche,' they declaimed, 'moins elle a besoin de secours; plus elle est supérieure à toutes les autres villes, moins on doit lui fournir des moyens nouveaux pour achever de les étouffer.' And if that plea for a more egalitarian distribution of resources were not sufficient, they went on to denounce the Marseillais in the roundest of terms: Marseille, they claimed, was a parasite, a city which 'pompe l'or, les habitants, l'industrie de la province. C'est une espèce de fléau sous lequel cette province gémit'.[33] Rivalries of this kind were common. They served to quench both the spirit of fraternity and any sense of regional unity or solidarity.

Yet, at a much more local level, the evidence of these petitions

---

[32] Ibid. 5 (Aubagne).   [33] Ibid. (Marseille et Provence).

and counter-petitions to the Comité De Division tells a very different story.[34] If there was only limited evidence of solidarity across whole provinces of France, there were clear indications of localized loyalty, by small towns to their natural regional centre, by hamlets and outlying villages to the market town to which their people would gravitate on business. We have, for instance, petitions from the smaller communes of their immediate hinterland to support the claims of Salers (Cantal) for a District, or Saintes over La Rochelle for primacy in the Charente-Inférieure, of Bazas for a department of the Bazadais. In such petitions economic motives played a major part: some communities would offer their support to a larger neighbour in the hope that they in their turn might glean some reward. And there is no doubt that aspiring towns indulged in electioneering among their nearest neighbours; in the Ariège, indeed, there were allegations that a 'model' document had been circulated among the villagers in a bid to whip up support. But most of these petitions would seem to have been genuine expressions of local feeling, the kind of loyalty that stemmed from habit and convenience and reflected the natural position held by the town in its regional context. This very localized focus for rural loyalty should not surprise us. As Fernand Braudel has stressed, eighteenth-century France was less a country of provinces than a country of *pays*, historic groupings of villages and valleys which often kept their own customs and folklore, their weights and measures, their distinctive dialect. The true *pays*, for Braudel, is not a province but a historic part of a province—the Vallespir rather than Roussillon, the Brionnais rather than Burgundy; in the far south-west he sees the mountain river valley that is the Gave de Pau not as a single entity but as an 'assemblage de sept pays différents'.[35] People travelled little and rarely in a country where communication remained slow and cumbersome: in 1789 it still took six days to get to Paris from Bordeaux, eight from Aix or Marseille.[36] Regional identity could still be very localized indeed.

---

[34] The evidence that follows is taken from ibid. 1–18. I have discussed this subject at greater length in a paper on 'Le Découpage administratif de la France' to a colloquium on 'Espace et temps' held at Marseille in 1989 (papers to be published during 1990).

[35] F. Braudel, *L'Identité de la France* (Paris, 1986), i. 40.

[36] Arbellot and Lepetit, *Atlas de la Révolution française, Routes et communications* (Paris, 1987).

Such local loyalties were often heightened during the revolutionary years by insensitive and at times crass actions by central government which served to underline the huge gulf that separated Paris from many of the ordinary people of provincial France. Provincials were repeatedly made aware that Paris was more than just the largest city in France, more than the capital city of the infant Republic.[37] A revolutionary imagery was created in these years, and especially during the months of the Jacobin dictatorship, which saw Paris as something different in kind from other towns and which portrayed Parisians as a rare breed in committed revolutionaries. Paris came to be seen as the most republican city in France, the most patriotic city, the most virtuous city, whose example should therefore be followed by all good republicans. Paris was the patriotic city which selflessly sent its sons to fight for the Revolution on the frontiers; Paris was the centre of vigilance which defended the whole country against the cancer of counter-revolution. In Year II, the Jacobin myth of Paris as the fulcrum of the Revolution was omnipresent, and it could only cast the provincial achievement in an unfavourable light. *Commissaires* and deputies on mission heaped praise on Parisian achievements during their tours of duty in the provinces, trying to stimulate a similar level of political commitment in the towns and villages through which they passed. Jacobin tracts and speeches pointed to Paris as a shining example for others to follow. Plays, sons, and popular festivals sang the praises of the 'braves Parisiens'. Parisian soldiers from local garrisons harangued popular societies on the achievement of the Parisian sansculottes and even, on occasion, tried to subvert the clubs for their own ends.[38] The implicit assumption could scarcely be avoided: that the Parisians were more committed to the cause of the Revolution, that they were better informed and enjoyed a better political education than their fellows in other parts of France. It was a message that aroused sullen resentment in the provinces, both among those who had no love for the Parisian revolution and among provincial patriots who saw no reason to be self-deprecating about their own patriotic achievement.

This resentment was only deepened by the lack of regard that

---

[37] R. Monnier, 'L'Image de Paris de 1789 à 1794: Paris capitale de la Révolution', in M. Vovelle (ed.), *L'Image de la Révolution française*, i (Paris, 1989).
[38] E. Leleu, *La société populaire de Lille* (Lille, 1919), 94–106.

was often shown for what local people were doing. The attitudes expressed from the centre—by *conventionnels* tainted by their years in Paris as much as by men who had been born and bred there—often confirmed the blackest suspicions of provincial communities. At best they were understanding but patronizing; at worst, like Carrier in the Loire-Inférieure or Javogues in the Loire, they were openly contemptuous.[39] But even the most gentle of deputies on mission demonstrated the cultural gulf that existed between Paris and the French country-side. If the local peasantry were not agents of counter-revolution, they were gullible fools ignorant of their civic responsibilities. Take, for instance, this report from Bô, on mission in the Cantal in 1794. Describing the state of public opinion in the District of Murat, he wrote, not without a certain perspicacity, that if local people were not carrying out the Republic's laws, it was for lack of information, not of good will. In Murat, he explained, he found the administrators 'plus faibles qu'infidèles' and the people 'disposé à entendre la vérité'. When he outlined the political situation to them, they listened patiently and thanked him for his words. The image is one of a patient administrator faced with a simple, rather childlike flock, devoid of political ambition and unburdened by even the most elementary education:

J'ai convoqué dans ce district, comme dans les autres, les agents nationaux, et j'en ai renouvelé plusieurs. Aucun n'avait connaissance de la loi du 14 frimaire; je la leur ai expliqué, je les ai engagés par leur propre intérêt à s'en pénétrer, à entretenir avec les agents nationaux des districts une correspondance exacte, et je crois qu'ils feront tout ce qu'on peut attendre d'un cultivateur illettré.[40]

Such paternalism was, of course, less detestable than the imposition of a revolutionary tribunal or the arrival on the town square of a *guillotine ambulante*, but it could still be bitterly resented. For it implied that there were two classes of citizens—the educated and the uneducated, the virtuous and the sinners. The provincial could easily form the impression that he was

---

[39] G. Martin, *Carrier et sa mission à Nantes* (Paris, 1922); C. Lucas, *The Structure of the Terror: The Example of Javogues and the Loire* (Oxford, 1973).
[40] J. Roberts and J. Hardman (eds.), *French Revolutionary Documents*, ii (Oxford, 1975), 179.

condemned for ever to be an innocent in the revolutionary Babylon.

It should be emphasized that if the Jacobins were the clearest advocates of centralized administration, the image of an unsympathetic and rather supercilious government in Paris did not die with Robespierre on 10 Thermidor. Those who served the Thermidorians and the Directory were often just as insensitive in their handling of local people; nor was the situation greatly improved by the increased use of professional bureaucrats during the Directorial years. They were appalled by the extent of local inefficiency and graft, which they deemed to be incompatible with the values of the revolutionary regime. They complained of the avarice and self-interest which they encountered among local mayors, and of the superstition and widespread illiteracy which still characterized the countryside. Increasingly Paris intervened to root out the worst abuses, dismissing mayors who could not meet even the most basic standards of literacy and replacing justices of the peace who could not distance themselves from local pressure. In the Oise a retired judge complained in 1798 that the law was simply not being enforced, because many of the *juges de paix* preferred to ignore the more minor offences committed in their area of jurisdiction. And why? Because of 'la crainte de se compromettre, d'éprouver les funestes effets des vengeances, les liaisons de parenté et d'amitié'.[41] In the villages of the Ariège, a traditional area of smuggling and lawlessness, the problems of law enforcement were predictably more serious. Here both *juges* and mayors conspired with local people to allow their sons to escape conscription, rigging ballots, omitting names from the *scrutin*, falsifying and even destroying the *état civil*.[42] Even after ten years of revolution Paris had not begun to establish habits of smooth or honest administration in such areas. Yet the government had no choice but to employ local people to carry out tasks of day-to-day administration, even where, as in the Ariège, they spoke a completely different language from that of the capital. They had no time to train them, no time to offer them the most rudimentary political education. Friction was bound to follow.

[41] R. C. Cobb, *Paris and Its Provinces* (Oxford, 1975), 92.
[42] A. Forrest, *Conscripts and Deserters: The Army and French Society during the Revolution and Empire* (New York, 1989), 190–1.

That revolutionary government aroused acrimonious opposition in many regions of the French provinces there is no doubt. In many areas this acrimony was itself localized, confined to immediate neighbourhoods, to the conflicts which set peasants against the local Jacobin 'bourgeois' or the countryside against the nearest administrative town. Such conflicts could assume a town–country character or could use the language of social antagonism, the language of class. They could also push rural communities into the arms of the counter-revolution. As Tim Le Goff and Donald Sutherland have shown, much of the anti-republican feeling in the departments of the west was expressed in attacks on the towns of the region, towns like Vannes and Auray, Fougères and Pontivy. But this should not be taken literally to mean that peasants disliked those who lived in towns, who worked and consumed as townsmen. Many of the townsmen, after all, were former members of the village community, and there is little reason to suppose that those who remained in the countryside felt any burning hatred for those who had left. Where towns were the object of hatred or even of physical attack, it was not urban culture as such that was at issue, but rather the role which towns had come to play in the Revolution's administrative order. The Revolution, as we have seen, had increased that role, giving a whole range of powers to the literate, politically sound burghers, powers which they proceeded to exercise over the people of the countryside. What made matters worse was that the men who formed this new *classe politique* were often indistinguishable from the class of bourgeois landowners whom the peasantry could identify as their principal rivals in the battle for land in their own village. Many were landlords themselves; many used their wealth and standing in the community to enrich themselves by the purchase of *biens nationaux*. Even more than the old seigneurs, they aroused the concerted hostility of the local peasantry.[43]

Of course, it must not be imagined that the peasantry were in a permanent state of insurrection, nor yet permanently dissatisfied. They, too, made gains from revolutionary policy, and they, too, enjoyed the rights of citizenship. But the conflict between town and country in the 1790s is not a figment of

[43] T. Le Goff and D. Sutherland, 'The Social Origins of Counter-Revolution in Western France', *Past and Present*, 99 (1983).

historians' imagination. It was very real, and it was sustained by the fact that revolutionary government and administration were so firmly implanted in the France of towns and cities, in a France which did not empathize with peasant culture and which made little effort to understand it. The local revolutionary officials were in this respect every bit as unpopular as the national politicians or the deputies sent down on mission from Paris. Even more markedly than in Paris, they tended to be drawn from the ranks of political militants—the Patriots, republicans, or Jacobins who attended local clubs and popular societies, men whose ideas of progress and civic duty often conflicted with the more conservative custom of the rural hinterland. They were associated with policing and with provisioning, two areas of government which brought countrymen into conflict with the state; and they were often accused of carrying out their role with an ill-concealed contempt for those less 'patriotic' than themselves. In the west, for instance, it was the local urban Jacobins who pushed ahead with policies of dechristianization, denouncing the superstition and fanaticism of the peasantry, ordering the closure of churches and the public humiliation of priests—in short, going far beyond the limits prescribed by the law. The sense of moral superiority displayed by these revolutionary townsmen and the backing they appeared to receive from the government turned whole communities against the Revolution and its agents.[44]

Religion was not, of course, the only issue which brought peasant and administrator into bitter conflict. If dechristianization outraged peasant faith, taxation, requisitions, and military levies all affected his welfare and security. Taxes were perhaps the least burning of these issues: after all, for much of the Revolution tax collection remained grossly insufficient and many peasants escaped taxes altogether.[45] The demands of the war were quite another matter. After the declaration of hostilities in the spring of 1792 the issue of recruitment and the accompanying requisitions of horses, mules, and carts came to

[44] T. Tackett, 'The West of France in 1789: The Religious Factor in the Origins of Counter-Revolution', *Journal of Modern History*, 54 (1982).

[45] Just how inefficient revolutionary tax collection was is shown in Patrick, 'French Revolutionary Local Government', 408–10.

be especially resented—evidence, if country people still needed it, that the towns did not understand their needs and made no effort to accommodate to their culture. There were suspicions of favouritism and of fraud, and there were constant allegations that townsmen protected their own and sent only the rural poor to the butchery of the front. There were protests that the rich and well-to-do of the towns were escaping service by buying replacements, leaving the poor *cultivateur* to shoulder an unfair burden. There were continued complaints that a service that involved little more than personal inconvenience for the urban artisan could ruin the lives of peasant families by depriving them of much-needed labour, thus making their smallholdings unviable.[46] Almost everywhere there was a veiled suggestion that in matters of recruitment the interests of the Revolution and those of the peasantry were locked in conflict.

In some areas of rural France draft-dodging was almost universal, as families connived with their sons, mayors protected their neighbours, and farmers employed deserters in a gesture of collective defiance of the state. In the South-west and the Massif, areas where peasant communities refused to provide volunteers for the army and where entire communities sought to escape from the levies of 1793, it was again urban officials who cajoled and denounced the villagers for their *incivisme*. There was nothing new in this: peasants had complained of their treatment at the hands of the 'privileged' towns from the earliest months of the Revolution. In the most extreme cases, like that of Avignon and the Comtat, Patriot townsmen turned to violence and terror in their attempt to cow and convert recalcitrant villagers: the excesses committed by Jourdan Coupe-Têtes and his motley Avignonnais army during 1790 would help determine the attitudes of whole communities towards the Revolution in the new department of the Vaucluse.[47] The response to such excesses could be a specifically peasant response, or it could be a rural response that united whole communities against the tyranny of the cities. It could also—as in the Vendée, where the insurrection was triggered by the recruitment laws of the spring of 1793—be the response of an

[46] Forrest, *Conscripts and Deserters*, 43–73.
[47] R. Moulinas, 'Le Plus Célèbre des Révolutionnaires avignonnais: Jourdan Coupe-Têtes, histoire et légende', *Provence historique*, 148 (1987), 275–86.

entire region, united against the government by a sense of common grievance and common interest.

But how far were collective responses endowed with a recognizably regionalist sentiment? Can Bretons who rejected military service or Marseillais who rose in rebellion against the Jacobin Convention be said to have done so out of a sense of their own distinct identity as Bretons or as sons of the *cité phocéenne*? These are never easy questions to answer, given that regionalist language could often be used where the real dispute lay elsewhere—over landownership, for instance, or the economy. The issue is even more complex in that opinion within a region was rarely united during the revolutionary period, while in some regions—most notably the Midi—the existence of bitter political divisions within the community concealed any sense of overall interest. These divisions, as Colin Lucas has observed, may have had some ideological point or may have reflected social antagonisms within local society. But in the violent and vengeful Midi these issues soon became blurred, till the object of the local power game was simplified into the sole issue of survival. Those in power wanted to keep it in order to thwart their rivals and rub home to the maximum their own advantage; their opponents sought to seize control in order to save their own skins and to persecute their former oppressors. 'Aux yeux des deux groupes la fonction primordiale de la politique est d'accéder au pouvoir local afin de s'empêcher de redevenir victimes.'[48] Nor were such divisions unique to the south. In the federalist cities there was always a minority of the sections that remained loyal to Paris. In their hinterland there would generally be at least one town or city eager to support the Paris Jacobins and act as a base for a counter-assault.[49] Terrorist killers could always hope to find a haven in a rival community.[50] Even in the counter-revolutionary west, indeed, the government was reassured to find towns and villages close to the war zone which

---

[48] C. Lucas, 'Le Jeu du pouvoir local sous le Directoire', in *Les Pratiques politiques en province à l'époque de la Révolution française: Actes du colloque de Montpellier* (Montpellier, 1988), 283.
[49] Examples are La Réole (in opposition to Bordeaux) and Aubagne (to Marseille).
[50] R. C. Cobb, *The Police and the People: French Popular Protest, 1789–1820* (Oxford, 1970), 352.

continued to harbour republican sentiments.[51] Local rivalries would die hard, even in the midst of a civil conflict sought in the name of starkly opposed political ideologies.

These squabbles and divisions do not, however, destroy the case for some sort of regional loyalty or sense of common identity. Local rivalries had always existed—over shrines and centres of pilgrimage, over the location of markets or the use of common grazing. But the existence of such tensions within and between communities does not exclude the existence of a stronger, less autarkic mentality, which assumed that Bretons or Basques or Savoyards had more in common than divided them, that their common identity was important and should be allowed to thrive. Differences might conceal this collective mentality just as they might mask a commonly-held dislike or distrust of Paris and national government. Yet some form of collective mentality—however apolitical in its expression—did exist, most visibly during the Jacobin period, when government centralism was at its peak. It was a largely cultural phenomenon rather than a part of organized politics. It could never be identified with any counter-revolutionary or royalist ideological line. And it never became the dominant force that some Jacobins pretended: the federalist cities of the south never seriously dreamed of secession or of establishing a 'République du Midi', even if Barbaroux may briefly have toyed with the notion.[52] For this reason, perhaps, regionalism has been largely discounted as a force in the counter-revolution, even although regionalist sentiments were to recur in many of these same regions in the more placid, romantic mood of the nineteenth century. This is, I believe, rash, since there are many hints of a regional expression during the revolutionary period and many reasons why regionalist appeals could seem powerful. Ill-defined as they undoubtedly were, regional loyalties often played a more considerable part than did precise ideologies in explaining the levels of support which the counter-revolution was able to muster.

The increasingly intolerant centralism of the Revolution itself created a provincial reaction. The strong legislative emphasis of

---

[51] C. Tilly, 'Local Conflicts in the Vendée before the Rebellion of 1793', *French Historical Studies*, 2 (1961).

[52] E. Bire, *La légende des Girondins* (Paris, 1881), 353 n.

the period meant that political decisions were concentrated in
the capital, with provincial clubs and sections, like provincial
towns and tribunals, responding tó outside initiatives rather
than accepting responsibilities for themselves. Increasingly their
role seemed to be to petition, to react, rather than to innovate,
and many saw the promised benefits of the Revolution—the
new liberties and civic responsibilities—removed from under
their noses. National priorities determined whether the local
economy would flourish or slip into a rapid decline, and once
the war was declared there was little that the great merchant
ports like Bordeaux and Nantes could do to save themselves
from economic strangulation. Privateering seemed a less desperate fate than bankruptcy and ruin; and the merchants took a
smaller and smaller part in politics and administration, confining
themselves to their balance-sheets and to the agonies of keeping
their businesses afloat.[53] Those who did devote themselves to
local government found that their freedom of manœuvre was
increasingly circumscribed. Local councils were purged and
local decisions overturned by deputies sent down from the
Convention. Courts dealing with political cases found themselves similarly restricted, as the criminal law was redefined and
sentencing policy determined from Paris. Prosecutors became
national agents, answerable to Paris rather than to local elected
bodies; and special military tribunals replaced the ordinary
courts for the trial of political offenders. Clubs looked to the
mother society in Paris for guidance on matters of policy; and
censorship seriously curtailed local press freedom. The needs of
the 'Patrie en danger' appeared to justify almost any act of
arbitrary centralization. By the end of the decade elected bodies
had given up much of their power to prefects and sub-prefects.
In Alfred Cobban's phrase, 'the decade that began with a
spontaneous outburst of communal liberty ended with the
creation of a far more ruthlessly centralised system of local
administration than even the *ancien régime* had known'.[54]

The rhetoric of the Revolution reflected this move to a
centralist philosophy, a centralism that was intolerant of
opposition and even of diversity. At the very heart of this

[53] F. Crouzet, 'La Ruine du grand commerce', in F.-G. Pariset (ed.), *Bordeaux
au dix-huitième siècle* (Bordeaux, 1968), 485–510.
[54] A. Cobban, *Aspects of the French Revolution* (London, 1968) 130.

philosophy was the idea that France was a nation, and that sovereignty was vested in the nation. That idea, as Pierre Nora rightly insists, was born from the moment when the National Assembly was formed, when Frenchmen ceased to be organized by legal estates, and when sovereignty ceased to lie with a hereditary monarch whose authority was justified by divine right. France was henceforth a political community devoted to the service of the nation, a social community assured of the benefits of citizenship, of equal rights in law.[55] The Nation had a special place within the Revolutionary canon, a place that was already ascribed to it in the writings of the Enlightenment. The Abbé Sieyès expressed it succinctly in 1789 in his famous pamphlet, *Qu'est-ce que le Tiers État?* 'La nation', he stated, 'existe avant tout, elle est l'origine de tout. Sa volonté est toujours légale, elle est la loi elle-même.'[56] If the Nation were sovereign, moreover, that sovereignty was absolute; it could not be shared or partitioned, and it was the foremost duty of free men to nurture it. It was to prove a useful way of discrediting the Revolution's enemies. Louis XVI would be charged with the crime of *lèse-nation*, of permitting the Nation to be 'blasphemed'. The federalist cities of 1793 would be ruthlessly suppressed on the grounds that the safety and integrity of the Nation had been put at risk. The Nation was a sort of totem round which good citizens were expected to unite, a totem that would be celebrated in many of the rather sterile set-piece festivals that marked the Revolutionary Calendar.

War, of course, gave a new meaning to the Nation, allowing the Revolution to capitalize on the nationalist sentiment created by the simple fact of being under attack. It also entitled the state to demand a higher level of sacrifice from the individual citizen in the sacred name of *salut public*. The entire population was bound to its service, not just the young men who were designated to fight in its name: as the Convention decreed in August 1793, the *levée en masse* was intended to encompass the entire community:

Tous les Français sont en réquisition permanente pour le service des armées. Les jeunes gens iront au combat; les hommes mariés forgeront

[55] P. Nora, 'Nation', in Furet and Ozouf, *Dictionnaire critique*, 804.
[56] E. J. Sieyès, *Qu'est-ce que le Tiers État?*, ed. R. Zapperi (Geneva, 1970), 180.

les armes et transporteront les subsistances; les femmes feront des tentes, des habits, et serviront dans les hôpitaux; les enfants mettront le vieux linge en charpie; les vieillards se feront porter sur les places publiques pour exciter le courage des guerriers, prêcher la haine des rois et l'unité de la République.[57]

With the war, too, nationalism became more emotive, at times verging on sentimentality. Frenchmen were urged to think of France as the Nation of Liberty, as the Nation towards which all free men must gravitate, while the spread of revolutionary values throughout the continent swiftly became confused by the imperialist ambitions of the 'Grande Nation'. Already the word *Patrie* had come to replace the more functional *Nation* in revolutionary speeches and calls to arms. And patriotism had become the supreme good: since the *patrie* was in danger, since the Revolution was under attack from foreign tyrants, from the two-headed monster that was Pitt–Cobourg, no sacrifice could be too great in the cause of ensuring its safety. Love of the *patrie* was demanded of every Frenchman, together with the eternal vigilance which alone could protect it from its enemies.[58] At home Robespierre repeatedly warned of the dangers posed by counter-revolution, alerting republicans to the threat posed by their neighbours, their employers, their workmates. In the armies the propaganda was even more insistent, against aristocrats, priests, even their own officers. The second issue of the soldiers' newspaper, *La Soirée du camp*, singled out for particular treatment 'tous ces viédazes, ces faquins à talons rouges, ces donzelles à tabouret, ces prélats crossés et à crosser, ces donneurs d'eau-bénite d'église et d'eau-bénite de cour'.[59] Under the Terror it was not just counter-revolutionaries who were called to account, but the indifferent, the apathetic, the *tièdes*. The *patrie* was becoming selective and exclusive, restricted to those who embodied Republican virtue.

In the adoration of the Republican *patrie* there was little place for regional diversity. Unlike Barrès and the romantic nationalists of the late nineteenth century, the revolutionary Patriot attached little importance to the individual *pays* within the Republic; rather he emphasized the unity and integrity of the *patrie*, talking of it in abstract and increasingly vacuous terms. The

---

[57] Quoted by J.-P. Bertaud, *La Révolution armée* (Paris, 1979), 115.
[58] N. Hampson, 'La patrie', in Lucas, *Political Culture*, 129–36.

patrie was, almost tautologically, 'une et indivisible'. The 'autel de la patrie' made its ritualistic and unifying appearance in almost every popular festival, stressing the common identity of all France's 'enfants'. The 'patrie' was evoked, with varying degrees of lyricism and increasing banality, in every political speech of the period—in Robespierre's last great ideological speech, on the cult of the Supreme Being, Norman Hampson notes that he used the word, often utterly vacuously, on twenty-four separate occasions.[60] But it is not the vacuousness that matters. It is the contempt for regionalism and the fear of diversity which the repeated calls to unity conceal which made the rather chauvinistic nationalism of the Revolution—and most particularly of the Jacobin Revolution—so very hard for provincial opinion to live with.

Contempt for regional sensibilities was nowhere more flagrant than in the Revolution's attitude to regional languages and local dialects. Not only was the *patrie* 'une et indivisible'; but it had a language, French, which was declared to be the language of free men. Legislative, administrative, and military centralism were soon matched by an intolerance of regional language and regional culture: the intrusion of Paris seemed complete. This in turn posed problems for the legislators, whose work was conducted in a language that was foreign to some six million of France's citizens, and exceptions were soon made where it was clear that the message of the Revolution was failing to get across to the local population. As in so many spheres, linguistic centralism was part of the ideological baggage of the later Revolution, the Revolution of the Convention, and the Committee of Public Safety. In the early months diversity had been tolerated, with decrees not only translated into the various languages of the *hexagone*—in Flanders, Alsace, Brittany, Corsica, and elsewhere—but rendered in many of the regional dialects as well. Dugas, for instance, planned to produce versions of the decrees of the Assembly in patois for all the departments of the south and south-west.[61] But this initiative proved short-lived. The report of the Abbé Grégoire was already indicative of a new

---

[59] *La Soirée du Camp*, issue 2 (3 Thermidor II).

[60] Hampson, 'La Patrié', 135.

[61] M. de Certeau, D. Julia, and J. Revel, *Une Politique de la langue: La Révolution française et les patois* (Paris, 1975), 288.

intolerance towards diversity: his enquiry collected data on the use of a dialect throughout France, but it was drawn up by an educated provincial bourgeoisie, through the filter of the Jacobin clubs, and the whole exercise reflected the belief that patois was symptomatic of backwardness and rural superstition, whereas enlightened and modern Frenchmen spoke only French.[62] Bertrand Barère, reporting to the Committee of Public Safety in 1793, went even further, urging that patois be eradicated as a means of educating the general public and of imposing revolutionary principles on the entire population. The deputy for Tarbes made no secret of his contempt for dialect, even the dialect of his own constituents. There was, he believed, more at stake than the luxury of linguistic diversity: 'Le fédéralisme et la superstition parlent bas breton; l'émigration et la haine de la République parlent allemand; la contre-révolution parle l'italien; et le fanatisme parle le basque.'[63] A good Republican, in Barère's view, must necessarily express his Republicanism in French.

Both the federalist centres and the regions of counter-revolution reacted against what they saw as the overbearing pride and pretension of the centre. With their strong traditions of regional autonomy, many provincial cities looked on Paris with suspicion and resentment, and though federalism generally had its roots in local politics and local power struggles, the federalist authorities were united in the use of a strongly anti-Parisian political discourse.[64] In particular, they saw the Paris sansculottes as a threat to the stability which they craved and as a form of anarchy that put property rights and Republican unity at risk. Paris in their eyes was not the city of virtue and patriotism: rather it was the city of murder and violence, of Marat and Hébert, of anarchic crowds and uncontained killing. Paris was the city that had produced the wild, untamed blood-letting of the September Massacres; and Paris was now the city which, through its undisciplined sections and the influence of the Commune, was challenging the sovereign authority of the Convention. The federalist leaders, in short, saw themselves as the true Republicans, and they took overt pleasure in emphasizing the solidity of their provincial roots. At Barcelonnette they

[62] Ibid. 11–49. [63] Ibid. 10–11.
[64] A. Forrest, 'Le fédéralisme et l'image de la Révolution parisienne', in Vovelle, *Image de la Révolution française*, i. 68–71.

Alan Forrest

denounced Paris as 'cette cité orgueilleuse qui a trop longtemps abusé de son pouvoir';[65] and a number of cities took up the cry that central government should be moved away from Paris to a genuinely central location, like Bourges. The Girondin Guadet urged the Convention in May 1793 to convoke all the *suppléans* to Bourges, where an alternative assembly could be held in readiness in the likely event that Paris threatened the integrity and liberty of deputies. His motion was defeated, but it was a fair reflection of provincial apprehensions and helps explain the degree of preparedness that already existed in the provinces when the Jacobins launched their assault on power.[66]

If federalism was anti-Parisian in tone, it was rarely, in any literal sense, federalist in its ambitions. Individual towns were much too ingrained in their own traditions to co-operate effectively with others, and if cities in revolt against Paris felt sufficiently vulnerable to seek alliances with neighbouring authorities, there was no plan to break down the unity of the Nation in favour of regional states or provinces. In the south-east, it is true, Marseille enjoyed such a firm reputation as the regional bulwark of Republicanism that many of the towns and villages of the neighbouring region rushed to pledge their support, trusting implicitly in Marseille's political judgement, denouncing the Jacobins in refrain to Marseille's denunciations and meekly converting their clubs into popular sections at Marseille's behest.[67] But that level of support was rare, even among the people of the cities' immediate hinterland. Similarly, no one city claimed to speak for all those in revolt or generalized its particular grievances into those of a whole province. At most they would emphasize the scale of discontent to boost their own morale, claiming that sixty-six or sixty-nine or even seventy-two departments shared their principles. Or they would indulge themselves in a regional rhetoric that suggested the power of collective strength. Arbanière in Toulouse talked of the 'torrent' that was being formed by 'les eaux de la Garonne, du Gers, de l'Aude, du Tarn, du Lot, de la Corrèze, de l'Ariège, de l'Hérault,

---

[65] Archives Départementales Rhône, 1L375, Adresse des autorités constituées du District et de la ville de Barcelonnette (Basses-Alpes), 25 June 1793.

[66] Convention Nationale, 18 May 1793.

[67] Cameron, *Revolution in Marseille*, 35–7; A. Forrest, 'Le Mouvement fédéraliste dans le Midi de la France', *Provence historique*, 148 (1987), 189–90.

de la Durance et du Rhône pour engloutir cette monstrueuse ville de Paris'.[68] But it remained at the level of rhetoric. Little was done to link forces or to present a common front against Paris. And nothing was done to take advantage of peasant insurrection in the west. Bordeaux, for instance, was careful to dissociate itself from any links with the Vendée and kept its troops in the Vendean campaign. Most of the federalist cities continued to help the national war effort.[69]

In the heartlands of rural counter-revolution there was a more conscious appeal to popular tradition and popular culture, a more specific link between counter-revolution and regional identity. Here the French Republic was viewed with intense suspicion, as an intruder in a familiar and trusted milieu where traditions were jealously defended and a strong degree of autarky was maintained. In many of these areas, and most especially the west, local tradition assumed the cloak of Catholicism as communities looked to their faith as a source of protection against an external threat. Refractory priests were welcomed and sheltered as part of the traditional community, while their constitutional replacements were shunned and rejected. *Chouan* soldiers were blessed before they left their villages for action, just as families would say prayers and shed tears for their sons when they were called up for military service by the state.[70] Church services and religious festivals remained central to everyday life, and the police knew very well that even men on the run—refractories and army deserters, bandits and Vendean soldiers—could often be surprised at mass on Christmas Eve or at a *fête votive* in the village.[71] For the foot-soldiers of the counter-revolution remained what the Republican troops could never claim to be—the defenders of their own local *pays*, a *pays* which, in the majority of cases, they had never left. Among them were many who had thrown in their lot with the *Chouans* out of deep community loyalty rather than out of fear or terrorization. Their songs, sung plaintively in Breton after the hard labour of the day's fighting, reflected both their rejection of

[68] M. Lyons, *Révolution et Terreur à Toulouse* (Toulouse, 1980), 67.
[69] W. Edmonds, 'Federalism and urban revolt in France in 1793', *Journal of Modern History*, 55 (1983), 26.
[70] J. Waquet, 'La Société civile devant l'insoumission et la désertion à l'époque de la conscription militaire, 1798–1814', *Bibliothèque de l'École des Chartes*, 126 (1968), 191. [71] Forrest, *Conscripts and Deserters*, 230–2.

the state and their fierce pride in their own Breton traditions. They sang of their native Brittany and of its dying culture, of its crosses and *pardons,* its vigils and confessions; they condemned the vandalism of the Republic and the destruction wreaked by its armies.[72] For them the nationalist discourse of the Revolution had little meaning: their consuming passion was for their *pays* rather than for France as a whole. And whatever the economic and social divisions which helped motivate their revolt, its Breton character cannot be brought into doubt. Theirs remains the true voice of counter-revolutionary regionalism.

[72] C. Emsley, 'Nationalist Rhetoric and Nationalist Sentiment in Revolutionary France', in O. Dann and J. Dinwiddy (eds.), *Nationalism in the Age of the French Revolution* (London, 1988), 51.

8

The French Revolution and Europe

T. C. W. BLANNING

THE last essay in this volume also has the most general title, its
generosity of scope posing a problem of focus. Bearing in mind
that Albert Sorel managed to write well over a million words in
the eight volumes of his *L'Europe et la Révolution française*,[1] it is
clear not only that I must be highly selective but also that even
then the breadth and depth of analysis that can be achieved in
an essay of this length can only be limited. I have decided not to
conduct a country-by-country tour of Europe, enumerating as I
go the Revolution's achievements in the manner of Leporello's
immense list of Don Giovanni's conquests—although my own
treatment, I suspect, would make it seem more like Ko-Ko's
little list of society offenders. There never has been a shortage of
historians seeking—and, of course, finding—ideological soul-
mates, whether conservative, nationalist, liberal, or radical. I
have written about this exercise on more than one occasion,
albeit not to everyone's liking.[2] Nor do I intend to deal with the
French Revolution and Europe at the level of what might be
called 'high intellect', by which I mean the way in which the
intellectual élites of Europe responded to or reacted against the
Revolution. Although there is no general survey, there is an
ample sufficiency of national studies, many of them of high
quality.

Instead, I have decided to take advantage of the opportunity
presented by this essay to try to redirect attention to a dimension
which was of central importance to contemporaries—and

[1] Albert Sorel, *L'Europe et la Révolution française*, 8 vols. (Paris, 1885–1905).
[2] T. C. W. Blanning, 'The German Jacobins and the French Revolution',
Historical Journal, 23, 4 (1980).

indeed to nineteenth-century historians—but which in more recent times has faded from view until it has become almost invisible. I refer to power politics, the intercourse between states, conducted sometimes by diplomacy but more usually, during the revolutionary-napoleonic period, by war. There is no space here and no need to review the richly various directions taken by revolutionary studies in this century. The heterogeneity of current historiography has been demonstrated very well by the previous essays in this collection. It can safely be said, however, that the international dimension of the Revolution, in the sense of international relations, is not so much neglected as ignored. To confirm the accuracy of that observation, one need only look at the many otherwise excellent general histories of the Revolution published in recent years. The last to give anything like adequate attention to foreign policy was that of Georges Lefebvre—and even he relied largely on Sorel.[3]

The proposition which lies at the heart of this essay is that the French Revolution and power politics were born together. I do not believe that I am creating an Aunt Sally when I say that French Revolution is commonly regarded as endogenous. The prerevolutionary crisis, the outbreak of the Revolution, and its first three years are all presented within a framework which is exclusively French. Of course, it is recognized that the Revolution went to war on 20 April 1792 and that 'the war revolutionized the Revolution' but this external force erupts on to the scene as a *deus ex machine*—or rather as a *diabolus ex machina*. The interaction is then recognized, but the two entities—the Revolution and the foreign intrusion—are kept conceptually separate. These remarks are not intended to be the prelude to a resurrection of the 'Atlantic' thesis advanced by R. R. Palmer, Jacques Godechot, Franklin Ford, and others.[4] I do not believe that the French Revolution was just one episode in the 'age of the democratic revolution' and am fully persuaded of its unique power. What I shall argue is that right from the start, from the prerevolution,

[3] Georges Lefebvre, *The French Revolution*, 2 vols. (New York, 1962, 1964). These are translations of a work first published in 1951.
[4] R. R. Palmer, *The Age of the Democratic Revolution*, 2 vols. (Princeton, NJ, 1959, 1964); Jacques Godechot, *La Grande Nation: L'Expansion révolutionnaire dans le monde 1789–1799*, 2 vols. (Paris, 1956); Franklin Ford, *Europe, 1780–1830* (London, 1970). I have discussed their views in *The French Revolution in Germany: Occupation and Resistance in the Rhineland 1792–1802* (Oxford, 1983), 11–12.

the French Revolution and European power politics were intertwined and that their relationship developed dialectically. I shall try to show that adopting a perspective of the Revolution which is international rather than French can be enlightening. In what follows—and, indeed, what has gone before—the need to be concise may well give a dogmatic impression, but I do not intend to suggest that this is the only valid approach to the Revolution. I am all in favour of pluralism and admire and envy the achievements of all the other methods employed; I can even grasp, albeit rather dimly, the sense of applying semiological tools to the study of the Revolution.

Expressed most generally, the Revolution and European power politics could never be separate simply because France was a great power. More specifically, not the least important force shaping the nature and course of the Revolution was the fact that at the time that the Old Regime was collapsing, Europe too was sliding into chaos. In August 1787, as a belated reaction to Catherine the Great's unilateral annexation of the Crimea four years earlier, the Turks declared war on Russia. That activated the defensive alliance between Russia and Austria concluded in 1781. Joseph II recognized at once the *casus foederis*, although he did not declare war on the Turks until February 1788. By that time, the certainty that Austria would be involved in a Balkan war had allowed Frederick William II to invade and conquer the United Provinces, to restore the Stadtholder William V and to destroy the existing alliance with France and to replace it with dependence on Prussia and Great Britain. In July 1788 Gustavus III of Sweden launched an attack on Russia in the hope of regaining the Baltic empire lost at the beginning of the century. With the Russians diverted in the north, the Turks were able to throw their full weight against the hapless Joseph II, thus precipitating a crisis in the Habsburg Monarchy which led to the revolt and independence of Belgium, and to apparently imminent revolt in Galicia and Hungary. Also taking advantage of Russian preoccupations, the Poles began a bid for national renewal and independence. In August 1789, Frederick William II of Prussia decided to invade Bohemia in the following spring, in alliance with the Poles and the Turks. With the Habsburg Monarchy apparently in its death throes, the Spanish and the Sardinians made ready to pick over the carcass in Italy. In short, as the revolutionary crisis developed in France, all Europe was ablaze with war or rumours of war, from the North Sea to the Black Sea, from the Baltic to the Mediterranean. Insularity saved the British from direct or immediate involvement in this imbroglio, but even they were affected eventually by the wave of bellicosity. They nearly went to war with Spain over Nootka Sound and nearly went to war with Russia in 1791 over Ochakov—not the first nor the last time that Britain has offered combat over places of uncertain location and even less certain importance.

It is into this international maelstrom that the French Revolution needs to be inserted, not the other way round. For Europe, what was most important about 1789 was not the eruption of a new ideological force but the final collapse of an old power. It was no sudden catastrophe. Ever since the disasters of the Seven Years War the decline of French power and prestige had been plainly and painfully evident. Exclusion from the affairs of Eastern and Central Europe was dramatized by the partition of Poland in 1772, the Russian guarantee of the Peace of Teschen in 1779, the annexation of the Crimea in 1783, and Frederick the Great's formation of the League of Princes in 1785, just to name the more humiliating revelations of French impotence. What little prestige was regained by participation in the American War was compromised by French failures during its last year in India, the West Indies, and at Gibraltar, the correspondingly unsatisfactory nature of the treaty of Versailles, and the swift post-war recovery of British trade with the American colonies.

So for Europe, the importance of 1787 was not the meeting of the Assembly of Notables or the fall of Calonne, but the events in the United Provinces. This was not just a domestic dispute between the country's endlessly warring factions: as contemporaries saw it, nothing less than the future control of the world was at stake. If the French alliance with the Dutch of 1785 had become permanent, if the French protégés had taken permanent control of the country, if the French had gained mastery of the Channel approaches and the Dutch navy, if the French had been able to add Dutch bases at the Cape and in Ceylon to their existing possessions in the Indian Ocean, then it could only have been a matter of time before the French did to the British in

India what they had done already in America. The invasion of
1787, carried out by the Prussians but to the exclusive benefit of
the British, put an end to these dreams once and for all. By the
time the French were able to regain control of the United
Provinces, this time by direct conquest in the winter of 1794–5, it
was too late: the British had consolidated their hold on the
world overseas and could not now be dislodged.

The French Revolution did not precipitate a crisis in Europe: it
was part of that crisis. Of course, many of the forces and
accidents making for the collapse of the Old Regime were
peculiar to France and unaffected by shifts in international
power. At the risk of provoking the scorn of specialists in the
domestic history of France, however, I venture the suggestion
that it might be fruitful to reconsider the nature of kingship in
prerevolutionary France. The first task of the king of France, and
indeed of any other country, was to see to the country's
security, to conduct its foreign policy, and to command its
armed forces. It was when monarchs failed in that elemental
task that their thrones tottered. George III's problems in the
early 1708s and Joseph II's problems at the end of that decade
were both created and solved by international relations. Similarly,
in France the sharpest wedge driven between state and society
was the common belief that French interests had been sacrificed
by the Austrian alliance of 1756 and had then been systematically
disregarded during the next three decades. The discovery in
1787 that Louis XVI was no longer capable of maintaining
French interests even in Western Europe was a catastrophic and
possibly mortal blow to his regime's credibility. I shall return
later to this question of the relationship between failure abroad
and instability at home.

Before I do so, I need to return to the international crisis of the
late 1780s. The main contribution of the Revolution was to
withdraw France from the European states-system for the best
part of five years, from 1787 until 1792. Of course, her absence
could only be temporary, as the more sharp-sighted of contemporary observers appreciated, but the effects were not temporary.
On the contrary, it was between 1787 and 1792 that a decisive
and permanent shift in the configuration of power in Europe
took place. I have suggested already that the decisive victory for
Great Britain in the struggle for control of the world overseas

was achieved in 1787, by proxy. A similar development occurred in Central and Eastern Europe. Of course, if one takes a properly macroscopic view of this development, one can see that its origins date back far beyond the eighteenth century and that it is part of that waxing and waning of empires which defy satisfactory explanation.

However deep-seated the causes, however protracted the transition, there come certain critical periods when the action suddenly accelerates and irreversible shifts occur. The period after 1787 was one such, perhaps the most important in the modern period. For it was then that Eastern Europe was reconstructed in a manner which in broad outline was to remain permanent for a century or more. Nothing could have suited the Russians better than a total elimination of French influence, for France had been the traditional ally of all of their three rivals for the domination of the East—Sweden, Poland, and the Ottoman Empire. Sweden was crushed definitively in 1788, never to try again. The defeat of the Turks took longer, required Austrian assistance, and was less final, for they did try again, but it also marked a decisive shift. The treaty of Jassy of 1792 confirmed Russia's possession of the Crimea and advanced her frontier to the Dniester, thus establishing her as the major Black Sea Power and opening the way for the domination of the Balkans. The third traditional rival, Poland, was expunged from the map of Europe in the second and third partitions of 1793 and 1795 respectively, which also advanced the Russian Empire's frontier more than 300 miles to the west.

By this time the war in the west was well under way and was providing further evidence of the interdependence between events inside and outside France. The collapse of French power that was the French Revolution allowed Russia to achieve hegemony of Eastern Europe; yet that same hegemony ensured the Revolution's survival. For Russia's move against Poland after the conclusion of the Turkish war came just as Austria and Prussia were preparing to intervene in France. The war in the west began on 20 April 1792; Russian troops invaded Poland on 18 May.[5] As a result, the two allies entered the war with one eye on what was happening in the east and one arm tied behind

[5] R. H. Lord, *The Second Partition of Poland* (Cambridge, Mass., 1915), 280.

their backs. It was not long before the opportunity presented by Poland persuaded the Prussians to disengage from the war and eventually to accept a separate peace with revolutionary France in 1795.

They were encouraged to do so by the fact that they had achieved their war aims. They had gone to war to make territorial gains, not at the expense of their enemy, France, but at the expense of their ally, Poland,[6] and that—the *non plus ultra* of Old Regime power politics—was just what they got, through participation in the second and third partitions, which increased Prussia's territory by more than 50 per cent. Quite apart from the intrinsic value of the territory acquired, this dismemberment confirmed that a centuries-long struggle for control of the Baltic littoral had been settled in Prussia's favour. Knowledge of Poland's unhappy history during the past two centuries naturally tends to obscure appreciation of the threat Poland was thought to pose to Prussia. It was real enough: East Prussia had been under Polish suzerainty from 1466 until 1660; until the partitions, the Polish–Lithuanian Empire was vastly greater in extent, stretching as it did from the Baltic almost to the Black Sea; and its resources were similarly greater, especially when linked to the prosperous and economically advanced Electorate of Saxony, as it was from 1697 until 1763.

Although the twenty years separating the death of Frederick the Great and the defeats at Jena and Auerstedt are usually regarded as a period of ossification and decline, it is worth remembering that more territory was added to Prussia during the reign of Frederick William II, usually depicted as the gross voluptuary who squandered his inheritance, than during the reign of his uncle.[7] Never mind the width, feel the quality, one might object; but in the crude currency of power politics, width counted for a lot. Perhaps it was more by luck than judgement, but Frederick William II did stabilize Prussia's position as a great power and also, by accepting compensation through secularization, helped to initiate the dissolution of the Holy Roman Empire. With the advantage of hindsight, we can see that Prussia's eventual conquest of Germany was made possible by

---

[6] Ibid. 237.
[7] Gerd Heinrich, *Geschichte Preussens: Staat und Dynastie* (Frankfurt-on-Main/Berlin/Vienna, 1981), 263.

the settlement of 1815. Of course, those crucial gains at the Congress of Vienna could not have been made without the extraordinary exertions during the wars of liberation; but the drama of the defeat of 1806 and the revival which followed have obscured the significance of the events of the 1790s.

For Russia and Prussia, therefore, the elimination of French influence in Eastern Europe brought the opportunity to achieve a decisive shift in the distribution of power. Their victims numbered not only the Swedes, Poles, and Turks but also the Austrians. The transformation of France from Old Regime ally to revolutionary enemy left the Habsburgs dependent first on Russia and then, after 1792, on Prussia, and consequently unable to resist effectively their aggrandizement. The obvious answer was a resurrection of the old alliance with Great Britain. The British did indeed oppose Russian gains at the expense of the Turks and the partitions of Poland, but their ability to intervene in Eastern Europe was limited by geography and their will was eroded by Prussian services in the United Provinces and in the war against France. The new constellation of forces, exacerbated by some flat-footed diplomacy, left the Austrians with little room for manœuvre. Excluded from the second partition altogether, from the third they took territory which was more a liability than an asset.

What I have been trying to suggest in the first part of this essay is that it was not French strength unleashed by the Revolution which affected Europe so profoundly but French weakness. From the European perspective, not only at the time but throughout the subsequent century and even beyond, what was most important about the French Revolution was not its principles but its elimination of France from the European states-system during a crucial phase of its development. That allowed a fundamental and permanent shift of power in the world overseas in favour of Great Britain, and in Eastern Europe in favour of Russia and Prussia.

Europe repaid the compliment by exercising an equally profound influence on the development of the Revolution inside France. Most importantly, the war stopped the modernization of France in its tracks. In the course of 1789–91 the National Assembly had set about creating a governmental, administrative, social, and economic system which, of course, would be free and equal (or rather meritocratic) but above all would *work*. The legislative programme was very similar to that introduced some time previously by the more enlightened autocrats elsewhere in Europe, the main difference being that, as an elected body, the National Assembly could afford to be a good deal more absolutist in its pretensions and effective in its achievements.

This exercise was brought to a halt by the intransigence of the king and the ambitions of the Brissotin Left. Both of these extremes turned the Revolution outwards, diverting it from its proper concerns at home. The court did this by appealing to the Old Regime powers for counter-revolutionary intervention, the Brissotins did it by launching a drive for war. As a result, the Revolution fell into the hands of the backwoodsmen, preaching the rhetoric of radicalism but in reality deeply conservative, especially in their attitudes to social structure and economics. The Revolution was not so much 'blown off course', as Furet and Richet put it,[8] it was shipwrecked. Out of the chaos created by the Revolution's adoption of an aggressive foreign policy came a France which was even more firmly anchored to a land-based economy, land-based society, and land-based values than in the past. The development was partly the result of conscious policy but mainly the result of the generation of warfare which now began. The economic effects of the Revolution upon France are discussed by Louis Bergeron elsewhere in this volume.[9] Certainly, they are such a contentious issue that a consensus among historians is hardly to be expected. I can only advance my own opinion that François Crouzet's general conclusion still holds good, namely: 'France was not disastrously behind [in the 1780s], and the Industrial Revolution might well have taken off there with only a few years' delay in relation to England. But the "national catastrophe" which the French Revolution and the twenty years war meant to the French economy would intensify the discrepancy and make it irremediable.'[10]

[8] François Furet and Denis Richet, *The French Revolution* (London, 1970), ch. 5.
[9] See also Louis Bergeron, 'L'Économie française sous le feu de la Révolution politique et sociale', in Pierre Léon (ed.), *Histoire économique et sociale du monde*, iii. *Inerties et Révolutions (1730–1740)*, ed. Louis Bergeron (Paris, 1978).
[10] François Crouzet, 'England and France in the Eighteenth Century: A Comparative Analysis of Two Economic Growths', in R. M. Hartwell (ed.), *The Causes of the Industrial Revolution in England* (London, 1967), 173. I have discussed

There is no time and no need for me to rehearse the arguments about the economic impact of the war. I do propose, however, to look at the political consequences, which are not so often considered these days. The first proper parliament of the Revolution was the Legislative Assembly (the Constituent Assembly, after all, was just the rump of the Estates-General) which met for the first time on 1 October 1791. Almost at once, a faction led by Brissot began a drive for war with Austria, as part of its plan to unmask the treason of the court, to push the Revolution left, and to bring themselves to power. The need to convince the Assembly and public opinion that war was not just inevitable, not just necessary, but positively desirable led to psychological extremism. The Brissotins had to present the impending conflict as a terminal struggle between good and evil. In doing so, they built the scaffold on which they themselves would eventually perish. The Terror is sometimes presented as a temporary aberration, an exceptional response to exceptional conditions in Year II. Yet the necessary psychological conditions were being created much earlier—two years earlier, indeed—when the Brissotins were stoking up the Legislative Assembly's nationalism, Austrophobia, and nihilism.[11]

All three of those explosive forces lay deep within the collective revolutionary psyche, but they could not have been brought to the surface with such explosive force without development elsewhere in Europe. The war of 1792 was not inevitable; all that was inevitable was France's eventual reassertion as a great power. Given the profound unpopularity of the Austrian alliance, however, and its personification in the shape of Marie Antoinette, the foreign dimension could not have been kept out of domestic politics, even if the revolutionaries had wanted to. With the unwitting co-operation of the Old Regime powers and their maladroit attempt to bully the Revolution into submission, the war party in the Legislative Assembly was able to direct the sense of betrayal and humiliation which had been festering since 1756 not only against Austria but also—and indeed primarily—against the court.

this point in *The French Revolution: Aristocrats versus Bourgeois?* (London, 1987), 49–56.

[11] T. C. W. Blanning, *The Origins of the French Revolutionary Wars* (London, 1986), 111.

By playing on the deputies' pride, prejudice, and paranoia with dazzling eloquence, the Brissotin hawks had their way, but in the process they had dealt not only the Revolution but their country a deadly blow. For the drive to war brought an end to pluralism and the criminalization of dissent; it set in train a process of polarization which has burdened French politics to this day. The Brissotin deputy Gensonné told the Assembly on 26 December 1791 that in the good old days of 1789, it had been possible for men of good faith to join all manner of parties—but no more; now there could be only two parties: for the Revolution, and against it, right and wrong.[12] Of course, the counter-revolution was not invented in the autumn of 1791 and, of course, France would have been deeply divided even without the war (the antics of the émigrés were sufficient to ensure that), but I do believe that it was the war—or rather the drive for war—which turned disagreements into divisions.

A case in point is the fate of the Church. The Civil Constitution of the Clergy, and even the oath of loyalty required, might just have been absorbed without civil war. The non-jurors and their supporters were, after all, protected in theory by the guarantees of religious liberty contained in the Declaration of the Rights of Man and the Citizen. At first, it looked even as though the National Assembly might respect it: on 7 May 1791 it confirmed that nonjuring priests would be allowed to hire church buildings for their own ceremonies and even stated that they would be allowed to celebrate Mass in constitutional churches.[13] But the drive for war identified the nonjuring clergy as traitors—the enemy within conspiring with the enemy without. Now the persecuting decrees came thick and fast, as the revolutionaries moved from what was really only a Josephist programme into the uncharted territory of a state attack on religion. Within two years, Notre Dame was a Temple of Reason, violent dechristianization was under way and between 30,000 and 40,000 refractory clergy had fled into exile. Somewhere between 2,000 and 5,000 of the less nimble were slaughtered during the course of the Terror and many thousands more were imprisoned. Anticlerical and anti-Christian

[12] *Archives parlementaires de 1787 à 1860: Recueil complet des débats législatifs et politiques des chambres françaises*, 127 vols. (Paris, 1879–1913), xxxvi. 406.
[13] John McManners, *The French Revolution and the Church* (London, 1969), 61.

atrocities neither began nor ended with the Terror: whenever the Revolution lurched to the left, as it did following the *coup d'état* of Fructidor in 1797, for example, another bout followed. I do not need to spell out the problems which this caused for the Revolution at home and abroad—and for France ever since.[14]

The Manichaean approach to politics induced by the war also led to other extremist acts and policies, notably the execution of the king and queen and the repression of the Vendée, which produced a degree of polarization, both social and regional, that became a permanent and destabilizing force in French political life. It would be, of course, unacceptably reductionist to blame it all on the war. Sectarian violence in the Rhône valley, for example, began long before the war was even a twinkle in Brissot's eye and would have continued without international conflict. But of all the polarizing forces in revolutionary France, the war was the most ubiquitous and the most powerful. Moreover, it produced polarization not just between revolutionaries and counter-revolutionaries, but also between different kinds of revolutionaries. There were many possible views of what the Revolution actually stood for, but only one that could be considered correct at any particular time; all the others had to be regarded as treasonable—and dealt with accordingly.

The end of pluralism brought the politics of *coup d'état*. The party which believes it has a monopoly of political virtue and which therefore sees its opponents as enemies of the Revolution is a party which feels authorized to do anything. Without wishing to downgrade the importance of the social and economic grievances of the Paris crowd—who would dare to do that?—I have to say that it seems to me that each of the violent changes of regime which occurred during the 1790s was largely the result of the war. The most important—the *journée* of 10 August 1792—was part of the crisis unleashed by the disastrous opening to the war, the imminent Austro-Prussian invasion and the duke of Brunswick's manifesto (news of which arrived in Paris on 1 August). The Brissotin regime fell at the beginning of

---

[14] For the domestic dimension, see ibid. *passim*, and for the foreign reaction, see my *French Revolution in Germany*, ch. 6, and my essay on 'The Role of Religion in European Counter-Revolution, 1789–1815', in Derek Beales and Geoffrey Best (eds.), *History, Society and the Churches: Essays in Honour of Owen Chadwick* (Cambridge, 1985).

June 1793, following yet another collapse at the front and the renewed threat of invasion. The revolutionary dictatorship established by Robespierre and the Montagne in the name of military necessary was destroyed on 9 Thermidor (27 July 1794) after the victory of Fleurus had rendered it unnecessary. The Directory succumbed to General Bonaparte not least because of the discredit inflicted by the defeats of 1799. The Bourbons were restored not by any shift in political culture but by the victories of the allied armies.

Persistent political instability was not the only domestic wound inflicted by the war. The wild optimism and nihilism of the rhetoric employed by the Brissotin hawks during their campaign for war had raised expectations so high that nothing less than total victory would suffice. This was one of the penalties for conducting foreign policy in public. The orators who played to the gallery in the Manège and to the public outside were concerned less with rational argument than with exploiting uncompromising emotions. And woe betide anyone who argued for moderation or compromise in the excited atmosphere thus created. The few warnings that the war would be long, difficult, and unpredictable in its effects were blown away by the gale of bellicosity. The Brissotins did not create nationalism, but it was greatly intensified by the war they engineered with its help. Once that particular genie was out of the bottle, only total victory or total defeat could put it back.

This popular and populist war brought militarization, by which I mean the elevation of military virtues, the permeation of civilian life with military values, and the subordination of political objectives and interests to those of the army. Prussia has often been regarded as the epitome of militarism but in fact it was revolutionary France which became the most militarized state in Europe. The most chilling expression of militarism in this period was the declaration of total war on 23 August 1793:

Dès ce moment jusqu'à celui où les ennemis auront été chassés du territoire de la République, tous les Français sont en réquisition permanente pour le service des armées.

Les jeunes gens iront au combat; les hommes mariés forgeront les armes et transporteront les subsistances; les femmes feront des tentes, des habits, et serviront dans les hôpitaux; les enfants mettront le vieux linge en charpie; les vieillards se feront porter sur les places publiques, pour exciter le courage des guerriers, prêcher la haine des rois et l'unité de la République.[15]

The invasion of the civilian sphere by the military did not happen overnight, but it did happen quite quickly. When General Lafayette or General Dumouriez got out of step with the civilian government in Paris, in 1792 and 1793 respectively, they were obliged to defect to the enemy. When General Bonaparte got out of step with the civilian government in Paris, he first ignored it—and then took it over. Together with the militarization of public opinion, this supersession of civilian interests created the Revolution's most intractable and ultimately fatal problem: perpetual warfare. Between April 1792, when the war began, and April 1814, when the allied armies occupied Paris, forced Napoleon to abdicate, and put Louis XVIII on the throne, France was at peace for less than a year. If the war 'revolutionized the Revolution', it also destroyed it. That is why the best pictorial illustration for any history of the period is not such favourites as David's *Marat* or even Gros's *Napoleon at Eylau*, but Goya's *Saturn Devouring One of his Children*.

The reasons for the longevity of the war were, of course, manifold, but the most important dates right back to those few years in the late 1780s and early 1790s because it was then that there developed that mutual misunderstanding which proceeded to govern relations between the Revolution and the rest of Europe. It was then that stereotypes were created which bore little relation to reality, leading to the formation of attitudes which were based on correspondingly erroneous assumptions. To say that great powers are incapable of appreciating each other's strengths may be a banal truism, but it is one which is seldom taken into account by historians and even less by politicians. I have written about what I call the 'Coppelia effect' elsewhere and shall not belabour the point again.[16] In the present context, what is important is that its effect was intensified by the fact that the French Revolution erupted and developed during an international crisis, indeed was part of that crisis.

---

[15] Article 1 of the National Convention's decree proclaiming the *levée en masse*.
[16] Blanning, *Origins of the French Revolutionary Wars*, 73, 103, 116, 209.

As a result both the Old Regime powers and the revolutionaries arrived at what proved to be a wholly erroneous assessment of each other's capabilities. They saw all the problems and weaknesses of their opponents but very few of the assets and strengths. To the Old Regime, revolutionary France seemed to be paralysed by political instability, social anarchy, economic dislocation, and financial bankruptcy. It was a country which could safely be left to stew in its own juice until 1792, while the affairs of Eastern Europe were being sorted out. It could then be bullied and harassed with impunity, for it was deemed unable to strike back. No matter if it did—the Prussians had encountered a patriot army in the United Provinces in 1787, and it had run away; the Austrians had encountered a patriot army in Belgium in 1790, and it too had run away. The French patriots were expected to behave no differently.

The error made by the revolutionaries was just as egregious. Their review of Europe found only Old Regimes apparently in their death throes, decadent feudal relics struggling to control restive subjects seeking to emulate the French. They looked at the civil war in the United Provinces, at the Belgian revolt, at the other problems in the Habsburg Monarchy, at the events in Poland, and at all the other disturbances, and they drew quite a different lesson. They were encouraged to do so by the large number of political refugees in Paris, especially the Belgians and the Dutch among them, who were quick with assurances that as soon as a French army loomed into view, their oppressed compatriots would rise in its support.

Consequently, both sides began the war confident of a quick victory. The main reason for their inability to achieve it was their inability to achieve a decisive victory. That may seem an astonishing claim in view of the great roll-call of revolutionary victories—Valmy, Jemappes, Fleurus, Marengo, Hohenlinden, Ulm, Austerlitz, Jena, Auerstedt, Friedland, Wagram, just to mention the more spectacular. Yet the obvious question is not often posed: if each of these was so overwhelming a victory, why did there have to be so many of them?

The answer lies, of course, in the simple fact that the decisive quality of any battle is more a subjective than an objective concept. The decision-makers of the Old Regime just refused to believe that all was lost, even after the most catastrophic of defeats. They had good reason for their obstinacy, which only a close reading of the military history of the period will reveal. The Austrians, in particular, kept coming back for more, rather like those infuriating lead-weighted toys which always right themselves after being knocked over, with the same fatuous grin painted on their faces. Napoleon observed contemptuously that the Habsburgs were always one idea and one army behind the rest of Europe, but—as Albert Sorel remarked—they always had an army and they always had an idea.[17] It was Napoleon who ran out of both.

What kept the Habsburgs plugging on was the cheering knowledge that every now and again they won. They lost at Jemappes in 1792 but they won at Neerwinden in 1793; they lost in Italy in 1796, but they won in Germany in the same year; they lost at Marengo and Hohenlinden in 1800, but had won at Stockach and Ostrach in 1799; they lost at Wagram in 1809, but had won at Aspern earlier in the campaign. Occasional military success was reflected in the peace settlements. At Campo Formio in 1797 the Austrians had to cede their Belgian possessions and the duchy of Milan, but they received in exchange Venice and a large part of its Adriatic empire. Even after the crushing defeats of 1805 they kept their Polish territories and Salzburg. The same point could be made with even more emphasis about the Prussians. When they left the war in 1795, they did not feel that they had been defeated by revolutionary France: on the contrary, in terms of acquisition of territory, they had done wonderfully well.

Once again, we can see that the real problem was not the Revolution's strength but its weakness. Even in its Napoleonic version, it was never able to convince Old Regime Europe that it had come to stay. Its successes, however dazzling, were thought to be ephemeral—just one more push, its enemies thought, and down it would come. In the event, many more pushes were needed, but in the end they were right. Although the operation took twenty-three years longer than had been

[17] Kurt Peball, 'Zum Kriegsbild der österreichischen Armee und seiner geschichtlichen Bedeutung in den Kriegen gegen die Französische Revolution und Napoleon I in den Jahren von 1792 bis 1815', in Wolfgang v. Groote and Klaus-Jürgen Müller (eds.), *Napoleon und das Militärwesen seiner Zeit* (Freiburg, 1968), 139.

hoped or expected, the allies did eventually achieve their war aims. This is not always appreciated, because the counter-revolutionary nature of the war of 1792 is so often exaggerated. The Prussians and Austrians did not go to war in 1792 to restore the Old Regime, they went to war to induce the revolutionaries to maintain a constitutional settlement which would keep France monarchical but weak (a kind of western version of Poland) and also, of course, to gain territory. That was exactly what they got in 1815.

By that time both sides were poorer but wiser. They had had to learn the error of their ways in a school where discipline was exceptionally brutal and the terms were exceptionally long. Paradoxically, the revolutionaries proved to be much less adaptable than the Old Regime, even after many painful visits to the headmaster's study. When Napoleon asked: 'What people will wish to return to the arbitrary rule of Prussia once it has tasted the benefits of a wise and liberal administration?'[18] or when he blamed his misfortunes in Russia on the fortuitous intervention of the weather, he was showing that it was not only the Bourbons who had proved unteachable.

Both the revolutionaries and Napoleon proved to be that much less adaptable because they were that much more ambitious. They were encouraged to undertake the conquest of Europe by the belief that what they had to offer—liberty, equality, and fraternity in the case of the revolutionaries and 'wise and liberal administration' in the case of Napoleon—would prove irresistibly attractive. That might well have been the case, if that was what they really had offered, although even then loyalty to the values and institutions of the Old Regime might have proved too strong. In the event, what they brought was not liberation but exploitation. It was forced on them by a problem as simple as it was insuperable: numbers. Revolutionary-napoleonic France suffered from both an excess and a shortage: its armies were too big for a war of liberation, but its demographic base was too small to support an empire based on permanent occupation.

The size of the armies—somewhere between 800,000 and a million men were under arms by the summer of 1794—and the

---

[18] Elisabeth Fehrenbach, *Vom Ancien Régime zum Wiener Kongress* (Munich/Vienna, 1981), 77.

inability of the revolutionaries to supply them from French resources meant that the war was of necessity a war of exploitation from the moment the first French soldier crossed into foreign territory and proceeded to loot to stay alive. For all their good intentions and liberationist rhetoric, what the French brought for the ordinary Belgian, German, Italian, Spaniard, or whomever was levies, requisitions, forced labour, looting, and all the other horrors of war.[19] As it turned out, there could have been no less appropriate instrument for the propagation of revolutionary ideals than the revolutionary armies. As Robespierre correctly predicted in two celebrated epigrams: 'Personne n'aime les missionnaires armés', and 'On ne peut jamais fonder la liberté par l'emploi d'une force étrangère.'[20]

The high-water mark of liberationism was quickly reached, with the celebrated 'fraternity' decree of 19 November 1792 promising assistance to any people seeking to regain its liberty—and was even more quickly passed. Disappointment with the response from the liberated masses, dramatized by the failure of the elections in Belgium and the Rhineland in early 1793, and disappointment with the course of the war during the winter and spring of 1793, prompted the revolutionaries to adopt a much more hard-headed attitude towards the rest of Europe. The decree of 19 November was revoked just five months later and on 15 September 1793 the National Convention decreed that henceforth the French armies would renounce all previous 'philanthropic' ideas and 'se conduiront envers les ennemis de la France, de la même manière que les puissances coalisées se conduisent à son égard'.[21] From now on, it was to be a war of conquest and exploitation in theory as well as in practice.

Of course the revolutionaries could not have hoped to rule the great tracts of Europe they had conquered without the co-operation of at least part of the native population. They achieved this, in the short and medium term at least, by their inspired invention of the satellite republic. They were always able to find a sufficient number of locals who preferred the

[19] I have discussed and illustrated this point in 'Occupation and Resistance in Europe in the 1790s', the final chapter of my *French Revolution in Germany*.
[20] Quoted in Blanning, *Origins of the French Revolutionary Wars*, 113, 138.
[21] *Archives Parlementaires*, lxii. 3 and lxxiv. 231.

modicum of independence permitted by the French to the rule of the Old Regime. This was an especially easy task in regions which had been plagued by civil strife in the past—in the United Provinces, in Switzerland, and in parts of Italy. The more intense that strife had been, the more eager were the opposition parties to accept a helping hand from the French to lift them into the driving seat.

Political ambition and a wish to settle old scores were not the only reasons for serving in the satellite republics: some collaborated out a sense of duty to their fellow citizens; many collaborated because they needed a job; a few collaborated out of attachment to the ideals of the Revolution. What they all had in common was dependence on the presence of French armed force; when that was removed—in 1799, for example—the satellite republics fell like ninepins; when it returned, in 1800, they obediently stood up again. This is not to deny their very real achievements, especially in the fields of social, economic, and cultural reform. Their programme of modernization was often, however, fiercely unpopular, especially when it impinged on traditional religious beliefs and ecclesiastical institutions. Moreover, any good will generated was dissipated by the continuing weight of the French military presence. The only groups to have benefited unequivocally and to have been suitably grateful were ethnic or religious minorities: Protestants in Catholic regions, Catholics in Protestant regions, and Jews everywhere.

The satellite republics worked reasonably well so long as the French armies could maintain their dominance and so long as French ambitions were confined to Western and Southern Europe. Strain began to appear when Central Europe was added to the list. This was masked for a while by Napoleon's development of the concept of the satellite republic into the satellite kingdom. When he closed down the Holy Roman Empire he created a dependent class of princely satraps, bound to him personally by his grant of fancy new titles and greatly expanded territories, and kept loyal by their fear of losing what they had and the hope of getting even more. But there was a price to be paid, of course, in the shape of men for Napoleon's army and the money to pay for them. 'The benefits of a wise and liberal administration' which Napoleon had expected to prove so attractive were more than counterbalanced by increased taxation, conscription, and political repression.

The satellite states, whether republican or monarchical in form, eventually foundered on France's inadequate demographic base. When Louis XIV had established—briefly—hegemony in Europe, France was incontestably the most populous state in Europe. By the outbreak of the revolutionary wars, that was no longer the case, thanks to the much faster growth rates achieved by the other major powers in the course of the eighteenth century. As Pierre Goubert observed, in 1789 France's demographic hegemony was over.[22] So the revolutionary-napoleonic bid for a degree of hegemony never even dreamed of by Louis XIV had to be manned by overexertion both at home and in the occupied territories. Belgians had to be used to conquer Germany, Bavarians had to be used to conquer the Habsburg Monarchy, Italians had to be used to conquer Spain—and just about everyone had to be used to conquer Russia. Long before that catastrophe, the strains imposed by almost a quarter-century of overexertion were becoming apparent, not least in the growing restiveness of the subject populations.

However, it was not tax-strikes or anti-conscription riots which put an end to the French Empire, although they certainly accelerated its fall. What brought the revolutionary-napoleonic era to a close was the operation of the European states-system and, in the final section of this essay, we must direct our attention to what seems to me to have been its most important aspect. As before, my starting-point is the crisis of the late 1780s and early 1790s. The most serious failure of understanding which arose from it concerned the relationship between Eastern and Western Europe. As I argued earlier, what had saved the Revolution in the 1790s had been the turmoil in the east. When the Austrians and Prussians went to war in 1792, they were concerned at least as much with Poland as with France. The continuing imbroglio there not only diverted Prussia at a crucial moment but also kept Russia neutral. That this was malevolent neutrality mattered not: Catherine the Great wished to avoid

[22] Pierre Goubert, 'Les Fondements démographiques', in Fernand Braudel and Ernest Labrousse (eds.), *Histoire économique et sociale de la France*, ii. 1660–1789 (Paris, 1970), 20.

joining the German powers in their western intervention for as long as possible, so that she could have a free hand in redrawing the map in the east. It is not much of an exaggeration to say that the Poles saved the Revolution.

Russia was both the most vociferously counter-revolutionary of the great powers and also the last actually to enter the war. That is not difficult to understand. It was of little or no concern to the Russians whether it was the Austrians or the French who dominated the Low Countries, the left bank of the Rhine, or even Italy. So long as that was the limit of revolutionary ambitions, they were content to stay out of the war, digest their massive gains in Poland, and watch with ill-concealed *schaden-freude* as their Prussian and Austrian neighbours exhausted themselves fighting the Revolution. East and West could remain separate.

The situation was transformed at once when General Bonaparte took his expedition to Egypt in 1798. By doing so, he took the West to the East and thus impinged on what the Russians now considered to be a vital zone of interest. As I argued earlier, by the annexation of the Crimea and the acquisitions made at the treaty of Jassy in 1792, Russia had become a major Black Sea power to rival the Turks. The creation of new ports, such as Sebastopol in 1783 and Odessa in 1793, and the expansion of old commercial centres announced that Russia also intended to become a major Mediterranean power.[23] Until Bonaparte's fleet actually landed in Egypt, the Russians were convinced that it was directed at them and would land in Albania, Macedonia, or even the Crimea.[24] Such was their anxiety that they even joined forces with the Turks, an alliance which for sheer improbability put even that between Prussia and Austria in the shade.

The result of this first incursion by the Revolution into Eastern Europe was a Russian declaration of war and the dispatch of a Russian expeditionary force to Western Europe, which in the course of 1799, together with the Austrians, expelled the French from Italy, Switzerland, and Germany and threatened the invasion of France itself. At that point, the Russian effort

---

[23] A. M. Stanislavskaya, *Russko-angliyskie otnosheniya i problemy sreidizem-normor'ya 1798–1807* (Moscow, 1962), 25–40.

[24] Blanning, *Origins of the French Revolutionary Wars*, 191.

faltered, not least because the threat of French hegemony in the eastern Mediterranean had been lifted. Bonaparte, however, did not read the writing which had just flickered across the wall. After a brief pause, he resumed his efforts to expand his empire to the Levant and once again, in 1805, brought a Russian army to the west.[25] Partly because he dealt with that threat so easily, at Austerlitz, he was unable to curb his eastern ambitions and consequently unable to avoid Russian hostility. The point of no return came after the defeat of Prussia in 1806. By deciding to go further east, Napoleon plunged into the mire of Eastern European politics and was never able to extricate himself.

As Napoleon was the initiator of these thrusts to the east, it is tempting to draw a distinction between his personal megalomania and the apparently more modest—and more rational—ambitions of the Revolution. But essentially the aims of the Revolution and of Napoleon were the same—unlimited. No more than Napoleon did the Revolution ever define its war aims.[26] Like him, it just unleashed its armies and waited to see what happened, raising or lowering its sights depending on the current state of combat. The supporters of the *'anciennes limites'*, led by Carnot, who favoured limited acquisitions and a stable peace, were never able to gain control of revolutionary policy and were eventually eliminated at Fructidor in September 1797.[27] It was in the wake of that *coup d'état* that General Bonaparte won approval for his Eastern adventure, aided and abetted by Talleyrand. Condemned by their own unlimited aims to perpetual warfare, the revolutionaries provided as good an illustration as did Napoleon for the validity of Clausewitz's warning against allowing war to become anything more than the conduct of policy by other means. It was Napoleon himself who observed that the Directory had come to rely on war for its continued existence in the same way that other regimes required peace for their survival.[28]

In appreciating the need to see the European states-system as

[25] Derek McKay and H. M. Scott, *The Rise of the Great Powers 1648–1815* (London, 1983), 305–6, 309–10.

[26] Godechot, *La Grande Nation*, i. 76.

[27] Georges Lefebvre, *The Thermidorians and the Directory: Two Phases of the French Revolution* (New York, 1964), 258.

[28] Denis Woronoff, *La République bourgeoise de Thermidor à Brumaire 1794–1799* (Paris, 1972), 193.

a whole, to formulate war aims which were both limited and realistic, and not to underestimate the enemy, the Old Regime powers proved to be more adaptable. As Lord Rosebery put it with his customary elegance: 'the instinct of self-preservation guides the European powers with the same certainty as weather moves sheep on the hill.'[29] The crucial conversion was that of the two German powers. Slowly and painfully they got the point, not so much wafted into their minds by the breeze of self-interest as drummed into their thick skulls by repeated blows from the French armies. The punitive peace treaties imposed on Austria in 1805 and 1809 and on Prussia in 1807, together with Napoleon's growing penchant for reshuffling the thrones of Europe, eventually persuaded the two hereditary enemies that the need for a strong centre in Europe could not be satisfied without *both* of them being strong.[30] When Russia was brought west yet again, after Napoleon's latest and last foray to the east, for the first time since the revolutionary wars began all the other major powers were allied against France. The end had come.

In conclusion, I wish to draw attention to one final paradox of great importance. The war which the French revolutionaries unleashed in April 1792 was intended to be the most universal war there had ever been, a war for the liberation of all humanity.[31] Their jaunty confidence was soon frustrated by what Hegel called 'the cunning of reason', which 'sets the passions to work in its service, so that the agents by which it gives itself experience must pay the penalty and suffer the loss'.[32] By the spring of 1793 the war had ceased to be universal and had become national; as Danton told the National Convention on 13 April: 'Il faut, avant tout, songer à la conservation de notre corps politique, et fonder la grandeur française.'[33] The next stage in this ideological contraction took

---

[29] Lord Rosebery, *Pitt* (London, 1892), 104.

[30] Leopold von Ranke, *Preussische Geschichte 1415–1871*, ed. Hans-Joachim Schoeps (Munich, 1981), 404; Paul R. Sweet, *Wilhelm von Humboldt: A Biography*, i. *1808–1835* (Columbus, Ohio, 1980), 121–3.

[31] See the speech of Mailhe in the debate in the Legislative Assembly preceding the declaration of war: *Archives Parlementaires*, xlii. 208.

[32] Georg Wilhelm Friedrich Hegel, *Lectures on the Philosophy of World History*, trans. H. B. Nisbet (Cambridge, 1975), 89.

[33] *Archives Parlementaires*, lxii. 3.

much longer because it had so much further to go: by 1808 the war was being fought for the benefit of one family, the Bonapartes.[34] Yet even then the spirit of negation had not yet completed its work; by the end, Napoleon had lost interest even in promoting his family: it had become a war for one man.

Meanwhile, the Revolution's enemies had been moving in exactly the opposite direction. Their aims in 1792 had been as limited and precise as the means they sought to employ. They did not even suppose they were embarking on a full-blown war in the spring of 1792; rather they thought they were organizing an armed demonstration which would send the revolutionary *canaille* skulking back into submission. In fits and starts, prodded and pushed by the revolutionary challenge outside and their more far-sighted advisers at home, the 'cunning of reason' took them from the particular to the universal. As napoleonic France slipped into military dictatorship, it was the Old Regime states which introduced programmes of modernization, mobilized citizen militias, declared total war and used the rhetoric of liberation.[35] So I wish to end by making explicit a maxim of Hegel's which has underpinned everything I have had to say in this essay: 'contradiction is the root of all movement and vitality; it is only in so far as something has a contradiction within it that it moves, has an urge and activity.'[36]

[34] Jean Tulard, *Napoléon ou le mythe du sauveur* (Paris, 1977), 448.
[35] See e.g. the proclamation 'An die Deutschen!' issued by Kutuzov from his headquarters at Kalisch on 25 Mar. 1813, reprinted in F. Förster, *Geschichte der Befreiungskriege: 1813, 1814, 1815*, new edn., i (Berlin, 1889), 161–2. There has been some dispute as to the identity of its author; it appears to have been the Prussian bureaucrat Karl Niklas Wilhelm Baron von Rehdiger: Franz Wiedemann, 'Zur Geschichte des Aufrufs von Kalisch 1813', *Forschungen zur Brandenburgischen und Preussischen Geschichte*, 45 (1933), 266. On Russian use of liberationist propaganda, see B. S. Abalikhin, 'Voennopublitsicheskaya deyatel'nost russkogo komandovaniya sredi soldat i naseleniya Germanii v 1812–1813 gg.', in A. L. Narochnitsky and H. Scheel (eds.), *Bessmertnaya epopeya: K 175–letnyu otechestvennoy voyny 1812 g. i osvoboditel'noy voyny 1813 g. v Germanii* (Moscow, 1988), 243–60.
[36] *Hegel's Science of Logic*, trans. A. V. Miller (London/New York, 1969), 439.

Index

DATE DUE

OCT 1 5 1991			
APR 0 3 2003			